# DAILY LIFE DURING

# THE FRENCH REVOLUTION

**Recent titles in**
**The Greenwood Press "Daily Life Through History" Series**

# DAILY LIFE DURING

# THE FRENCH REVOLUTION

## JAMES M. ANDERSON

The Greenwood Press "Daily Life Through History" Series

**GREENWOOD PRESS**
Westport, Connecticut • London

**Library of Congress Cataloging-in-Publication Data**

Anderson, James Maxwell, 1933–
   Daily life during the French Revolution / James M. Anderson.
      p. cm. — (The Greenwood Press daily life through history series, ISSN:
1080–4749)
   Includes bibliographical references and index.
   ISBN 0–313–33683–0 (alk. paper)
   1. France—History—Revolution, 1789–1799.  2. France—Social conditions—
18th century.  I. Title.
   DC148.A656   2007
   944.04—dc22     2006034084

British Library Cataloguing in Publication Data is available.

Library of Congress Catalog Card Number: 2006034084
ISBN-10: 0–313–33683–0
ISBN-13: 978–0–313–33683–6
ISSN: 1080–4749

First published in 2007

Greenwood Press, 88 Post Road West, Westport, CT 06881
An imprint of Greenwood Publishing Group, Inc.
www.greenwood.com

Printed in the United States of America

The paper used in this book complies with the
Permanent Paper Standard issued by the National
Information Standards Organization (Z39.48–1984).

10  9  8  7  6  5  4  3  2  1

The publisher has done its best to make sure the instructions and/or recipes in
this book are correct. However, users should apply judgment and experience
when preparing recipes, especially parents and teachers working with young
people. The publisher accepts no responsibility for the outcome of any recipe
included in this volume.

For Viv
welcome to the world

# Contents

# PREFACE

For everyone in France, from the king to the lowliest peasant, July 1789 was either exhilarating or ominous. A rare person indeed would have been apathetic or unruffled by the social turmoil enveloping the country, for the July events and those that followed laid the foundations of a new society, a new state.

The decisive actions that led to the overthrow of the old order were staged mostly in Paris, although the provinces, where most of the population resided, played no small part in an escalating crisis.

The day-to-day life of the people of that time and place forms the major component of this book. Each chapter adds to a portrait of France before, during, and after the revolution.

The book begins with a geographical overview, followed by a description of the country's diverse political, social, and cultural influences and of the major historical events that led to the revolution. Subsequent chapters deal with the economy; courtly, aristocratic, urban, and rural life; and details about people of all classes—their anxieties, pleasures, living conditions, health care, ethics, charity, and personal experiences; what they wore and ate; what they did to entertain themselves; and the influence of the church, crime, and revolutionary propaganda.

The author owes a debt of gratitude to Sherry Anderson, whose perseverance, encouragement and plain hard work made this book possible. Others who contributed in no small measure were Dr. Siwan Anderson, Dr.

Katherine Connors, Dr. Patrick Francois, Richard Dalon, Georges Gottlieb of the Bibliothèque National de Paris, Howard Greaves, Dr. Rodney Roche, Drs. Bernard and Herbie Rochet. Thanks also go to Michael Hermann of Greenwood Press, who suggested the topic, and Sarah Colwell, assistant editor, Greenwood Press.

Storming of the Bastille by citizens with guns and pikes. The heads of "traitors" were carried on pikes. Courtesy Library of Congress.

# CHRONOLOGY

| | |
|---|---|
| October 5–6 | King and National Assembly move to Paris. |
| November 2 | Church property nationalized. |
| December 11 | Assignats introduced. |

**1790**

| | |
|---|---|
| February 13 | Monastic vows forbidden. |
| May 21 | Paris sections established. |
| June 19 | Noble titles abolished. |
| July 12 | Civil Constitution of the Clergy. |
| July 14 | Feast of Federation. |
| August 16 | Parlements abolished. |
| August 31 | Mutiny at Nancy. |
| November 27 | Oath of the clergy. |

**1791**

| | |
|---|---|
| January 2 | Roll-call on clerical oath. |
| March 2 | Guilds dissolved. |
| April 13 | Pope condemns Civil Constitution. |
| June 10 | Royal family's flight to Varennes. |
| July 16 | Reinstatement of Louis XVI. |
| September 14 | Annexation of Avignon. Louis XVI accepts Constitution. |
| September 30 | National Assembly dissolved. |
| October 1 | Legislative Assembly convenes. |
| October 20 | Call for war. |
| November 9 | Decree against *émigrés.* |
| November 12 | Louis XVI vetoes decree against *émigrés.* |
| November 29 | Decree against refractory priests. |
| December 19 | Louis XVI vetoes decree against priests. |

**1792**

| | |
|---|---|
| April 20 | War declared on Austria. |
| April 25 | First use of guillotine. |

| | |
|---|---|
| May 27 | New decree against refractory priests. |
| June 13 | Prussia declares war. |
| June 20 | Sans-culottes invade the Tuileries. |
| July 22 | Legislative Assembly declares the country in danger. |
| July 25 | Brunswick Manifesto. |
| July 30 | Marseilles *fédérés* enter Paris. |
| August 3 | Paris sections demand dethronement of king. |
| August 10 | Storming of the Tuileries; monarchy overthrown. |
| August 19 | Prussians cross frontier. Defection of Lafayette. |
| September 2 | Fall of Verdun. |
| September 2–6 | September massacres. |
| September 20 | Battle of Valmy. |
| September 21 | Convention meets. |
| September 22 | Republic proclaimed. |
| December 3 | Decision to try Louis XVI. |

**1793**

| | |
|---|---|
| January 21 | Execution of Louis XVI. |
| February 1 | War declared on England and Holland. |
| February 21 | Line and volunteer regiments joined. |
| February 24 | Decree conscription of 300,000 men. |
| February 25–27 | Food riots in Paris. |
| March 7 | War declared on Spain. |
| March 10 | Revolutionary tribunal created. |
| March 11 | Revolt in the Vendée. |
| April 5 | Defection of Dumouriez. |
| April 6 | Committee of Public Safety created. |
| April 11 | Assignats made sole legal tender. |
| April 29 | Federalist uprising in Marseilles. |
| May 4 | First Maximum decreed. |

| | |
|---|---|
| May 31 | First anti-Girondin uprising in Paris. |
| June 2 | Purge of Girondins from Convention. |
| June 7 | Federalist revolt spreads to Bordeaux and Caen. |
| June 9 | Vendeans capture Saumur. |
| June 24 | Constitution of 1793 accepted. |
| July 13 | Marat assassinated. |
| July 17 | Final abolition of feudalism. |
| July 26 | Death penalty for hoarding. |
| July 27 | Robespierre joins Committee of Public Safety. |
| August 23 | Decree of *levée en masse*. |
| August 25 | Marseilles recaptured. |
| August 27 | Toulon surrenders to the British. |
| September 5 | Government by terror begins. |
| September 17 | Law of Suspects. |
| September 29 | General Maximum introduced. |
| October 3 | Girondins sent for trial. |
| October 5 | Revolutionary calendar introduced. |
| October 9 | Fall of Lyon. |
| October 10 | Revolutionary government declared. |
| October 16 | Marie-Antoinette executed. |
| October 17 | Vendeans defeated at Cholet. |
| October 31 | Execution of Girondins. |
| November 10 | Festival of Reason at Nôtre Dame. |
| November 22 | Parisian churches closed. |
| December 4 | Revolutionary government created. |
| December 12 | Vendeans defeated at Le Mans. |
| December 19 | Fall of Toulon to French. |

**1794**

| | |
|---|---|
| February 21 | Price controls revised. |
| February 26 | Confiscation of *émigré* land. |

| March 3 | Distribution of *émigré* land among the poor. |
| March 13 | Arrest and execution of Hébertists. |
| March 27 | Revolutionary armies disbanded. |
| April 5 | Danton and Desmoulins executed. |
| June 8 | Festival of the Supreme Being. |
| July 5 | Wage controls introduced in Paris. |
| July 28 | Robespierre sent to guillotine. |
| September 18 | State renounces all subsidies to religion. |
| November 12 | Jacobin club closed. |
| December 8 | Surviving Girondins reinstated. |
| December 24 | Maximum abolished; invasion of Holland. |

**1795**

| February 17 | Pacification in the Vendée. |
| February 21 | Freedom of worship restored. |
| April 1 | Uprising of Germinal (12 Germinal). |
| May 20 | Uprising of Prairial (1 Prairial). |
| May 31 | Revolutionary tribunal abolished. |
| June 8 | Death of Louis XVII. |
| June 27 | Royalists land at Quibéron; defeated three weeks later. |
| July 22 | Peace concluded with Spain. |
| October 1 | Annexation of Belgium. |
| October 5 | Uprising of Vendémiaire. |
| October 26 | End of Convention. |
| November 3 | Directory constituted. |
| December 10 | Forced loans from the wealthy. |

**1796**

| February 19 | Withdrawal of assignats. |
| March 2 | Napoleon appointed commander in Italy. |
| June 12 | Papal territory invaded. |

**1797**

| | |
|---|---|
| July 25 | Political clubs closed. |
| August 24 | Laws against clergy repealed. |
| September 4 | Coup d'état against royalist deputies. |

**1798**

| | |
|---|---|
| May 11–12 | Extremist deputies removed from office. |
| July 1 | Napoleon lands in Egypt. |
| September 5 | General conscription law. |
| November 25 | Napoleon takes Rome. |

**1799**

| | |
|---|---|
| March 12 | Austria declares war. |
| July 12 | Law of Hostages. |
| November 10 | Napoleon overthrows Directory. |
| November 13 | Law of Hostages repealed. |
| Maps | |

PHYSICAL MAP OF FRANCE

Physical map of France.

PROVINCES OF PRE-REVOLUTIONARY FRANCE

Provinces of prerevolutionary France.

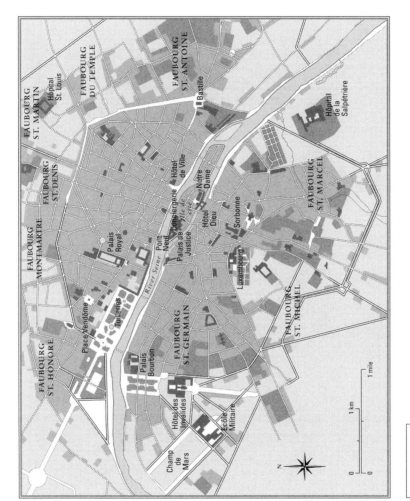

Paris 1789.

## DEPARTMENTS OF POST-REVOLUTIONARY FRANCE

Departments of postrevolutionary France.

# 1

# THE SETTING

## GEOGRAPHY

Mainland France presents a diverse landscape that stretches for 600 miles from north to south and for 580 miles east to west, with a total land area of 211,208 square miles. The plains, the most extensive area of the country, are a projection of the Great Plain of Europe and consist chiefly of gently undulating lowlands and the fertile valleys of the rivers Seine, Somme, Loire, and Garonne. The south central plateau, the Massif Central, is an elevated terrain rising gradually from the plains on the north and is characterized by volcanic outcroppings and extinct volcanoes. Farther south lie the Cévennes, a series of highlands rising from the Mediterranean coast. These regions are separated from the eastern highlands by the valley of the Rhône River.

Along the entire Spanish border lie the Pyrenees Mountains, a climatic divide; the French slopes receive abundant rainfall, while the Spanish side experiences little. They extend from the Bay of Biscay to the Mediterranean Sea, and some peaks reach heights of more than 10,000 feet. The north of France borders Luxembourg, Belgium, and the North Sea, and in the northeast, partly separating Alsace from Lorraine, lies the Vosges mountain range, running parallel to the Rhine and extending about 120 miles from north to south. The highest summits rise to about 4,700 feet. The Jura Mountains straddle the border between France and Switzerland, and, further south, the French Alps dominate the region from the Rhône to the Italian border. The highest peak, Mont Blanc, 15,771 feet, is on the Franco-Italian frontier.

## PRINCIPAL CITIES AND POPULATIONS

There were about 28 million inhabitants in France in 1789; today, there are about 60 million. Some three-fourths of the population are currently classified as urban, but in the eighteenth century the overwhelming majority were rural and engaged in agriculture. The capital and largest city of France—Paris—had more than half a million inhabitants at the time of the revolution. Today, in the Paris metropolitan area, there are well over 10 million.

The second largest city in 1789 was Lyon, with about 140,000 people, followed by Marseille, with 120,000, and Bordeaux, with 109,000. Once independent feudal domains, the regions of France were acquired throughout the Middle Ages by various French kings, a process that continued into the eighteenth century. For example, Brittany was incorporated by marriage to the French crown in 1532, and the duchy of Lorraine was added in 1766. The papal enclave of the city of Avignon and its surroundings was acquired in 1791.[1]

## SOCIAL AND CULTURAL DIVERSITY

Before the revolution, French society was organized into three estates: the clergy, the nobility, and the rest of the people. The two top tiers of society, the First and Second Estates, dominated the Third and monopolized education, the high posts in church and government, and the upper echelons of the military. Within these privileged classes, there were wide differences: wealthy nobles idled away their time at the king's court at Versailles, while others were often poor, dwelling in rundown châteaux in the countryside, living on the fees they collected from the peasants who tilled their land. Similarly, bishops and abbots, also of noble strain, enjoyed courtly life, owned land and mansions, and lived well off peasant labor and royal subsidies. The village priest or curate, on the other hand, was often as poor as his flock, living beside a village church and surviving on the output of his small vegetable garden and on local donations.

The upper crust of the Third Estate comprised a broad spectrum of nonnoble but propertied and professional families that today we refer to as the upper middle class (the bourgeoisie). They were between 2 and 3 million strong and included industrialists, rich merchants, doctors, lawyers, wealthy farmers, provincial notaries, and other legal officials such as village court justices. Below them in social status were the artisans and craftsmen, who had their own hierarchy of masters, journeymen, and apprentices; then came shopkeepers, tradesmen, and retailers. They, in turn, could look down on the poor day laborers, impoverished peasants, and, finally, the indigent beggars.

Throughout the history of France, as distinct historical divisions were brought together under one crown, the king generally accepted the institutions of each locale, such as local parlements, customs, and laws. Hence, no commonly recognized law or administrative practices prevailed throughout the realm, and, with the exception of certain royal edicts, each area relied on its own local authorities and traditions to maintain order. In northern France, for example, at least 65 general customs and 300 local ones were observed.[2] Such laws relating to inheritance, property, taxes, work, hunting, and a host of trivial matters differed from one district to another, as did systems for weights and measures, in which even the same terms could have different meanings depending on where they were used.

## LINGUISTIC DIVERSITY

The backward conditions under which many peasants lived and toiled and their generally illiterate state were only some of the factors that made them objects of amusement and jokes in high society. Another was the fact that many did not speak French in their everyday lives, if at all. On the fairly densely populated rocky Brittany peninsula, the generally poor native inhabitants spoke Breton, the Celtic language of their ancestors, who had arrived there from southwest England in the fifth and sixth centuries. Totally different from French and Breton, Basque, a language of unknown provenance, was spoken by the people of the southwest. The Basques occupied the western Pyrenees Mountains long before Roman times.[3]

Also in the southwest, Gascon, which developed from Latin, as did French (but which was very different), was spoken in the former Duchy of Gascony, annexed by France in 1453, while at the eastern end of the Pyrenees, Catalan, another Romance language, seemingly an early offshoot of Provençal, was spoken in the villages and on the farms.

Although French derived from Latin, the languages spoken north and south of the Loire began to diverge, the former influenced by the speech of early Germanic invaders. Two distinct languages emerged during the Middle Ages, the *langue d'oïl* of the north and the *langue d'oc* of the south. (The terms derive from the words for "yes" in each of the languages at the time.) In the south, Provençal (sometimes referred to as Occitan), derived from *langue d'oc*, became the language spoken by about one-fourth of the population of the entire country. Many local dialects developed within its orbit. One, Franco-Provençal, for example, refers to a distinctive group of dialects spoken northeast of the Provençal area, extending slightly into Switzerland and Italy.

By the time of the revolution, the French of *langue d'oïl*, with Paris as its social status symbol, was making inroads in the south and reducing Provençal to the status of a rustic and socially inferior dialect. Patois, dialects particular to a small region or hamlet, as in the Pyrenees valleys and other remote places, continued relatively free from Parisian influence.

In the east, a German dialect persisted in Alsace, a formerly German-speaking region that came under the sovereignty of France in 1648, and another language, Flemish, related to Dutch, was spoken by a small population near the Belgian border.

In most villages where French was not the language or where the inhabitants were illiterate, there was usually a priest with enough education to read and write when a villager needed someone with these skills. Visitors to France, although speaking good French, reported many difficulties with the language. Mrs. Thrale, who spent several months there in 1775 and visited again in 1786, noted that when peasants in Flanders were addressed, they did not understand a word of French and that most signs in French had the Flemish translation as well.[4]

The English agriculturist Arthur Young found the language barrier a serious obstacle in his research just before and during the revolution. He writes about Flanders and Alsace: "not one farmer in twenty speaks French." In Brittany, he had a similar experience. Henry Swinburne, who climbed in the Pyrenees Mountains, came across an incomprehensible language—Basque—and Sir Nathaniel Wraxal, writer and parliamentarian, wrote in 1775 that even in Bayonne, "they speak a jargon called the Basque, which has scarce any affinity either with the French, Spanish, or even the Gascon dialect."[5] At the eastern end of the Pyrenees, Young declared, "Roussillon is in fact a part of Spain; the inhabitants are Spaniards in language and in customs; but they are under a French government."

As travelers ventured down the Rhône valley toward Avignon, they encountered *langue d'oc*. It was in this region, after leaving Le Puy de Montélimar and heading for Aubenas, that Young barely escaped injury in August 1789 when his horse backed his chaise over a precipice. If he had been injured, he mused:

A blessed country for a broken limb … confinement for six weeks or two months at the Cheval Blanc, at Aubenas, an inn that would have been purgatory itself to one of my hogs: alone, without relation, friend or servant, and not one person in sixty that speaks French.[6]

## MONARCHY, VENAL OFFICES, AND DEVELOPMENT

A major issue dating back to the Middle Ages was the notion of the absolute and divine right of kings to rule over their subjects. Such power reached its zenith under Louis XIV, who died in 1715, and it remained the case, at least in theory, under his successors.

Through negotiations with the papacy, French kings won the right to fill all bishoprics and other benefices with persons of the king's choice, instead of the pope's, thus assuring a pliable clergy dependent on the monarch's will.

French kings were obliged to supplement the royal income from taxes by selling government offices to pay for the interminable wars and for the expenses of the royal court. The purchaser, noble or not, paid the crown a sum of money and derived the financial benefits and privileges of the office. These positions, such as secretary to the king, of which there were many (Louis XVI had 800), or magistrate of a court, became the individual's private property. Wealthy bourgeois who secured such a position were often elevated to the noble class, creating a new type of nobility that did not derive its legitimacy from family and birth; these new nobles were referred to as Nobility of the Robe, as opposed to the old Nobility of the Sword, which scorned the newcomers. These offices remained a source of money for the monarchy until the revolution when, it has been estimated, there were 51,000 venal offices in France.

The eighteenth century was nonetheless one of the great ages in the country's history, with France the richest and most powerful nation on the European continent. French taste and styles in architecture, interior decoration, dress, and manners were copied throughout western society. The political and social ideas of French writers influenced both thought and action, and French became the second language of educated people around the world. Excellent roads were constructed in the vicinity of some of the larger cities, although they remained poor in other places. The French merchant marine expanded to more than 5,000 ships that engaged in lucrative trade with Africa, America, and the West Indies and enriched the merchants of the French seaports. The income of urban laborers and artisans, however, barely kept pace with inflation, and most peasants, with little surplus to sell and heavily burdened by taxes, tithes, and, for some, leftover feudal obligations to their lord of the manor, continued to eke out a miserable existence. The advocates of badly needed governmental fiscal and social reform became increasingly vocal during the reign of Louis XVI but were resisted by those who wielded power.

## AGE OF ENLIGHTENMENT

It was taken for granted that even a bad king was better than none at all, and alternative forms of government were not discussed, at least publicly, until the eighteenth century, when intellectual opposition to the monarchy was led by French writers who focused on political, social, and economic problems. Points of view expressed in letters, pamphlets, and essays ushered in an age of reason, science, and humanity.

Such men argued that all mankind had certain natural rights, such as life, liberty, and ownership of property, and that governments should exist to guarantee these rights. Some, in the later part of the century, advocated the right of self-government. These ideas resonated both among nobles discontented with the centralization of power in the king and within the growing bourgeoisie, which wanted a voice in government.

Men of reason often viewed the church as the principal agency that enslaved the human mind and many preferred a form of Deism, accepting God and the idea of a future existence but rejecting Christian theology based on authority and unquestioned faith. Human aspirations, they believed, should be centered not on a hereafter but rather on the means of making life more agreeable on earth. Nothing was attacked with more intensity and ferocity than the church, with all its political power and wealth and its suppression of the exercise of reason.

Proponents of the Enlightenment were often referred to by the French word *philosophes*. Charles de Montesquieu, one of the earliest representatives of the movement, began satirizing contemporary French politics, social conditions, and ecclesiastical matters in his *Persian Letters* (1721). His work *The Spirit of Laws* (1748) examined three forms of government (republicanism, monarchy, and despotism). His criticism of French institutions under the Bourbons contributed significantly to ideas that encouraged French revolutionaries. Similarly, the works of Jean-Jacques Rousseau, especially his *Social Contract* (1762), a political treatise, had a profound influence on French political and educational thought.

The *Encyclopedia*, in which numerous philosophers collaborated, was edited by the rationalist Denis Diderot in Paris between 1751 and 1772 and was a powerful propaganda weapon against ecclesiastical authority, superstition, conservatism, and the semifeudal social structures of the time. It was suppressed by the authorities but was nevertheless secretly printed, with supplements added until 1780.[7]

There was always a price to pay for enlightened ideas considered irreverent and blasphemous to church and crown. Voltaire, for example, one of the most celebrated writers of the day, known in Paris salons as a brilliant and sarcastic wit, spent 11 months in the Bastille and was often exiled for his satires on the aristocracy and the clergy. The language of the Enlightenment entered the vocabulary and the words "citizen," "nation," "virtue," "republican," and "democracy," among others, spread throughout France.

The Seven Years War ended in 1763 with Great Britain's acquisition of almost the entire French empire in North America and shattered French pretensions to rule India, resulting in abject humiliation for France, while the costs greatly increased the country's already heavy debt. By 1764, the country's debt service alone ran at about 60 percent of the budget.[8] The unpopular Louis XV died at Versailles on May 10, 1774. His reported prophecy "After me, the deluge" was soon to be fulfilled.

## LOUIS XVI

Home to about 50,000 people, the town of Versailles, primarily a residential community, lies 12 miles southwest of Paris and is the site of the royal palace and gardens built by Louis XIV, who, along with his court and departments of government, occupied it beginning in 1682. Louis XV lived here, and Louis XVI, his grandson, was born here on August 23, 1754. The deaths of his two elder brothers and of his father, the only son of Louis XV, made the young prince dauphin of France in 1765. In 1770, he married Marie-Antoinette, the youngest daughter of the archduchess Maria-Theresa of Austria. In 1774, upon the death of his grandfather, Louis XVI ascended the throne of France.

Twenty years old and inexperienced when he began his reign, Louis XVI ruled over the most populous country in Europe, where millions belonged to a fluid population in search of work or were involved in lawlessness. The country was burdened by debts and heavy taxation, resulting in widespread suffering among the ordinary people. If there was ever a time for a strong and decisive king, it was now. Louis XVI was indecisive and easily influenced by those around him, including his wife, who intervened to block needed reforms, especially the pressing problems of taxation. Matters of state were not high on his agenda. He preferred to spend his time at hobbies such as hunting and tinkering with locks and clocks or gorging himself at the table.

## AMERICAN WAR OF INDEPENDENCE

The ideals of the American struggle for independence, coupled with those of the Enlightenment—liberty, justice, equality for all—resonated strongly among many educated French people, some of whom went to fight on the side of the American colonies. These included the marquis de La Fayette (anglicized as Lafayette), who in 1777 left French military service to enter the American continental army, where he was commissioned major general and became an intimate associate of George Washington. In the minds of many, the American Declaration of Independence signaled, for the first time, that some people were progressing beyond the discussion of enlightened ideas and were putting them into practice. To those who clamored for a voice in their own government and who detested the abuses of the monarchy, the American republic appeared an ideal state. French philosophy had prepared segments of society to receive with enthusiasm the political doctrines and the portrait of social life that came from across the Atlantic.

Bitter over the results of the Seven Years War and with a profound dislike of the English, Louis XVI granted aid to the American colonies. By intervening in support of the Americans, he hoped to weaken England and recover colonies and trade lost in the war. The price of aiding the budding United States of America was about 1.3 billion livres.[9] The French government could ill afford the expense and hovered on the brink of bankruptcy.

## JACQUES NECKER

In August 1774, the king appointed a liberal comptroller general, the economist Turgot, baron de L'Aulne, who instituted a policy of strict economy in government expenditures. Within two years, however, most of his reforms had been withdrawn, and his dismissal, forced by reactionary members of the nobility and clergy, was supported by the queen.

Turgot's successor was a Swiss banker, Jacques Necker, who was made director general of finance in 1777 and was expected to bring stability to the chaotic finances of the state. Idolized by the people for attempting to bring about much-needed reforms, he was disliked by the court aristocracy and the queen, whose wildly extravagant spending he tried to curb. Weak-willed and irresolute, Louis XVI, who made erratic decisions based on the interests of officials ingratiated at court, dismissed Necker in 1781, only to recall him in September 1788 as the state sank deeper into bankruptcy. Continuing depression, high unemployment, and the highest bread prices of the century alienated and incensed the people of Paris, but their faith in Necker persisted. He was acclaimed by the public as the only man capable of restoring sound administration to the hectic French financial system. In the following year, his popularity was further increased when, along with others, he recommended to the king that the Estates-General, a representative assembly from the three estates, which had not met since 1614 and which was the only body that could legally sanction tax increases, be convened. The assembly met in Versailles on May 5, 1789.

Opposed by aristocrats at court for his daring reform plans, which included both the abolition of all feudal rights of the aristocracy and the church and support for the Third Estate, Necker was again dismissed, on July 11, 1789. This act of dismissal and rumors that royal troops were gathering around the city aroused the fury of the populace of Paris.

## ESTATES-GENERAL AND *CAHIERS DE DOLÉANCES*

Just prior to the meeting of the Estates-General, censorship was suspended, and a flood of pamphlets expressing enlightened ideas circulated throughout France. Necker had supported the king in the decision to grant the Third Estate as many representatives in the Estates-General as the First and Second Estates combined, but both men failed to make a ruling on the method of voting—whether to vote by estate, in which case the first two estates would certainly override the third, or by simple majority rule, giving each representative one vote, which would benefit the Third Estate.

The representatives brought to the Assembly *cahiers de doléances* (notebooks of grievances) produced by every parish and corporation or guild in the country. These provided the information needed by the 1,177 delegates, consisting of 604 representatives of the Third Estate, mostly lawyers; 278 nobles (the vast majority nobles of the sword); and 295 clerical delegates,

FUSILLADE AU FAUXBOURG Sᵗ ANTOINE,
Le 28 Avril 1789,

Troops firing on rioting workers at Faubourg St.-Antoine. Bibliothèque Nationale de France.

three-quarters of whom were parish priests sympathetic to the misery of their parishioners.[10]

All three estates expressed their loyalty to and love for the king in the *cahiers,* but all declared that absolute monarchy was obsolete and that meetings of the Estates-General must become a regular occurrence. The royal ministers were chastised for their fiscal inefficiency and arbitrary decisions. The king was urged to make a full disclosure of state debt and to concede to the Estates-General control over expenditures and taxes.

The belief was also widespread that the church, whose noble upper echelon lived in splendor but whose parish priests often were mired in poverty, was in dire need of reform. The *cahiers* expressed the need for fiscal and judicial changes, demanding that the church and the nobility pay their share of taxes and that justice be uniform, less costly, and more expeditious and the laws and punishments more humane. The abolition of internal trade boundaries and free transport of goods throughout the country were also generally considered to be highly beneficial to the realm.

There were sharp differences among the three estates, especially in the countryside, where peasant, bourgeois, church, and noble interests

Opening of the Estates-General at Versailles, May 5, 1789. Courtesy Library of Congress.

conflicted. The Third Estate wished to see the abolition of all exemptions, such as those concerning taxes and lodging of soldiers in peasant homes, for which the poor carried the brunt. It also hoped to see the end of seigneurial justice and to have all cases settled before the nearest royal judge. The clergy hoped for a rejuvenated social order and a monopoly on morality and worship, while the lower clergy supported making high positions in the church available to men of talent, noble or otherwise. The bourgeoisie and the nobility each wanted a larger say in running a government in which the power of the king would be far from absolute.

## REVOLUTION AND CONSTITUTION

The deadlock on voting procedure persisted for six weeks, but finally, on June 17, the Third Estate, led by abbé Emmanuel-Joseph Sieyès and the comte de Mirabeau, proclaimed itself the National Assembly. This display of defiance of the royal government, which had given its support to the clergy and the nobility, was followed by the passage of a measure vesting the National Assembly with sole power to legislate taxation. In swift retaliation, Louis deprived the National Assembly of its meeting hall, and it responded, on June 20, by gathering at a Versailles tennis court and swearing what is known as the Tennis Court Oath, a pledge that it would not dissolve until it had drafted a constitution for France. At this juncture, serious divisions split the ranks of the upper two estates, and numerous representatives of the lower clergy and a number of liberal nobles broke off to join forces with the National Assembly.

Prominent factors leading to this display of disobedience to the established order were the indecisive and immature nature of the monarch; the inability of the ruling classes to cope successfully with the problems of state; the demands of the middle class (bourgeoisie) and the nobility for more influence in government; the oppressive taxation that fell on the Third Estate, especially the peasantry; the impoverishment of workers; the intellectual ferment of the Age of Enlightenment; and the example of successful rebellion by American colonies. Unequal distribution of land under the seigneurial system and the unending cycle of wasteful government spending were causes of discontent, as were the remnants of feudal obligations in some areas. Perhaps most important of all was the shortage and the rising cost of bread and the inability of the common people to afford the prices, which led to hunger and further poverty. There were also a host of minor grievances, from hunting rights to the right to gather firewood and to use open land.

On the morning of July 14, 1789, incensed by the dismissal of Necker yet again, Parisian mobs roamed the streets in search of weapons and finally attacked the dominant symbol of despotic royal authority, the fortress prison of the Bastille, on the eastern edge of the city, an institution that epitomized injustice and arbitrary rule. Citizens of every class and profession had been arrested by secret warrants *(lettres de cachet)* and imprisoned indefinitely in the fortress without formal accusation or trial. The bloody battle to take the Bastille heralded the violent onset of the revolution. Even though only seven prisoners were incarcerated there on July 14, the commander of the military garrison was beheaded by the mob. Two days later, the dismantling of the stronghold was begun amid public rejoicing.

Shortly thereafter, Necker was again recalled by the king, but he was unable to resolve the financial crisis. Frustrated in his efforts at reform and at curbing court extravagance, and especially over the issuance of the disastrous assignats (a new form of government bond), he resigned, in September 1790, to retire to his estate in Switzerland.[11]

Meanwhile, during the last two weeks of July and the first week of August 1789, provincial unrest and disorder, known as the Great Fear *(Grande Peur),* swept the countryside as the rumor spread that aristocrats were sending brigand bands to destroy peasant holdings and put an end to the revolution. Châteaux were set alight by peasants, and nobles fled the country. As news of destruction and chaos reached Versailles, the National Constituent Assembly was spurred into action. During the night session of August 4, 1789, the clergy and nobles renounced their privileges; a few days later, the Assembly passed a law abolishing feudal and manorial prerogatives. Parallel legislation prohibited the sale of public offices and of exemptions from taxation and abolished the right of the Roman Catholic

Church to levy tithes. The Assembly then proceeded to deal with its primary task—the drafting of a constitution.

In the preamble, known as the Declaration of the Rights of Man and Citizen (see Appendix 1), the delegates formulated the revolutionary ideals later summarized as *liberté, égalité, fraternité* (liberty, equality, fraternity). While the Constituent Assembly deliberated, the food-deprived population of Paris (a hotbed of anger and of rumors of royalist conspiracies) clamored for bread and lower prices. Reports of a bountiful banquet at Versailles given by the royal guards in which the tricolor of the revolution was said to have been trampled underfoot propelled the political ferment in Paris into a frenzy. On October 5, 1789, a large body of Parisians, mostly women, many from the market place, marched on Versailles and laid siege to the royal palace. Louis and his family were rescued by Lafayette's National Guard, but the crowd demanded that they be escorted to Paris and lodged in the palace of the Tuileries. The Constituent Assembly, following suit, also moved to Paris. The court and the Assembly, more readily accessible within the capital, became increasingly subject to pressure from the citizens.

While the draft of the constitution of 1791, the first such written document in French history, was in preparation, indignation, anger, and mistrust grew as reports circulated that Marie-Antoinette was in secret communication with her brother Leopold II of the Holy Roman Empire, a

*Prise de la Bastille*

July 14, 1789, the storming of the Bastille. Bibliothèque Nationale de France.

man who, like all monarchs of the time, had no desire to see the revolution succeed and who offered sanctuary to the French *émigrés*. Suspicions that the king and queen were devising a means to overthrow the revolution with foreign and *émigré* support were confirmed when, on June 21, 1791, the royal family was apprehended at Varennes, near the Belgian border, while attempting to flee the country. Belgium at the time was under the control of Leopold II. The royal family was brought back to Paris under guard.

After suspending the monarchy for a brief period, the moderate majority of the Constituent Assembly reinstated the king on July 16 in the interest of stemming the mounting radicalism and to forestall foreign intervention. The following day, July 17, 1791, the republicans of Paris massed in the Champ de Mars, a military parade ground, under the direction of the Cordeliers (more radical than the Jacobins) and demanded that the king be tried for treason. Lafayette ordered his troops to fire on the demonstrators, and the bloodshed widened the gulf between radical and moderate bourgeois sections of the population.

By the terms of the constitutional document, the provinces of France were eliminated and the country was divided into 83 departments, each provided with a local elective administration. Hereditary titles were abolished, and trial by jury in criminal cases was ordained. The constitution confined the electorate to men age 25 and older who paid taxes of at least three days' wages and vested authority in a Legislative Assembly elected by an indirect system of voting. While executive authority was in the hands of the king, strict limitations were imposed on his powers. He was given veto power over legislation, but his veto merely suspended the legislation for a time, rather than expunging it. The Assembly took effective control of the conduct of foreign affairs and placed severe restrictions on the power of the Catholic Church that were legalized on July 12, 1790 through a series of articles called the Civil Constitution of the Clergy, the most important of which confiscated all ecclesiastical property. The Civil Constitution of the Clergy also provided for the election of priests and bishops by voters, for remuneration of the clergy by the state, for a clerical oath of allegiance to the state (November 27, 1790), and for dissolution of most monastic orders.

Church matters were now settled to the government's satisfaction, and on September 14, 1791 the first written constitution of France was finished and reluctantly accepted by the king. Two weeks later, the Assembly dissolved itself, its work finished.

## THE GROWTH OF RADICALISM

Suspicion and discontent among the disenfranchised section of the population grew. The nonpropertied and working classes saw little in the revolution that promoted their welfare and had no trust that the bourgeois government would redress their misery. They steadily gravitated toward radical solutions for their problems. This process was expedited by the highly organized and powerful Jacobin clubs, among others.

The new Legislative Assembly began its sessions on October 1, 1791. It was composed of 750 members, all of whom were inexperienced, since members of the Constituent Assembly had voted themselves ineligible for election to the new body. This new legislature was divided into widely divergent factions, the most moderate of which was the Feuillants, who supported a constitutional monarchy as defined under the first constitution. In the center was the majority caucus, known as the Plain, which was without well-defined political opinions. The Plain, however, uniformly opposed the republicans who sat on the left, composed mainly of the Girondins, who wanted to change the constitutional monarchy into a federal republic similar to that of the United States of America. The Plain and the Girondins opposed the Montagnards (men of the mountain, because they sat in the highest seats), consisting of Jacobins and Cordeliers, who favored establishment of a highly centralized, indivisible republic.

Before these differences caused a serious split, the Assembly passed several bills, including stringent measures against clergymen who refused to swear allegiance to the government. Louis XVI exercised his veto against these bills, however, creating a crisis that brought the Girondins to power. Despite the opposition of leading Montagnards, the Girondist ministry adopted a belligerent attitude toward Frederick William II and Francis II, the Holy Roman emperor (who had succeeded his father, Leopold II, on March 1, 1792). The two sovereigns openly supported the *émigrés* and encouraged the opposition of the feudal landlords in Alsace to the revolutionary legislation. Sentiment for war spread among the monarchists, who hoped that foreign armies would destroy the revolutionary government and permit the restoration of the old order, as well as among the Girondins, who wanted a final triumph over reaction at home and abroad.

## REVOLUTIONARY WARS

On April 20, 1792, the Legislative Assembly declared war on Austria, beginning the series of conflicts known as the French Revolutionary Wars. On June 13, 1792, Prussia declared war on France. Successive defeats for France followed, threatening the revolutionary movement. As Austrian armies invaded eastern France, this threat produced major repercussions in Paris, where disorder erupted. On June 20, the sans-culottes and Paris mobs invaded the Tuileries palace and forced the king to don the red revolutionary hat. On July 22, the duke of Brunswick, commander of the combined Austrian and Prussian armies, issued a declaration stating that if any member of the royal family were harmed, Paris would be destroyed. Instead of fear, the Brunswick manifesto inspired an outburst of patriotic fervor in the capital.

Louis XVI forced to wear the red liberty bonnet of
the revolution. Bibliothèque Nationale de France.

The Legislative Assembly proclaimed the country in danger, and
reserves were hurried to the hard-pressed armies while volunteers were
summoned to Paris from all parts of the country. The *fédérés* contingent
from Marseille arrived on July 30, 1792, singing the patriotic hymn thence-
forth known as the "Marseillaise." On August 3, the militant sans-culottes
of the Paris sections (consisting mostly of the working class) demanded the
overthrow of the monarchy. On August 10, angry disturbances, combined
with the threat contained in the manifesto of the allied commander, precipitated a Parisian insurrection. Radical elements in the capital, strengthened by national volunteers passing through the city on route to the front,
stormed the Tuileries, massacring the king's Swiss Guards. Louis and
his family escaped to the nearby hall of the Legislative Assembly, whose

members promptly suspended the king and placed him and his family in confinement.

During the first week of September, more than 1,000 royalists and suspected traitors who had been rounded up in various parts of France were tried by mock courts in the prisons and summarily executed. These "September massacres" were induced by popular fear of the advancing allied armies and of rumored plots to overthrow the revolutionary government.

## NATIONAL CONVENTION

On September 20, 1792, a French army, commanded by General Charles Dumouriez, stopped the Prussian advance on Paris at the town of Valmy, east of the capital. The same day, the National Convention (the third National Assembly of the revolution) was elected by male suffrage.

This newly elected body convened in Paris, and its first official move, on September 22, 1792, was to abolish the monarchy and proclaim the establishment of the First French Republic. Agreement among the principal convention factions, the Girondins and the Montagnards, went little beyond common approval of these initial measures. In their euphoria, the Girondins promulgated a decree, on November 19, that promised French assistance to all oppressed peoples of Europe.

Reports arrived almost weekly from the army, which, after the battle at Valmy, had now assumed the offensive, forcing the enemy back on all fronts. In the meantime, however, strife steadily intensified in the National Convention, with the Plain vacillating between support for the conservative Girondins and support for the radical Montagnards.

In the first major test of strength, a majority approved the Montagnard proposal that Louis be brought to trial before the Convention for treason. On January 15, 1793, the monarch was found guilty as charged, but, on the following day, when the nature of the penalty was determined, factional lines were sharply drawn. By a vote of 387 to 334, the delegates approved the death penalty, and Louis XVI went to the guillotine on January 21, 1793.

Girondist influence in the National Convention diminished markedly after the execution of the king. The lack of unity within the group during the trial had damaged its national prestige, already at low ebb among the Parisian populace, which favored the Jacobins. Their influence was further diminished as a consequence of the military reversals suffered by the revolutionary armies after the French declaration of war on England and the United Netherlands on February 1, 1793. The French situation was again becoming desperate. Line regiments and volunteers were amalgamated on February 21, and, three days later, the Convention voted to conscript 300,000 men, dispatching special commissioners to the various departments for the purpose of organizing the levy.

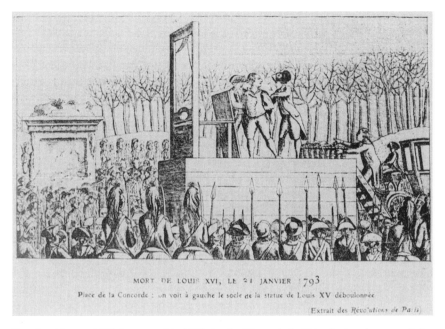

MORT DE LOUIS XVI, LE 21 JANVIER 1793

Place de la Concorde : on voit à gauche le socle de la statue de Louis XV déboulonnée

[Extrait des *Révolutions de Paris*]

Death of Louis XVI, January 21, 1793, in the Place de la Révolution (renamed the Place de la Concorde in 1795), Paris. To the left is the pedestal of the toppled statue of Louis XV. Courtesy Library of Congress.

War was declared on Spain on March 7, 1793, and, along with several smaller states, the Spanish entered the counterrevolutionary coalition. A tribunal was established on March 10 in which Jacobin proposals to strengthen the government for the crucial oncoming struggles met resistance from the Girondins, while royalists and clerical foes of the revolution stirred up the anticonscription and pro-Catholic feelings of peasants in the Vendée, leading to open rebellion on March 11, 1793. Civil war quickly spread to neighboring departments. On March 18, the Austrians defeated the French army of General Dumouriez at Neerwinden, and on April 5, the General, a Girondin, deserted to the Austrian enemy. On April 6, the Committee of Public Safety was created as the executive organ of the republic.

The defection of the leader of the army, mounting civil war, food riots due to mediocre harvests, the falling assignat, and the advance of enemy forces again across the French frontiers inevitably led to a crisis in the Convention, the factions with the more radical elements stressing the necessity for bold action in defense of the revolution. On April 29, 1793, a Federalist uprising (by those against centralized authority in Paris) took place in Marseille. The political situation was going from bad to worse.

To keep prices down and the people calm, the first Maximum (price controls on wheat and flour) was decreed on May 14, 1793, and, desperate for money, the government forced the rich to contribute. Following anti-Girondist uprisings in Paris, the Girondins were purged from the Convention on June 2. In the meantime, Federalist revolts spread to Bordeaux, Lyon, and Caen, while the rebels of the Vendée captured Saumur. The 1791 constitution creating a limited monarchy was defunct, as was the monarch, and a new constitution of 1793 was accepted on June 24.

Leadership of the Committee of Public Safety passed to the Jacobins on July 10, 1793. On July 13, Jean-Paul Marat, a radical politician, was assassinated by the aristocrat Charlotte Corday, a Girondist sympathizer. Public anger over this crime considerably enhanced Jacobin influence, and Federalism (the objective of the Girondins) was declared illegal on July 17. By now, the food shortage was desperate, and the death penalty was decreed on July 26 for hoarders. The next day, Robespierre, a lawyer from Arras, joined the Committee of Public Safety.

On August 23, 1793, the National Convention, facing a dwindling supply of recruits for the army and under pressure from the sans-culottes of Paris, decreed a *levée en masse,* or total mobilization of the populace for the war effort. Unmarried men and childless widowers between the ages of 18 and 25 were ordered to enlist. Married men were ordered to work in the manufacture of arms, while women were to volunteer for work in military hospitals or make uniforms and tents for the army, which now had grown to 750,000 men. Meanwhile, on September 8, 1793, the French army scored a victory at Hondschoote, near the Belgian border, raising morale, but the levy further alienated the Vendean rebels, as well as inhabitants of large parts of the west and other rural districts who were already angry over the treatment of their priests and who needed their sons, destined for the army, to help work the land.

## GOVERNMENT BY TERROR

Functioning as the executive power of the government once held by the king, the Committee of Public Safety was endowed with immense authority. The Jacobin leader Maximilien Robespierre, the dominant power on the Committee, aided by Louis Saint-Just, Lazare Carnot, Georges Couthon, and other prominent Jacobins, instituted extreme policies to crush any possibility of counterrevolution. Their mandate was renewed monthly by the National Convention beginning April 1793.

The committee began implementing government by terror on September 5, followed by the Law of Suspects, which was passed on September 17. The law, vague and draconian, decreed that all suspect persons were to be arrested and tried by the tribunal. Suspect persons were defined as anyone who, by thought, word, or deed, had opposed the revolution. So-called enemies of liberty could also be arrested if they could not prove that they were engaged in some civic duty. Relatives of the *émigrés* were the first to be rounded up for trial. The sentence was usually death with no benefit of appeal. Antoine Fouquier-Tinville, the prosecutor for the Revolutionary Tribunal, earned a reputation as a bloodthirsty extremist and became the most feared and hated man in France.[12]

On September 29, 1793, the General Maximum to control food prices was introduced, extended now to all grains and to many staple goods. The revolutionary army was sent to various districts to enforce price controls and to requisition grain from farmers. A portable guillotine went with them. By this time, royalist and Roman Catholic insurgents controlled much of the Vendée and Brittany. Caen, Lyon, Marseille, and Bordeaux were in the hands of the Girondins.[13]

The government of terror acted ruthlessly toward everyone who did not adhere to its political ideals. It even took revenge on people who played no prominent role in politics but who had committed past sins in the eyes of the revolutionary zealots, who had little compunction about executing men of talent and international fame and who were a credit to France.

Antoine-Laurent Lavoisier, now recognized as the father of modern chemistry, had been a Farmer General (tax collector) and had spent the income from this post on science, sharing his laboratory with colleagues and young researchers. James Watt, Benjamin Franklin, and Joseph Priestley, among others, had visited his laboratory. The salon run by his wife was one of the intellectual centers of Paris. The fact that he had carried out numerous experiments, coined the term "oxygen" and studied its role in human and plant respiration, discovered the chemical composition of water, made discoveries in human metabolism, and demonstrated that, although matter changes its state in a chemical reaction, the quantity of matter remains the same, had little effect on members of the Committee of Public Safety. Many other facets of science also came under the scrutiny of this remarkable man. As a member of the Academy of Science, Lavoisier had played a role in denying membership to Jean-Paul Marat, perhaps a fatal move. He was in favor of the revolution, for funds for the aged poor, as well as for the abolishment of the *corvée* (forced labor), but he had once assisted in the building of the much-resented wall around Paris whose gates controlled taxes on goods entering the city. In 1793, the Academy of Science was abolished. In November of that year, an arrest warrant was issued for all former Farmers General. Lavoisier was incarcerated and then sent to the guillotine, on May 8, 1794, his body thrown into a pit. In 1796, his name was resurrected, and a magnificent state funeral was given in his honor.

## FEDERALIST REVOLT

The reaction to the ejection of the Girondist deputies from the Convention in June 1793 led to the Federalist revolt. The two factions, Girondist and Montagnard, had long quarreled over most issues: the September massacres, the trial of the king, the constitution of 1793, and the influence of the Parisian sans-culotte sections in politics. Many departments objected to the ousting of the Girondist deputies, and 13 of them carried on prolonged resistance to the Montagnards (mostly Jacobins). They declared themselves in a state of resistance to oppression and withdrew their recognition of the National Convention, calling upon their citizens to take up arms, march on Paris, and restore the deputies. This bellicose declaration, lacking support, failed. With the revolt in the Vendée, the government nevertheless felt the hot breath of civil war. By October 1793, the Montagnards, now in control of the Convention, rounded up the Girondist deputies who had not fled Paris and arrested them. Armed forces were sent to suppress the revolt in the various regions. Lyon resisted a two-month siege, capitulating on October 9, 1793, and reprisals afterward cost the lives of 1,900 rebels. The government did not carry out its threat to destroy the homes of the wealthy and erase the city's name from the record.[14] About 300 rebels were executed in Bordeaux and Marseille.

In the three-day battle of Wattigenies, a little south of Lille, on October 15–17, the French defeated the main Austrian army. Marie-Antoinette, after a farcical trial, was beheaded on October 16, 1793, to the glee of many Parisians, and the next day the Vendeans were defeated at Cholet, east of Nantes; they subsequently resorted to scattered guerrilla warfare. On the last day of October 1793, the Girondins arrested some weeks before were executed. On November 10, the Festival of Reason was celebrated in Nôtre Dame, and on November 23, the Commune of Paris, in a measure soon copied by authorities elsewhere in France, closed all churches in the city and began actively to sponsor the revolutionary religion known as the Cult of Reason.

The factional struggle between the extremist publisher Hébert (a member of the Cordeliers) and his followers on one side and the Committee of Public Safety on the other ended on March 24, 1794, with the Hébertists meeting Madame Guillotine. Within two weeks, Robespierre moved against the Dantonists, who had begun to demand peace and an end to the Terror. Danton and his principal colleagues met the same fate on April 5. Due to purges and wholesale reprisals against supporters of these two factions, Robespierre also lost the backing of many leading Jacobins, especially those who feared their heads could be next on the block.

The committee had struck violently at internal opposition; thousands of royalists, nonjuring priests, Girondins, workers, and peasants, along with others charged with counterrevolutionary activities or sympathies, were brought before revolutionary tribunals, summarily convicted, and beheaded. Executions in Paris totaled 2,639 during the Terror. In many outlying departments, particularly the main centers of royalist insurrection, even harsher treatment was meted out to traitors, real and suspect. The Nantes tribunal, headed by Jean-Baptiste Carrier, which dealt most severely with those who aided the rebels in the Vendée, sent more than 8,000 persons to the guillotine within three months. The machine could not work fast enough to empty the overcrowded prisons, so batches of nonjuring priests were crammed into barges, hog-tied, and taken out into the Loire River and sunk. In all of France, revolutionary tribunals and commissions were responsible for the execution of about 16,000 individuals. Many other victims included those who died in overcrowded, disease-ridden prisons and others who were shot. More than 100,000 died in the brutal pacification of the Vendée.

Of those condemned to the guillotine, approximately one-third were nobles, priests, and wealthy members of the upper middle class, another third were propertied peasants and lower-middle-class townsmen, and roughly one-third were from the urban working class.[15] Workers or peasants were often charged with draft dodging, desertion, hoarding, theft, or rebellion. Meanwhile, the tide of battle against the allied coalition had turned in favor of France. By the end of 1793, the invaders in the east had been driven back across the Rhine, Toulon had been liberated from the British, and the Committee of Public Safety had largely crushed the insurrections of the royalists and the Girondins.

The general dissatisfaction with the leader of the Committee of Public Safety soon developed into full-fledged conspiracy. Robespierre and 98 of his colleagues were seized on July 27, 1794, and beheaded the next day, the day generally regarded as marking the end of the Terror. The Jacobin clubs were closed throughout France, revolutionary tribunals were abolished, and various extremist decrees, including one that had fixed wages and commodity prices were repealed.

## CONSTITUTION OF 1795 AND THE DIRECTORY

Peace was restored to the frontiers, and in July 1795 an inept invading army of *émigrés* was defeated in Brittany. The National Convention then completed the draft of a new constitution, which was formally approved on August 22, 1795. On November 3, the new fundamental law of France now vested executive authority in a Directory composed of five members. Legislative power was delegated to a bicameral legislature consisting of the Council of Ancients (with 250 members) and the Council of the Five Hundred. The terms of one member of the Directory and a third of the legislature were renewable annually, beginning May 1797. The franchise was limited to male taxpayers who could establish proof of one-year's residence in their voting district. The new constitution failed to provide a means of breaking deadlocks between the executive and legislative bodies, however, which led to constant intergovernmental rivalry and ineffectual administration of national affairs.

The Directory had inherited an acute financial crisis that was aggravated by disastrous depreciation of the assignats. Although most of the Jacobin leaders were dead, transported, or in hiding, their spirit still flourished among the urban lower classes. In the higher circles of society, royalist agitators boldly campaigned for restoration of the crown, while the bourgeois political groupings, determined to preserve their hard-won status as the masters of France, soon found it materially and politically profitable to direct the mass energies unleashed by the revolution into militaristic channels. Old scores remained to be settled with the Holy Roman Empire. In addition, absolutism, by its nature a threat to the revolution, still held sway over most of Europe. The Directory gave way to the next phase, the Consulate under Bonaparte, which opened the Napoleonic Wars.

The French revolutionaries had spent much time debating constitutions and formulating and approving them by plebiscite. The first, in 1791, resulted in the stillbirth of a constitutional monarchy. The second, in 1793, was never implemented. The third, in 1795, created the Directory, with the real power vested in the First Consul, Napoleon Bonaparte, who took up residence in the Tuileries on February 19, 1800. By 1802, he was proclaimed Consul for Life. A dictatorship was now established.

With the fall of Napoleon, a constitutional monarchy was instituted that survived until overthrown in 1848.

**French Political Structure, 1789–1804**

| *Legislative* | | | *Executive* |
|---|---|---|---|
| Estates-General (May 5–June 1789) | | | King 1774–92 |
| First Estate | Second Estate | Third Estate | |
| Clergy | Nobility | Common people (referred to itself as National Assembly June 17, 1789) | |

Three Estates merged June 27, 1789
National Constituent Assembly (June 1789–91)
Constitution
- Drawn up 1791
- Sanctioned by king, September 13, 1791
Legislative Assembly (October 1, 1791–September 20, 1792)
First French Republic declared
- Elected under 1791 Constitution
- Dissolved for republican Convention                    King overthrown, August 10, 1792

National Convention (September 20, 1792–October 26, 1795)
| Left: | The Mountain |
| Center: | The Plain |

Right:                    Gironde (to June 1793)

Election to establish new constitution

- Constitution June 24, 1793, never implemented
- Constitution of 1795 voted by the convention, August 22, 1795

King executed
January 21, 1793

Committee of Public
Safety (April 6, 1793–
October 26, 1795)

Thermidoreans

- Led coup that ousted Robespierre

Directory (October 26, 1795–November 9, 1799)          Five elected members

- Council of Elders 250 members

  Draft of 1795 constitution

- Council of 500 members
- Overthrown by Napoleon

Consulate (1799–1804)

- Napoleon appointed First Consul for life, August 1802
- France became a military dictatorship until 1812
- Napoleon defeated at Waterloo, 1815

Limited monarchy, Louis XVIII

---

## NOTES

1. The administrative departments of France set out during the revolution are those that remain today. The name France was derived from the Germanic tribe the Franks, which invaded the Roman empire across the Rhine River in the fifth century.

2. Doyle, 4.

3. Most Basques live on the Spanish side of the Pyrenees; fewer live in France.

4. Lough, 5.

5. Ibid., 6.

6. Young, 246.

7. The Enlightenment movement also had representatives in other countries, including Kant in Germany, David Hume in England, and Benjamin Franklin and Thomas Jefferson in the American colonies to mention a few. All maintained contacts with the French philosophers.

8. Schama, 65.

9. Ibid., 62.

10. Lewis (2004), 220.

11. Ministers of Finance under Louis XVI were Turgot (1774–76), Necker (1777–81), Calonne (1783–87), Brienne (1787-August 1788), Necker (September 1788–July 11, 1789), and Necker again from mid-July 1789 to September 1790.

12. Fouquier-Tinville served Robespierre during the Terror, then helped send him to the guillotine. He himself was arrested in Paris and executed on May 7, 1795, for his part in the Terror.

13. On February 24, the Convention passed a final version of the Maximum that introduced more uniformity and stricter punishments but kept the markets better supplied with food and curbed inflation. By December 1794, under the Thermidoreans, all price controls were lifted.

14. For this threat see Cobb/Jones, 200.

15. See Bosher, 192.

# 2

# ECONOMY

During the last decade of the old regime, new industries were emerging and old ones were being revitalized financed by bankers, wealthy noble entrepreneurs, and businessmen. The population was growing, and the wealth of the nation increased steadily. Wages did not keep up with rising prices, however, and the revenues of the government lagged far behind expenditures. Trust—a major factor in economic development—barely applied to the government under Louis XVI.[1] Investors in government securities could never be certain that interest would be forthcoming on the date due, or even that they would retrieve their money. To loan money to the government was, in effect, a speculative affair, since payment was based on the estimated future income of the crown derived from taxes. A poor harvest would, for example, reduce the amount received and thus the crown's ability to pay creditors. Private companies that built ships for the navy, supplied clothes to the army, or constructed or repaired roads and canals might wait years for payment. Treasury accounts were never audited, let alone published, and investors were always in the dark as to the crown's financial liabilities.

In 1789, the service of the public debt alone absorbed 300 million livres a year, or a little more than half the total revenue of the state. To its creditors, the government owed some 600 million livres, while many of these creditors were themselves in debt, having borrowed money to finance the enterprises they took on for the government.[2] The mismanagement of state finances, which in the past had affected only the crown and its administration, now began to ruin many private businesses, and, as a result, merchants, manufacturers, financiers, and businessmen began to demand reform of the country's monetary system.

## HEAVY INDUSTRY

In spite of economic growth, up to the time of the revolution industry was still in a rudimentary state. More than half of production was in textiles; other significant manufactures included metal working, glass-making, and construction. The process for the extraction of coal for both home heating and industrial furnaces was still primitive.[3]

Nevertheless, coal production throughout the country increased, rising from around 60,000 tons in 1700 to 600,000 tons by 1790.[4] The Anzin coalmines at Valenciennes employed 4,000 workers, who lived in miserable shacks and in unhealthy conditions and who worked long hours.

Philip Thickness, an English army officer, noted that many people in France thought coal was not only noxious but even dangerous to burn and that some servants refused to live with English families that burned it. The soap factories at Marseille used vast quantities of coal, much of it brought by ship from Newcastle for its better quality and price. One such factory employed between 800 and 1,000 people.[5]

By the time of the revolution, heavy industry was also producing more and more iron, although it did not meet domestic demand. Here, also, methods of production were outdated.

Another traveler to the area around Valenciennes remarked about the developing steel industry:

Wood is almost universally used throughout France for fuel, but in the neighbour-hood of the place coal is found, which they call charbon de terre. They have also some considerable works, which, upon inquiry, I found were steel ones; the French are daily gaining ground in the art of tempering this metal, and giving it that lustre and polish which has been carried to such perfection in this country [England].[6]

At Montcenis, another foundry visited by Arthur Young cast and bore cannon on a large scale, using steam engines, forges, and a horse-drawn railway. On August 3, 1789, he stated that the establishment was very considerable and employed from 500 to 600 men besides colliers.

Before the revolution, wood was the most important fuel, although it was rapidly becoming in short supply, which pushed the price up. In February 1787, an army officer wrote that wood was the most extravagant article both in Rouen and in Paris. A stick about two feet long and six inches in diameter, split in half, cost 12 sous. Keeping a moderate fire, the officer explained, used up 22 of these sticks in one day. Firewood was floated downstream on the Seine for many miles on rafts to reach Paris. Wading into the muddy water, men unloaded the precious fuel and carried it ashore on their backs.[7] It was obvious to many that as the forests declined, the population increased, and wood prices rose, coal would have to be used more generally for private use.

## LUXURY INDUSTRIES

A number of people found employment in industries whose products were bought by the wealthy. The famous glassworks at St. Gobain was seen by Young in October 1787.[8] The works employed some 1,800 men.

He described the procedure: when all was prepared for the running of the glass, an official entered and bolted the doors, and a man striking an iron bar on the ground gave the signal for silence. If anyone spoke thereafter, he was fined. The furnace was then opened and the 18-inch pots containing the melted glass were extracted. They were placed on a wheelbarrow and taken to the copper table by two men; a windlass was used to raise the pots and empty them onto the table. A great copper roller was then slowly pushed along over the glass, moving on two iron bars, flattening the glass by its weight. The thickness of the bars determined the thickness of the intended plate glass. The glass sheet was then pushed forward from the table into the oven that was heated to receive it for annealing (gradual cooling to prevent cracking). Young admired the simplicity and dexterity of the process. The abundance of wood for the fires was the reason the factory was established in the great forest owned by the duke of Orleans, from whom the company rented space.[9]

Mirrors were made in Paris on the rue St. Antoine and seem to have delighted many tourists, among whom was Alexander Jardine, who was very impressed with the process and commented on the superiority of the mirrors, whose manufacture employed 800 people.[10]

## TEXTILES AND OTHER PRODUCTS

The cities of Lyon and Nîmes became major centers of the silk manufacture in the eighteenth century. John Moore wrote that, after Paris, Lyon was the most magnificent city in France, enlivened by luxury industries that made it famous. Visitors or locals there could watch the making of gold and silver thread for the lace industry or the intricate making of velvet.[11] In other places of any size, smaller but numerous commercial enterprises seemed to thrive. Arthur Young mentioned that the town of Montpellier had "narrow, ill-built, crooked streets, but full of people, and apparently alive with business; yet there is no considerable manufacture in the place."[12] Products included verdigrease (a green or blue pigment), silk handkerchiefs, blankets, perfumes, and liqueurs.

Most small towns had a few artisans, bakers, shoemakers, harness makers, wheelwrights, and blacksmiths, but more important for the locals were rural industries, such as textile manufacture, located throughout the country, that employed thousands of people, working out of their own homes. Urban entrepreneurs, resorting to rural production to avoid high wages and the continuous labor strife in the cities, supplied the materials and yarn to the private weavers, who were paid by the piece. The cloth was then sent back to city workshops for finishing. Some of the major linen and woolen centers were Lille, Reims, Beauvais, and Amiens.

In Châteauroux, Young found some 18 private weavers working in their own houses, producing cloth that was sold on both the national and the international markets. Women and children were an essential part of these cottage industries, and the spread of manufacture to the countryside allowed many poor peasant farmers with small plots of land to supplement their incomes. How much improvement was made to their lives is debatable, however. The rural weavers were generally the poorest in the countryside, more so than the village blacksmith or baker or the general mass of cultivators.

An anonymous soldier, visiting Rouen in 1787 and walking in the surrounding countryside, noted women and children at work in the villages for the local linen factory. The fields were covered with linen of various colors, and some was twisted around the trees that lined the streets. Every rivulet turned two or three mills. The women and children all seemed to be employed, and all were very diligent. He looked into a number of their huts to see what benefits they derived from the labor and noted that they "were the picture of misery & famine."[13]

On the outskirts of many of the older cities, cottage industries proliferated. For example, in and around Grenoble, 60 master glovers employed about 6,000 men and women who cut, dressed, and scented hides and then stitched and embroidered the finished product.[14]

By the eighteenth century, cotton goods were manufactured in Rouen, where their production increased threefold around the middle of the century. A factory at Jouy-en-Rosas, near Paris, had 800 workers by the time of the revolution. Throughout the country, 300 printed cloth manufacturers employed 25,000 people by 1789.[15]

Arthur Young provided information on the state of French industry in Beauvais in 1787. He examined a tapestry works, a calico printing house, and a textile establishment where the primary fabric was wool. The industry in town and in the adjacent countryside employed 7,000 to 8,000 workers. Using French wool, they made "course stuffs for the clothing of the country people, for men's jackets and women's petticoats.... There are also stocking engines at work."[16]

He also visited the Normandy cloth factories at Louviers on October 8, 1788. This was one of the principal cloth manufacturing towns in the country, and at least one of the mills, according to him, produced the most beautiful and the finest materials he had ever seen. It came from pure, natural Peruvian wool, not from sheep (presumably from llamas). Other fabrics, such as Spanish wool, were spun in the nearby countryside, where a good spinner could do a pound a day.

Industry in Rouen had a boost from a few capitalists who imported English equipment and created modern spinning factories. By the end of the old regime, this city, with a reputation of being the worst-smelling and most unhealthy town in northern France, was producing woolen hose, hats, porcelain, paper, refined sugar, glass, soap, copper products, and sulfuric acid, among other items.[17]

In 1762, a Parisian merchant transferred his gauze factory from the capital to near Saint-Quentin, no doubt to find a cheaper and less unruly labor force. Here, 1,000 of his looms turned out mixed silk and cotton gauze. The manufacture of tapestries at the Gobelins factory attracted countless visitors, as did the producers of royal porcelain at Sèvres, owned by the crown. Both drew clients as well as the curious. Thomas Bentley was in Paris for about three weeks in the summer of 1776, and he left notes in which he states:

This manufactory [at Sèvres] was begun and is supported at the expense of the King in a very magnificent building about 5 miles from Paris, on the left hand side of the road to Versailles. I have been through the magazines and several of the workshops, and find a great many fine things and a great many people employed: about 1 dozen carvers or modellers and near 100 painters, and other workmen of course in proportion. The workshops are very commodious and well fitted up, and there are several fine appartments left for his Majesty when he chooses to visit the manufactory.[18]

By the time of the revolution, France was producing more porcelain, wine, and brandy than anywhere else. Philip Thickness advised English travelers that they need go no further south than Lyon, "a rich, noble and plentiful town, abounding with everything that is good, and more finery than even in Paris itself."[19]

Beer was popular in northern Europe, but less so in France. There was a huge decline in beer drinking between 1750 and 1780, and the number of brewers in Paris fell from 75 to 23. Production dropped from 75,000 hogheads (each containing 286 liters) to 26,000. Many brewers turned to producing cider, which depended on apples, most of which came from Normandy. There was no improvement in beer production up to the time of the revolution. Wine was the choice of the people. From 1781 to 1786, total wine consumption in Paris rose to 730,000 hectoliters (73 million liters), while beer consumption was about 54,000 hectoliters—a 1:13 ratio.[20]

## WAGES, CURRENCY, AND COST OF LIVING

In large cities, the majority of manual workers and artisans were engaged in the food, textile, and construction industries. Such workers made up about half the population of Paris. About 16 percent of the inhabitants were in domestic service, and about 8.4 percent were in the king's service. A mass of unskilled workers and beggars accounted for somewhere around 25 percent of the population. The census of 1791 recorded 118,784 paupers.[21]

A little prior to the revolution, there was a 65 percent increase in prices, primarily for food, and above all for bread, which seems to have made up half the expenses of the average household.[22] This rise in prices was occurring while the general wage increased only 22 percent. The population of France increased notably in the eighteenth century, and the resulting surplus of labor contributed to a reduction in workers' wages. It has been estimated that in the 1780s, coalface workers received 20 to 25 sous per workday, while those who removed the coal from the mine earned between 10 and 20 sous. Both the St. Gobain glassworks in Picardy and the Tubeuf coal-mining company in Languedoc were among those that used child labor (boys 7 to 12 years old) for menial jobs such as sweeping out the ashes from the furnaces of the glassworks or pulling baskets of coal along pathways like donkeys. The pittance they earned, five or six sous a day, helped in a small way with family expenses. At the glassworks, unskilled laborers could make up to 20 sous a day, semiskilled workers up to about 30, and skilled workers up to 60 sous. Often, entire families had to work to make ends meet, but women were generally paid about half as much as men.

In Paris, an exceptional journeyman printer earned about 680 livres per annum. A journeyman builder made around 472 livres a year if he managed to work 225 days. In most cases, work was not available every day, or other matters such as illness might keep workers at home, for which they received no pay. It has been estimated that journeymen silk workers in Lyon earned 374 livres a year in 1786; no provision for their lodging and meals was provided. It has also been reckoned that 435 livres annually was the minimum needed to maintain a family of four at subsistence level. Near the end of the eighteenth century, the unskilled worker made about 350 livres a year.

In the manufacture of printed fabrics, wages varied from 40 to 80 sous a day for skilled work, but unskilled workers, usually women, earned only about 10 sous, about enough for a four-pound loaf of bread. Any surplus went to rent and supper, if the woman was single, in a cheap cafe.[23]

The time people spent working was long by any standard. An Englishwoman, Mary Berry, traveled in France from February 1784 to June 1785[24] and left the following account:

Went in the morning to several manufacturers, to silk mills, and to see cut velvet wove—the most complicated of all the looms. A weaver working assiduously from 5 in the morning to 9 at night cannot make above half a yard and a quarter a day of a stuff for which they are paid by the mercers eight livres a yard. A weaver of brocade gold-stuff, working the same number of hours, cannot make above half a yard, and the payment uncertain. All these weavers, lodged up in the fourth and fifth stories of dirty stinking houses, surprised me by the propriety and civility of their manner, and their readiness to satisfy all our questions.[25]

Young reports a similar situation where a day's work in fabrics meant 15 or 16 hours; there was time off for meals.[26]

There were about 2 million domestic servants in France in 1789. They were paid low wages, but room, board, and uniforms were provided. Before the revolution, male servants in Aix were paid some 90 livres a year, whereas a woman servant earned only 35 to 50. A male cook made 120 livres per annum, a female cook half as much. Wages were higher in Paris, where some 40,000 servants worked. Stableboys there could earn anywhere from 120 to 450 livres a year; in provincial cities, however, their income might only be 60 or 70 livres. By 1789, wages had risen about 40 percent for women and only marginally for men,[27] but the daily wage for an unskilled worker was still little better than that of a peasant.[28]

## UNEMPLOYMENT AND MIGRATORY WORKERS

It was believed by most people that there was always work for those who wanted it. In the rural areas, work could be found in the fields, while in the urban environments there were jobs for doormen, street porters, water carriers, and couriers to pick up and deliver luggage, goods, or letters. Some institutions that hired men and boys for such tasks included the courts, the markets, and the prisons.[29] Street sweepers and bootblacks were common, the latter especially so since animal dung on one's shoes was a constant nuisance. All these people, however, were looked upon with suspicion by the police since they were not property owners. For almost anything unusual, they were likely to be detained and sometimes exiled from the locality.

It was common for the unemployed to migrate from rural to urban areas looking for work, and sometimes the movement went the other way around, but movement from one place to another was also suspect. Itinerant vendors and tinkers found it advisable to openly display their wares and tools to avoid police inquiries and made sure they were always able to show where they got their merchandise. Farm migrants and journeymen on the move needed to obtain papers from their local authorities to prove they were not vagrants and to avoid the charge of gens sans aveu, or people for whom no respectable person would vouch. Incarceration was always a definite prospect if identity papers were missing. The step from migrant to vagrant or vagabond in the eyes of the police and the general public was quick and easy; it often led to the next step, which everyone feared—brigandage. Beggars, often unfit for work, were especially mistrusted.

## AGRICULTURE

Eighteenth-century France was predominantly agricultural, as the country had been since Roman times. Of the population of about 26 million in the last decades of the century, some 21 million lived by farming. While about 40 percent of the land was owned by peasants, the great majority of them possessed fewer than 20 acres, about the size necessary to support a family.[30] The church, nobles, and rich bourgeoisie owned the remainder.[31]

At the time of the revolution, agriculture accounted for around three-quarters of the national product. Yet, grain surpluses were slight and hardly sufficed for feeding the towns and areas of low productivity. The people of Paris, of course, consumed an enormous amount of grain.

Peasants, seldom fully outright owners of land, had specific rights on it. While they might pass land on to their offspring, they owed obligations and dues to the seigneurial lords. The value of these dues had dropped considerably over the years, and landlords often tried to extract additional money from the peasants or to reinstitute manorial rights that had fallen into disuse. Another source of discord was the increasing curtailment of common land on which the inhabitants of a village could graze their livestock. As the commons were sold off, peasants had fewer places to feed their animals, leading to more poverty.

From his harvest the farmer had to deduct the tithe to the church, royal and seigneurial taxes, enough seed for the following year's planting and enough to feed his family until the next harvest. Then, if there was a surplus, it could be sold at market and the money used to buy supplies for the farm. The peasant-farmer's position was always precarious. If bad weather or other circumstances reduced his harvest by only 12.5 percent and he was used to having a 25 percent surplus, his surplus, and thus his income, would be cut in half, since his other obligations had to be filled first. The impact on the markets and in the cities would also amount to a 50 percent reduction in the availability of the product.[32]

Many peasants were forced to seek paid but low-wage work for part of the year on larger, more prosperous farms. When weather or disease destroyed the crops and animals, people died by the thousands from malnutrition or outright starvation.

The degree of agricultural growth in the eighteenth century has been a much-debated subject, but overall it seems that development was slow and methods outdated up to and beyond the period of the revolution. While more and more land was cleared for agricultural development, the growing population boosted consumption but did not provide greater surpluses for the cities and towns. Cereal accounted for about half the crop, with wheat in the vanguard.

## REGIONAL FAIRS

Fairs gave a boost to regional economies and attracted people from near and far. At one fair in Normandy, French, English, Dutch, and other merchants showed and sold their wares, endeavoring to open new markets for their goods. One of the largest of such fairs was at Beaucaire, at the southern end of the Rhône valley. It was visited by the dowager countess of Carlisle, who described it in a letter dated July 1779:

The addition of an hundred thousand people every day has not a little added to the heat, or rather suffocation, but if afforded me a most agreeable spectacle for the time, and I am very glad to have seen it. The Rhone covered with vessels; the bridge with passengers; the vast meadow filled with booths, in the manner of the race-ground at York; and the inns crowded with merchants and merchandize, was very entertaining, although it was impossible, after seven in the morning, to bear the streets. The kind of things the fair produced were not such as you could have approved of for Lady Carlisle. The only thing I liked was a set of ornamented perfumed baskets for a toilet, which were indeed very pretty, but which it would have been impossible for me to have got over [to England]. The fair, indeed, seems more calculated for merchants than for idle travelers; no bijouterie, no argenterie, no nick-nacks or china. For about thirty shillings, however, one can buy a very pretty silk dress, with the trimmings to it; muslins are also very cheap; painted silks beautiful; and scents, pommades, and liqueurs, very cheap.[33]

On his way to Nîmes in 1787, Arthur Young remarked on the fair at Beaucaire. Although he did not attend it, he wrote that the countryside all around was alive with people and many loaded carts going to or coming from it. The following day, at Nîmes, he described his hotel as being practically a fair in itself, with activity from morning till night. From 20 to 40 diners represented, in his words, the "most motley companies of French, Italians, Spanish and Germans, with a Greek and [an] Armenian." Merchants from many places were represented there, but they were chiefly interested in the raw silk, most of which was sold out within four days. The fair was still going on in the summer of 1789 and attracting crowds.

Edward Rigby, a doctor from Norwich, encountered great numbers of people on the road from Nîmes to Beaucaire on July 28, 1789. In the city,

The streets were full of people, every house was a shop, and a long quay was crowded with booths full of different kinds of merchandise. Besides these there were a number of vessels in the Rhone, lying alongside the quay, full of articles for sale, and no less crowded with people, access being had to them by boards laid from one to the other.[34]

## FOREIGN TRADE

In lean years of crop-destroying weather, grain was imported from the eastern Mediterranean through the port of Marseille. The prosperous city of Nantes was also a thriving seaport, and when Young arrived there in 1788, he described the commerce:

The accounts I received here of the trade of the place, made the number of ships in the sugar trade 120, which import to the amount of about 32 millions; 20 are in the slave trade; these are by far the greatest articles of their commerce; they have an export of corn, [grain] which is considerable from the provinces washed by the Loire…. Wines and brandy are great articles, and manufactures even from Switzerland, particularly printed linens and cottons, in imitation of Indian, which the Swiss make cheaper than the French fabrics of the same kind, yet they are brought quite across France.[35]

He was again impressed by the trade when visiting Le Havre in 1788. On August 16, he found the city "fuller of motion, life and activity, than any place I have been in France." He continued:

There is not only an immense commerce carried on here, but it is on a rapid increase; there is no doubt its being the fourth town in France for trade. The harbour is a forest of masts…. They have some very large merchantmen in the Guinea trade of 500 or 600 tons but by far their greatest commerce is to the West-India Sugar Islands…. Situation must of necessity give them a great coasting trade, for as ships of burthen cannot go up to Rouen, this place is the emporium for that town, for Paris, and all the navigation of the Seine, which is very great.[36]

A few days later, on August 18, Young was in Honfleur, seven and a half miles up the Seine from Le Havre on the south bank where the estuary is still wide enough for large ships. He noted: "Honfleur is a small town, full of industry, and a bason [sic] full of ships, with some Guineamen [probably slave ships] as large as Le Havre."[37]

From records and from observers' notes, it is clear that French commerce in foreign trade, employing many thousands of people, was flourishing up to the time of the revolution. In 1787, 82.8 percent of French exports went to European countries and the Ottoman Empire, while 57.5 percent of trade was in the form of imports such as sugar from the West Indies or spices from the East. The re-export trade of colonial goods also thrived. Of the 9,500 kilograms of coffee that arrived in 1790, 7,940 were exported.[38] Much of the country's commercial prosperity rested on the colonial economy, and very profitable trade was conducted with the French West Indies, especially in sugar. The cities of Bordeaux, Nantes, and Rouen were the major beneficiaries of this commerce.

May 1787 brought a blow to French industry in the form of the Eden Treaty with England, which removed many tariffs and angered French manufacturers and their workers, since they all knew that they could not compete in price with English products. Some French entrepreneurs wanted a war with England to cut off the importation of their goods and to save their own industries. The major problem was that England was buying very little in the way of French fabrics, pottery, grains, meat, or anything else, while English goods flooded into France and were readily sold. Some citizens of Paris held a more optimistic view that English competition would in the long run improve the quality of competitive French products and that eventually France would benefit more than England.

The revolution and subsequent war with England ended further conjecture on the subject.

## FISHING

The Loire was famous for salmon and carp, and the Rhine for perch; but fishermen had to be authorized to fish, even in the Seine. More lucrative perhaps was open-sea fishing. In 1773, records indicate there were 264 French boats of 25 tons and about 10,000 crewmen.[39] The boats were primarily cod boats used for fishing on the Grand Banks of Newfoundland and in Icelandic waters. Le Havre and Honfleur were the principal ports that supplied Paris with cod, while Nantes supplied the Loire region, St. Malo provided Brittany and Normandy with fish, and Marseille took care of the south. Two fleets went out each year, the first leaving in January and returning in July and the second leaving in March, to return in November. The fish was either salted or dried for preservation. Paris also received cod caught off English coasts by English fishermen and imported via Dieppe.

For Norman communities, especially St. Malo, cod was the "beef of the sea," and the French continued to fish from bases around the Gulf of St. Lawrence and St. Pierre and Miquelon in spite of growing English dominance. In northern regions, wet or salted cod was preferred, while the more thoroughly processed dried cod went to the south. In 1772, the largest distributor of cod in Europe was the port city of Marseille, which sent the fish throughout the region and to Spain, Italy, and other Mediterranean locations.

Besides cod, herring was imported and arrived in the large cities such as Paris by river and by the chasse-marées who carried them on horseback from the north coasts to the denizens of the city. They rode all night, horses weighted down with herring and oysters, so that those who could afford it could have fresh seafood. Imported herring from countries like Holland carried very high tariffs, and most people could not pay the price. Food from the sea was often supplanted inland by local fish from rivers and streams, sold on the market by licensed fishermen.[40]

## REVOLUTION AND THE ECONOMY

Figures show that the total value of the country's trade in 1795 was less than half what it had been in 1789; by 1815, it was still only 60 percent of what it had been at the beginning of the revolution.[41]

More than any other class of people, perhaps, the manufacturers felt the effects of the revolution the most profoundly. The rivalry with English textile makers, strong in 1787 and 1788; the revolutionary movement in 1789 in which so many landlords, clergy, and those in public employment lost income; the emigration of the wealthy classes, causing unemployment for many others; the falling value of the assignats—all combined to lower purchasing power and industrial output. Those whose investments were safe nevertheless restricted their buying and hoarded their money, apprehensive about the unsettled state and the prospect of civil war. The result was, predictably, immense unemployment and a starving population, especially in the big cities.

On December 29, 1789, Young visited Lyon and conversed with the citizens. Twenty thousand people were unemployed, badly fed by charity; industry was in a dismal state; and the distress among the lower classes was the worst they had ever experienced. The cause of the problem was attributed to stagnation of trade resulting from the emigration of the rich. Bankruptcies were common.

The Constituent Assembly's economic reforms were guided by laissez-faire doctrine, along with hostility to privileged corporations that resembled too much those of the old regime. The Assembly wanted to make opportunities accessible to every man and to promote individual initiative. It dismantled internal tariffs, along with chartered trading monopolies, and abolished the guilds of merchants and artisans. Every citizen was given the right to enter any trade and to freely conduct business. Regulation of wages would no longer be of government concern, nor would the quality of the product. Workers, the Assembly insisted, must bargain in the economic marketplace as individuals; it thereby banned associations and strikes. Similar precepts of economic individualism applied to the countryside. Peasants and landlords were free to cultivate their fields as they liked, regardless of traditional collective practices. Communal traditions, however, were deep-seated and resistant to change.

The Atlantic and Mediterranean port cities, all centers of developing capitalist activity, had suffered from antifederalist repression and from English naval blockades. In textile towns such as Lille, the decline was abrupt and ruinous. No matter what business they were in, tailors, wigmakers, watchmakers—all those engaged in businesses related to deluxe items or pursuits—lost their clientele. Even shoemakers suffered along with other lower-class enterprises, except for the very few who managed to get contracts to supply the military. In heavy industry such as iron and cannon manufacture, some opportunities were provided by the continuing warfare, which tended to focus capital and labor on the provision of armaments.[42] For most businesses, however, the situation appeared gloomy.

In 1790, while in Paris, Young learned that the cotton mills in Normandy had stood still for nine months. Many spinning jennies had been destroyed by the locals, who believed they were Satan's invention and would put them out of work. Trade, Young said, was in a deplorable condition.[43]

All cities were in a sad state and remained so throughout the revolutionary period. When Samuel Romilly returned to Bordeaux in 1802, during a period of peace with England, he was grieved to see the silent docks and the grass growing long between the flagstones of the quays. The sugar trade with the West Indies continued to flourish, but in port cities connected to the slave trade, people were alarmed over talk in the National

Convention about freeing the blacks, who provided the labor for the colonial sugar industry.

## THE ASSIGNAT

Preceding the revolution, the basic money of account was the livre, of which three made an écu, and 24 livres equaled one louis. The livre was made up of 20 sous (the older term was sols), and the sous was divided into 12 deniers. (The system was similar to that used in England—pounds, shillings, and pence—until the 1970s.)

On December 19, 1789, to redeem the huge public debt and to counterbalance the growing deficit, the revolutionary Constituent Assembly issued treasury notes or bonds called assignats, to the amount of 400

The value of the assignats depreciated rapidly. The beggar symbolizes the subsequent ruin of thousands of investors. Bibliothèque Nationale de France.

million livres distributed in 1,000-livre notes. These were intended as short-term obligations pending the sale of confiscated lands formerly owned by the nobility and the church and were distributed to creditors of the state to be exchanged for land of equal value or redeemed at 5 percent interest. The assignats were then to be liquidated, reducing government debt. Neither the economy nor the royal tax revenues increased as quickly as the deputies had hoped; assignats were made legal tender in April 1790, and subsequent issues bore no interest.

In the autumn of 1790, the government issued another 400 million in assignats. In following years, more and more were issued in smaller denominations of 50 livres, then 5 livres, and, finally, 10 sous. By January 1793, about 2.3 billion assignats were in circulation. The paper currency rapidly became inflated, and people hoarded metallic coins that had been used previously. By July 1793, a 100-livre note was only worth 23 livres.

The stringent financial measures put in place during the Terror temporarily stabilized the value of the assignat at one-third of its face value. However, by early 1796, under the Directory, inflation again increased dramatically, and the assignats in circulation were worth less than 1 percent of their original value. This did not even cover the cost of printing them. Severe inflation stopped only when all paper currency was recalled and redeemed at the rate of 3,000 livres in assignats to one franc in gold. On May 21, 1797, all unredeemed assignats were declared void.

## TAXATION

The company Farmers-General purchased the privilege of collecting taxes and paying state debts for the various government departments. Taxes thus passed through private hands, and some of it wound up in private pockets. There was no central bank to provide economic stability, only a group of businessmen who sought to find the best balance between a functioning government and their own profits. The tax farmer advanced a specified sum of money to the royal treasury and then collected a like sum in taxes. Given exceptional powers to collect the money, tax farmers bore arms, conducted searches, and imprisoned uncooperative citizens. The money collected over and above that specified in the contract with the government went to the tax farm. Tax farmers were usually rich men and hated by the general public.

There were various kinds of taxes levied in different parts of the country. The taille was a direct tax collected on property and goods; the clergy and the nobility were exempt from this levy, and the peasants bore the brunt. Indirect taxes included the *gabelle*, or salt tax, a duty on tobacco, the aides, which were excise duties collected on the manufacture, sale, and consumption of a commodity, and the traites, customs duties collected internally. There was no uniformity, and some sections of the country bore heavier tax burdens than others. The main direct tax, the taille, was levied by the crown on total income in the northern provinces but only on income from landed property in the south.

## SALT TAX

The government monopoly on salt went back as far as the thirteenth century; the salt was extracted from seawater ponds that were left to dry out. The detested salt tax (*gabelle*) had become a leading source of royal income and was levied at different rates in various parts of the country.[44] In some regions, everyone over eight years of age was required to purchase seven kilos of salt each year at a fixed government price. In other regions, people were required to purchase a fixed quantity of salt per household. There were other areas where the salt tax did not apply (*pays exempt*), such as the Basque country and Brittany. Fortunes were made in the illegal transport of salt.

The collectors and enforcers of the salt tax were often crude, abusive men who were allowed to carry arms and to stop and search whomever they pleased. They were not above looking for contraband by squeezing the choicest parts of women who had no recourse but to suffer the humiliation. Women sometimes did hide bags of salt in corsets and other places where they hoped not to be squeezed; some concealed it in false rears of their dresses. Salt rebellions were frequent, and battles sometimes erupted between smugglers and tax collectors.

The Loire River was notorious for the movement of contraband, since it separated tax-free Brittany from heavily taxed Anjou; the price for salt was 591 sous per minot (49 kilos) in Anjou but 31 sous in Brittany, which was exempt from the tax thanks to an agreement reached with the crown when Brittany became part of France. The large number of families working the salt ponds there were in the best position to ferry the salt across the river, so the government passed a no-fishing-at-night law to curb the illegal trade and stationed troops along the banks of the river in an attempt to end the smuggling. The *gabelle* was abolished by the revolution but was reinstated 15 years later; it continued in force until 1945.[45]

## NOTES

1. See Francois, Introduction.
2. De Tocqueville, in Greenlaw, 14.
3. Aftalion, 34.
4. For similar figures, see Lewis (2004), 179.
5. Lough, 88.
6. Quoted in ibid., 111.
7. Ibid., 108.
8. Young, 105.
9. Quoted in Lough, 107–8.
10. Ibid., 79.

11. Ibid., 84.
12. Young, 49.
13. Lough, 102–3.
14. Schama, 193.
15. Lewis (2004), 180.
16. Lough, 99.
17. Schama, 194.
18. Lough, 77.
19. Ibid., 84.
20. Braudel, 239.
21. See Aftelion, 35.
22. Greenlaw, 92.
23. See Lewis (2004), 124ff.
24. Lough, 85.
25. Ibid.
26. Ibid., 120.
27. Lewis (2004), 133.
28. For wages and costs, see Rudé (1959), Appendix VII, and Garrioch, 35, 48, 52–3, 307, 309.
29. Andress (2004), 56.
30. Hibbert, 29.
31. Aftelion, 32.
32. Ibid., 37.
33. See Lough, 117.
34. Ibid., 118.
35. Ibid., 97.
36. Quoted in Lough, 98.
37. Young, 116.
38. Lewis (2004), 181.
39. Braudel, 218.
40. Ibid., 215.
41. Schama, 185.
42. Ibid., 853.
43. Young, 295.
44. Kurlansky, 226.
45. For more on the salt tax, see Kurlansky, 231–33.

# 3

# TRAVEL

At the end of the Seven Years War, swarms of English people visited France, and some left accounts of their travels there. Later, hostilities between France and England during the American War of Independence nearly dried up the flow of English tourists to Paris and the provinces, but it still did not stop entirely, and the return to peace in 1783 brought another influx of Britons to French shores.

Travelers to France. especially those from England, were always surprised by the great distances and the plethora of internal customs houses. Further, they found that there was no national language either spoken or understood by a great many of the illiterate inhabitants and no uniform system of administration, laws, taxes, weights and measures.

Although French people did not seem to travel much within their own country, those who did, with interests different from those of foreign visitors, have also left accounts that help portray the daily life of the time. About half of the members of the Convention were sent out on assignments to the departments (administrative districts) or to the army, and some reports of their missions are available. For many, such as a representative from Paris, a journey to the south was like going to a foreign land.

## MODES OF TRANSPORT

Major rivers in France, such as the Seine, Loire, Saône, Rhône, and Garonne, had long been used as a means of transportation. To supplement the river system and move cargo, some important canals were built in the seventeenth century, including the Brienne, Orléans, and Languedoc. The Canal du Midi, running from Toulouse to Béziers, made it possible to link the Atlantic Ocean with the Mediterranean through southwest France. One could travel on riverboats pulled by horses along the banks that in Paris embarked from the Palais Royal or the bridge of Saint Paul. Arrangements for private travel on commercial barges or riverboats over long distances seemed not to appeal to many who, for whatever reason, preferred to go by horse and carriage. For this manner of travel, the transportation system was in place, with scheduled stops and prices. One could, for example, go to the Royal General Bureau of Coaches and Freight and book a trip to anywhere in the realm.

By the late eighteenth century, the region of the Ile de France had the best-constructed roads in Europe, greatly admired by foreigners. However, when traveling by horse drawn vehicles over large distances, travelers found that the roads sometimes became just bumpy tracks and that the journey was slow and tedious. Going to Bordeaux or Strasbourg from Paris took six days; traveling to Toulouse took seven or eight days, and to Marseille, nine days.

Most of the time, it was impossible to move heavy loads conveniently outside the well-paved postal roads, and, according to Adam Smith, to travel on horseback was difficult. Mules, he thought, were the only conveyance that could be trusted.[1]

Despite the fact that roads in some places were excellent by the standards of the day, others, such as the road from Aix to Marseille, were, in the words of Mary Berry, "abominable"; she wrote, "The narrow wheels of the loaded charrettes of this country would spoil the best road in a short time, and the more so from the heavy weights being placed upon two instead of upon four wheels."[2]

In 1780, the countess of Carlisle had a similar complaint when she wrote from Montpellier that after heavy rains she was compelled to delay her journey to Lyon, maybe for a month, and that the traffic in carts cut the roads to pieces.

Other travelers, among them Arthur Young, found very little traffic on the roads;[3] Doctor Charles Burney met not a single carriage, horse, or foot traveler between St. Omar and Paris the entire day; and the lawyer Harry Peckman found the road from Chantilly to Calais depressing partly because it had so little traffic. Some years earlier, the naturalist Thomas Pennant had spent a night in a wretched inn at Ecouen, fifteen miles from Paris. There were few people at the inn and even fewer on the road to the capital, where he saw only one coach.[4]

Variations of coaches included the light, one-horse, two-wheeled *cabriolet*, with a removable top and room for two passengers, that was often used as a taxicab in the cities, as was the four-wheeled *fiacre*, with a high chassis for better viewing, glass windows, and room for four people. The deluxe, four-wheeled *berline*, with good suspension, comfortable seats, and glass windows, was pulled by six horses and was often employed for long-distance travel, along with the six-horse *diligence,* a kind of stage-coach with room for passengers and goods, which traveled at about six miles per hour.

Some coaches were built for speed with space for merchandise and dispatches as well as a few passengers. Others were exceptionally sturdy and built to carry heavy loads of merchandise, such as the *fourgon.* The trip from Calais to Paris by *fourgon* took six days; by *diligence,* the travel time was two and a half days. How much a person was willing to spend decided on the manner of travel. The mail coaches, solid but elegant with a high chassis, windows, was pulled by four to six horses; it also took people and would make unscheduled stops along the route to pick up or discharge passengers. Anyone interested in taking a trip could go to the offices of the conveyer or look through the *divers* announcements in the newspapers:

### NOTICE

Proposed Voyage Monday, the 7th of this month, at 7.00 P.M. precisely, a superb berline with 8 new and solid seats, will be leaving Paris. Travellers are invited to come and see it at the following address: M. Rebut, manufacturer of soft drinks, rue Saint Denis, at the corner of rue Aux Ours. This berline can transport all luggage, packages, trunks, effects and other important things as well as the travellers, at the price set by the National Assembly. It is going to Angers; the driver will do all that is expected of him to take travellers who would like to go on to Nantes in a comfortable manner and at the lowest possible price.

CP 3 May, 1792.

### INNS

Tobias George Smollett arrived in Boulogne in June 1763 and proceeded to Paris on his way to the Mediterranean coast. Frustrated by the inso-lence of coachmen, he launched into a diatribe on the inconveniences of the road, complaining that in France

if you are retarded by any accident, you cannot in many parts of the kingdom find a lodging, without perhaps travelling two or three posts farther than you would choose to go, to the prejudice of your health, and even the hazard of your life, whereas, on any part of the post-road in England, you will meet with tolerable accommodation at every stage.[5]

Having crossed France on his way to visit the Pyrenees Mountains along the Spanish border, with the town of Luchon his ultimate destina-tion, Arthur Young also compared the lodgings he stayed in with those of England.[6] He found some French inns better than the English ones in two respects: the food and drink were superior in France, and the prices cheaper. Otherwise, he complained:

they roast every thing to a chip, if they are not cautioned: but they give such a number and variety of dishes that if you do not like some, there are others to please your palate. … We sometimes have met with bad wine, but upon the whole, far better than such port as English inns give.

He goes on to say that in the French inns, there was

no parlour to eat in; only the room with two, three, or four beds. Apartments badly fitted up; the walls white-washed; or paper of different sorts in the same room; or tapestry so old, as to be a fit nidus for moths and spiders; and the furniture such that an English innkeeper would light his fire with it. For a table, you have every-where a board laid on cross bars, which are so conveniently contrived, as to leave room for your legs only at the end.—Oak chairs with rush bottoms, and the back universally a direct perpendicular, that defies all idea of rest after fatigue. Doors give music as well as entrance; the wind whistles through their chinks; and hinges grate discord. Windows admit rain as well as light; when shut they are not so easy to open; and when open not easy to shut.

Other comments include,

Mops, brooms, and scrubbing-brushes are not in the catalogue of the necessaries of a French inn. Bells there are none; the *fille* must always be bawled for; and when she appears, is neither neat well dressed, nor handsome. The kitchen is black with smoke; the master commonly the cook, and the less you see of the cooking, the more likely you are to have a stomach to your dinner.… Copper utensils always in great plenty, but not always well tinned. The mistress rarely classes civility or attention to her guests among the requisites of her trade.[7]

Young found it awkward to live in his bedroom but observed that every-one, regardless of rank, did so. The price of the room at Luchon was about four livres a day; locating a place to stable horses was not always easy, and, while hay and oats could be found, straw was expensive, and often there was none at all.

"Horrible holes" was the way Young referred to the public spa or baths of the town:

the patients lie up to their chins in hot sulphureous water, which with the beastly dens they are placed in, one would think sufficient to cause as many distempers as they cure. They are resorted to for cutaneous eruptions.[8]

This intrepid traveler, leaving Gange on May 30, 1787, and arriving at Montadier, found it

a beggarly village, with an auberge that made me almost shrink. Some cut throat figures were eating black bread, whose visages had so much of the gallies that I thought I heard their chains rattle. I looked at their legs, and could not but imagine they had no business to be free. There is a species of countenance here so horridly bad, that it is impossible to be mistaken in one's reading.[9]

Alone, and unarmed, Young now wished he had his pistols with him. The master of the inn, not unlike his guests, procured for him some wretched bread, but there was no meat, eggs, or vegetables and only abominable wine. There was no corn, grass, hay, or straw for Young's mule, so he took a portion of the large loaf of bread for himself and gave the rest to his four-footed friend, to the disgust of the innkeeper.

From there Young moved on to Lodève, which he described as a "dirty, ugly ill-built town, with crooked close streets, but populous, and very industrious." Here he found "excellent, light and pleasing white wine." On another occasion, he had reason to complain about the inn at St. Geronds (St. Girons), where the Croix Blanche was, in his words, "the most execrable receptacle of fifth, vermin, impudence, and imposition that ever exercised the patience, or wounded the feelings of a traveller. A withered hag, the daemon [demon] of beastliness, presides there."

Young tells us that he lay, not rested, in a chamber over a stable whose odor, entering through the broken floor, was the least offensive of the perfumes afforded by this hideous place. An English hog would have turned from this place in disgust. He could get nothing to eat here but two stale eggs, for which he paid 20 sous. He did find some reasonable inns along the way, but the bad ones, which were the majority, seemed to stick in his mind the most. However, on September 22, 1788, Young discovered at Rennes what he considered to be one of the best hotels in France. He found the quarter of the *Comédie* most agreeable, with streets at right angles and of white stone, where the Hotel Henri IV contained 60 beds for masters and 25 stables. The rooms were clean and reasonably priced; for merchants the cost was five livres per diem for room, dinner, supper, and wine; the charge for a horse was 35 sous.[10]

In August 1789, he was in the Ardèche with the purpose of examining some volcanos in the region. Making inquiries about hiring a mule and a guide, he aroused suspicion among the local people. Why would anyone want to see mountains that did not concern him? He was refused both. A little later, he received a message from the marquis Deblou, seigneur of the parish, who cautioned him about taking any excursion away from the main road, as people in the area were suspicious of him. That night, at eleven o'clock, after he had fallen asleep, about 20 of the local militia burst into his room armed with muskets, pikes, and old swords. The commander demanded his passport. They had decided that he was a pretended Englishman and a spy for the queen and the count d'Artois, as well as for the count d'Entragues, who owned property in the area. They insisted he was there to measure the local fields in order to raise the people's taxes. With difficulty Young proved to them, through letters and papers, that he was English and quite harmless. Finally, they bade him good night and left.[11]

On December 2, 1789, having stopped at Nemours, Young met the most conniving innkeeper he had yet encountered. Supper consisted of a thin soup, a partridge, a roasted chicken, a plate of celery, a small cauliflower, two bottles of poor local wine, and a dessert of two biscuits and four apples. Including the room and fire, the bill was extortionate at 19 livres, 8 sous. He complained, but to no avail, and then asked the innkeeper to sign the bill, which he finally did under protest, writing a false name for both the inn and for himself. When his ruse was discovered, he ran off and hid until the guest departed.

Travelers, including Young, generally found good lodging in the major cities and sometimes on the rural roads, but too often the country inns were unpleasant even on the main roads. Young describes his experience at Guingamp, in Brittany, on his way to the naval port at Brest this way: "This villainous hole, that calls itself the *grand maison,* is the best inn at a post town on the great road to Brest."[12] The lack of reasonable inns suggests that the circulation of people around the country must not have been of great importance.

## CUSTOMS BARRIERS AND OTHER INCONVENIENCES

Not only were foreign travelers inconvenienced by the numerous custom stops, but also the French businessman, trader, migrant worker, or tourist had to waste time having bags examined by petty officials or reach deep into his purse. The country was plagued with such customs barriers, both official and private, and various fees on persons and goods passing from one region to another were collected in excise taxes or tariffs. Duties on goods shipped down the Saône and Rhône Rivers from Franche-Comté to the Mediterranean were paid at 36 separate customs barriers. The city of Paris was surrounded by no fewer than 54 customs stations linked by a stone wall.[13] Taxes were levied on all goods entering the city, and these detested houses were some of the first places to be attacked as the revolution got under way.

Smollett referred to customs officials as "those vermin who examine the baggage of travellers in different parts of the kingdom" and resorted to bribery to expedite his passage. On his arrival at Lyon, he noted, "at the gate [of the city] of which we were questioned by one of the searchers, who, being tipped with half a crown, allowed us to proceed without further inquiry."[14]

From people passing through Flanders we learn that at Péronne all persons on the road were thoroughly searched for contraband goods such as lace, fine linen fabrics, tobacco, and snuff, on which a very high duty was charged. Lady Mary Coke was many times in France, the latest in the 1770s. She described the strict custom searches in Calais and at Péronne and added: "I lay at Peronne in a terrible dirty Inn, & had again the pleasure of having all the boxes of the inside of my Coach search'd."[15] Her coach was scrutinized again at St. Quentin, but, with bribes, travelers could reduce inspectors' vigilance.

Many travelers, in spite of proper documents from the customs at Calais and bags closed with lead seals, were searched again upon entering Paris. Not only did unexpected delays at custom houses inconvenience people and cost them money, but also they caused havoc with internal trade conducted by legitimate businessmen right up to the time of the revolution. Even going down the Rhône from Lyon by boat, passengers were forced to wait at Vienne, only about 20 miles south, to be once again inspected by customs officers, recorded Lord George Herbert.[16]

An indignant Reverend William Cole refused to pay any more bribes to custom officials when he reached the gates of Paris in 1765, and his luggage was thoroughly searched for contraband goods. Found was a pair of new boots, and when the officials claimed that no new goods were allowed without payment, the reverend told them to take the boots at their peril, but he was not paying. After some time and probably an unpleasant altercation, they let him pass. Most travelers paid to avoid the inconvenience.

Philip Thicknesse, an English army officer who made many trips to France before the revolution, reported that there were ways to quickly get through the internal customs barriers—"a twenty-four sols piece and on assuring the officer that you are a gentleman and not a merchant, will carry you through without delay." He returned in 1801, well after the revolution, and wrote: "You are not now plagued, as formerly, by customhouse officers on the frontiers of *every* department, My Baggage, being once searched at Calais, experienced no other visit."[17]

Having reached Paris, many travelers found the buildings too tall and the streets too narrow and dirty; in addition, many of the streets lacked sidewalks, making them a danger to pedestrians. This was often commented on by both foreigners and French. There were other problems also: Dr. John Moore, who was there in 1792, complained that "Paris is poorly lighted" and that people "must therefore grope their way as they best can, and skulk behind pillars, or run into shops to avoid being crushed by the coaches."

Others reported that carriages clattered along at top speed, and it was the responsibility of those on foot to jump clear. There were many injuries and deaths in the city from passing coaches that often did not even bother to stop.[18]

## FRENCH TRAVELERS

When Fréron and Barras, two representatives of the revolutionary government, were sent on a mission to Marseille, Fréron sent back a letter to the Convention on December 12, 1793, to counter accusations that they were living in luxury. He claimed that they were not dining in the style of a tax collector and indeed ate only one meal a day, at four in the afternoon, and sometimes they gave a bowl of soup to hungry sans-culottes if they asked for it. Fréron also mentions how hard he worked, not going out for several days but instead sitting in his dressing gown writing his reports. If he did go out at all, it was only for a few hours to get some fresh air. He had no time to see any women because he was much too busy working for the nation (which he loved a hundred times more). The two men lived at an inn and dined alone to save money.

He wrote about Marseille and the work they were going to do there. Since there were no police in the city, he and Barras established a police force. They discovered four gaming houses where the people addressed each other as Monsieur and Madame and the louis cost 60 livres in paper money: "We are going to raid the gamblers tomorrow morning. Marseilles is going to be paved and cleaned up, for it is of a horrible filthiness. Moreover, this will give employment for many idle hands." To bring the city into line, one of the deputies stated, with regard to prostitutes, "all the public women who infect our volunteers and entice them away from the army shall, within two days be placed under arrest. The order has been signed and a place readied to receive them. Diseased girls will receive treatment and healthy ones will work at sewing uniforms or shirts for the brave defenders of the *Patrie*."[19]

As a result of a decree passed by the Convention on October 8, 1793, for the requisitioning of horses for the army, the country had been divided into 20 sections, each assigned to a representative. The deputy Goupilleau de Montaigu, from the west, made several trips to the south from 1793 to 1795. He did not depart on horseback or in a two-wheeled buggy but instead hired a four-wheeled carriage and three horses to pull it. On the roof he placed an enormous hamper for his personal effects. Horses and postilion were changed at each posting house, which were not far apart. Citizen Goupilleau spent enough just getting to his first destination: 25 sous for each horse, and another 10 for the postilion or guide; about 25 sous to cross rivers and streams by ferryboat, not to mention the charges for lodgings at inns and for meals. Bolstered with many cushions, he was able to travel comfortably, observe the countryside, and take notes.

Lyon was not to his liking: the narrow streets were badly paved and muddy, and the houses, in his opinion, were not as nice as those in Nantes. After passing Vienne, on October 15, he felt he had reached the south, for the weather turned warm. On his way to Valence, he remarked on the shallowness but the fast flow of the Isère River as he crossed it by ferry and noted that the life of the people seemed to change with the scenery, becoming more relaxed. The mulberry and almond trees and large, black swine seen along the side of the road suggested a more carefree existence than existed in the north. On October 17, at Mondragon, he saw more mulberries but also fig and olive trees. He found the food good and the wine excellent at Avignon, but the innkeepers, he said, were rogues who "lavish attention on you when you arrive and skin you alive when you depart." On October 19, at seven in the morning, he arrived at Arles complaining that the mosquitoes kept him awake all night and that he had been forced to close the window of the coach. Next stop was Aix, whence he went on to Marseille, which, contrary to Fréron, he found to be a beautiful city comparable to Nantes, although the theater was not as good and the port was only a large pool surrounded by rundown buildings. He complained about the prices of the inns whose keepers, as at Avignon, he claims were of "Italian" mentality.

Madame Simon, the mistress of the Hôtel de Beauveau, charged him extremely high prices, and he swore never to return there. He did find in his expensive room, however, a wonderful invention that allowed him to sleep well—a mosquito net draped around the bed.

He visited many other cities where he was grandly received by the town dignitaries. In the Jacobin town of Antibes, where patriotic fervor was at a high pitch, many of the streets were named after recent revolutionary events, such as July 14. Then, on to Nice where again he found the streets too narrow, but he admired the Place de la République. Generally he found the inhabitants of the south very honest and decent but fatiguing. A man from the more formal west, he complained that he could not walk a step without being surrounded by chatter. He was forced to eat and drink too much by amicable and generous southerners. On his return to Paris, he again stopped at Arles and remained there for a month, until December 6, attending to his mission of requisitioning horses. While there, he was dragged off to a bullfight but thoroughly disliked the spectacle of animals engaged in combat before they were slaughtered, simply for the amusement of people, comparing it to Roman barbarism. His other missions were also replete with festivals, gastronomic delights, and fine wine, the price of which was well out of reach for most Frenchmen. Apparently, for some, it was splendid to be a deputy *en mission*.[20]

## NOTES

1. Braudel, 425.
2. Lough, 20.
3. Traveling along a magnificent road in the vicinity of Perpignan, Arthur Young met one *cabriolet* and half a dozen carts in 36 miles.
4. Lough, 22.
5. Ibid., 24.
6. Young, 35ff.
7. Ibid.
8. Ibid., 37.
9. Ibid., 54.
10. Ibid., 133.
11. Ibid., 244.

12. Ibid., 126.
13. Andress (2004), 107.
14. Lough, 18.
15. Ibid.
16. Ibid., 19.
17. Ibid., 17.
18. Ibid., 74.
19. Robiquet, 178-79.
20. For further details, see Robiquet, chapter 20.

# 4

# LIFE AT VERSAILLES

## THE PALACE

The palace at Versailles was the wonder of Europe, a monument to Bourbon power and wealth. The main buildings, comprising decorated halls, galleries, apartments, state rooms, terraces, and courtyards, were surrounded by vast formal gardens that included lawns, bushes, trees, and sculpture intersected by broad gravel pathways. There were numerous secluded groves and a mile-long Grand Canal. The many fountains played all around, and manmade lakes were home to swans. North of the gardens stood the Grand and Petit Trianons, or royal villas. The Petit Trianon was a favorite retreat of Marie-Antoinette.

There was another side to the palace besides its intricate beauty and grandeur, however. The many chimneys did not draw well, and throughout the winter rooms were full of smoke and the upholstery, wall hangings and carpets smelled of soot, the odor permeating clothes and wigs. Servants and aristocratic visitors often relieved themselves on back stairs, along the darkened corridors, or in any out-of-the-way place.[1] The writer Horace Walpole agreed with other English visitors to Versailles that the approach was magnificent but the squalor inside was unspeakable.[2] The stench of urine and fecal remains wafted through corridors and gardens where waste water was often emptied from the windows. Sometimes garbage was dumped on the royal grounds by local peasants. Cats and dogs roamed freely, many wild, leaving their calling cards on paths and roads and in the shrubs.[3] Madame de Guéménée, governess of Louis XVI's two sisters, went about the palace with an escort of dogs that she kept in her rooms. She feigned communication with the spiritual world through them.

Just about anyone could enter the palace and wander about its broad hallways and spacious salons.[4] Visitors from Paris strolled through the corridors admiring the *objets d'art* and furnishings, watched by servants who, no doubt, looked on with dismay at the parade of muddy boots and dirty paws. Dignitaries and ambassadors from foreign courts brought their entourages to Versailles and filled rooms of the palace and town with servants, slaves, camp followers, and exotic pets. About 10,000 people lived or worked in the palace.[5]

## FINANCES

Debt was part of everyday life for the royal court and the nobles who lived there, but it was not of any great concern, and everyone reckoned that it would be paid off eventually.[6] Huge expenses were incurred when each of the royal children was born, with the usual fanfare in Paris of booming cannons, bonfires, pyrotechnics, music, and plenty of free wine. Many Parisians loved the celebrations but were not pleased when another palace, St. Cloud, was purchased for the queen. The money was said to have come from selling other crown lands, but Parisians were skeptical, assuming that more millions of livres had been added to the debt. They began calling the queen Madame Deficit, among other unsavory names.

Further, they were angry when Marie-Antoinette singled out the Polignacs for favors. In 1777, Yolande de Plastron, comtesse de Polignac, became a close and intimate friend of the queen, who lavished expensive gifts on her. Before long, her husband, who was not well off, began to attain high, lucrative offices. In one year (1780), he was made the first equerry to the queen, grand falconer of France, and governor of Lille. In a position to spread his largesse around, he made his portrait painter, Elisabeth Vigée-Lebrun, the most important artist at court and her brother one of the many secretaries of the king (which gave him noble status). Vigée-Lebrun's art-dealer husband also received a constant stream of wealthy customers.[7]

The list of Polignac appointments to the royal household grew and grew, and eventually the entire family and relatives had lucrative posts. An ample pension was given to a monk who happened to be related, and even remote members of the family received gifts and annuities, all of which amounted to tens of thousands of livres. This kind of extravagant spending, and the huge state pensions given to Marie-Antoinette's favorites, aroused a good deal of indignation among the people. In 1776, the entire annual household budget of the court amounted to about 30 million livres, of which about 3 million went to the Polignac clan. The average Parisian worker of the time received about two livres a day.

## DAILY LIFE

Well before the light of dawn, the palace hummed with activity. Footmen, pages, grooms, and kitchen personnel all emerged from their tiny, draughty rooms, washed, dressed in their distinctive clothes, and got ready to work. They had just enough time to sip a little coffee and swallow some morsels of bread before hurrying off to their posts. There were close to 900 noble officials at the court of Louis XVI, as listed in the *Almanach de Versailles*. They also rose early to prepare for the day, waited on by their own servants. While exalted by society for their high birth, they were little more than subordinate adjuncts to the monarch and his family. Their duties consisted of such things as arranging flowers in the queen's apartments, opening doors for their majesties, assisting them with their elaborate toilets, giving the king his rubdown with perfumed essence, holding their wigs for them to make a selection, or handing the king his cane or knotting his tie. They had to be prepared to perform these tasks as soon as the members of the royal family arose from bed. Each one had specifically defined duties and privileges. The one who combed the king's hair, for example, would never empty the king's chamber pot. That was another gentleman's job.

New members of the royal staff, both officers and servants, were hard pressed to master the numerous rules of etiquette that were demanded. On some doors one knocked; on others one scratched with one's fingernails. In some rooms the servants were allowed to sit; in others, such as the king's chambers, only standing was permissible, even if no one was present. The king's family and intimate friends could speak to him directly. Others used the third person: "Did His Majesty enjoy his dinner?" Servants had to learn which uniform to wear when the court went to other locations; they wore blue at the palace at Choisy and green at Compiègne. Absolute obedience to superiors was required, and any failure could result in a beating, extra duties, or discharge from service.

The position of royal page was open only to boys who could demonstrate aristocratic ancestry dating back at least 200 years. The young men were also required to have a pension from their families of no less than 600 livres annually for incidental expenses. Everything else—copious food, clothing, medical care, and education—was supplied. Not all young noble gentlemen were fortunate enough to become royal pages, which generally required having the right connections, such as an uncle or aunt already in royal service. At the court there were some 58 pages—the figure varied— but 8 of these were assigned directly to the king. They had to be present when he rose from bed, which was generally late morning, to attend his needs; they accompanied him to Mass, lit his way with torches when he arrived home after dark, often from hunting excursions, and fetched his slippers in the evenings. The duties of the pages were relatively light, but new ones were often treated with cruel disrespect by the older boys who

Louis XVI, King of France and Navarre. Bibliothèque Nationale de France.

had served several years and who punished the novice severely for any
mistake.

When not attending the king, these young men spent their time with
tutors studying mathematics, horsemanship, firearms, German (the native
language of the queen), and dancing. Sometimes, when tempers flared,
they fought duels with each other that generally resulted in few serious
wounds. All expected at the end of their term, at about age 17 or 18, to be
given a commission in the guards.

Fifty sons of noble families were assigned to the royal stables, where
up to 3,000 horses were kept. The boys lived in the stables in small rooms
and learned to groom and care for the animals under the supervision of
the prince de Lambesc of the royal house of Lorraine, a distant relative of
the queen. Their work began at five o'clock in the morning but the pages

were free to roam around the town of Versailles for much of the later day. Those who became superb riders were chosen to accompany the king on his frequent hunts to carry his guns, hand them to him, and take them back when discharged, giving them to the arquebusier, who loaded them again, after which the process repeated.

The queen's *ménage*, smaller than the king's but of greater complexity, contained about 500 officers and servants. Marie-Antoinette revived the office of Superintendent of the Queen's Household, appointing the princesse of Lamballe to the job in 1774. Under her was the chief lady-in-waiting, who oversaw the work of a host of servants. The loyal Madame Campan was one of two women in charge of all the bedchamber servants, as well as being responsible for the queen's private funds, including her jewels. Several secretaries handled the correspondence and paid the bills. Whenever the court moved residence, thousands of invitations were sent out for suppers, hunting parties, and balls. Overseeing the payment of pensions to former servants and others was a large job, as was maintaining the queen's carriages and the gilded sleds she kept to ride in if and when enough snow fell in the area. Apothecaries and surgeons were on hand to tend to the health of the household, and scores of other people looked after the glassware and silver, the ordering of food, and the cleaning and storing of underclothes, robes and dresses, shoes, bags, fans, gloves, and towels. Linen was replaced every few years, and the sheets and pillowslips on the queen's bed were changed every day.

## THE QUEEN'S DAY

When Marie-Antoinette awoke each morning around ten o'clock and said her prayers, a gaggle of ladies in waiting entered the queen's bedchamber with a basket of underclothes and towels, and she was presented with a choice of dresses to wear. She would select something for the morning, something for the afternoon, a gown for supper, and perhaps another for the evening entertainment. There were so many outfits that she made her choices from a picture book, and several ladies then scurried off to find those chosen in the immense wardrobe.

Next, the queen took her bath in a portable tub wheeled into the room, accompanied by another squadron of women armed with all the paraphernalia of soaps and perfumes. Antoinette bathed clad in a flannel gown buttoned up from ankles to neck. Emerging from the tub, she was shielded from curious eyes by a sheet as she slipped into a robe before returning to bed to await her breakfast of hot chocolate or coffee.

When she arose again, the bed was stripped and the sheets sent off to the laundry. Then four footmen entered the room, turned the heavy mattress, and quickly departed. The bed was remade with fresh linen, while the furniture was dusted and all was tidied up. The lady-in-waiting sat in an armchair watching that everything was done correctly.

The remainder of the morning was taken up by a few minutes with her husband followed by visits from those possessing the *petite entrée*—a bishop or two, the royal physician or surgeon, secretaries, and perhaps a reader with the news from Paris.

At noon came time for the ceremony of the *grande toilette,* when a large, ornate table was moved into the center of the room and chairs and sofas placed around it. The queen sat at the table, and dignitaries arrived, including the king's brothers, Artois and Provence, the princes of the blood, high court officials, and others possessing the *grande entrée,* which allowed them to visit the queen at any convenient time. Each received a nod, the inclination of which depended on their rank. The bedchamber women then retired to a nearby room, and the ladies of honor, accompanied by their maids, began the ceremony.

Portrait of Marie-Antoinette of Austria, Queen of France and Navarre, wife of Louis XVI. Bibliothèque Nationale de France.

First the queen had her coiffure completed. Then a chemise was put on, and the wide-hooped skirt of her gown was attached, a neckerchief adjusted, and jewels put in place. The long train came next. While she was being dressed, an usher stood in the doorway and announced the name of visitors to the lady of honor, who in turn announced them to the queen, who signed petitions and received notables, who, departing the palace, said their farewells. Much of the conversation dealt with the theater in Paris: how well did the actors and actresses do? How many people attended? What lords and ladies were there?

The formalities over and the queen fitted out, she returned to her bedchamber. There the ladies-in-waiting assembled, along with the bedchamber attendants, the maids, the first gentleman usher, and the clergy who had the duty that day to escort the queen and the royal princesses with their entire entourages to Mass. They went off together to the chapel, meeting up with the king and his large assemblage on the way.

This procession was most elaborate on Sundays, when the first gentleman of the king's bedchamber led the way, followed by the captain of the guard and then the king and queen. Behind them came the highest-ranking ladies and gentlemen of the aristocracy. Lesser individuals lined the hallways to bow and curtsy as the line, four abreast, passed by. Afterwards, the queen made a deep curtsey to the king before setting off with her entourage to her rooms.

Next came the midday dinner, and all of its ritual, which, again, was the most resplendent on Sundays. Surrounded by their servants, the king and queen dined together on silver dishes with gilded cutlery. They were given a menu card to choose from and dishes of fowl, meat, fish, and puddings were brought before them in great profusion. The wine was tasted by two lackeys before it was served. Behind the king's chair stood the captain of the guards and the first gentleman of the chamber. Behind the queen stood her first gentleman usher and the chief equerry. The meal began when the *maître d'hôtel* entered the room with a seven-foot staff crowned with a *fleur-de-lys,* followed by a legion of servants from the kitchens balancing an array of dishes for the royals to select from.

The sumptuous feast finished, the royal pair repaired to their separate rooms. The queen changed into something less formal and cumbersome, after which she spent the rest of the afternoon in conversation with friends and relatives, often playing and listening to harp music. Later she would take walks in the gardens or perhaps a coach ride in the forest. The evening was filled first by a splendid supper, the guests carefully selected for their wit, sociability, and polished manners. An orchestra entertained, the wine flowed generously, the talk and gossip went on sometimes late in the candlelight, and women stifled their yawns behind jewel-studded fans.

Afterwards, in a grand salon, the evening entertainment continued with various types of gambling. Billiards, card games, or throwing dice continued long after the king went to bed. Servants stood by to fulfill all needs, and, once more, the ladies-in-waiting were obliged to attend. The king retired to bed about eleven every night, and the queen's ladies were escorted back to their cell-like rooms to catch a few hours' sleep before the routine began all over again. At a late hour, Marie-Antoinette often went visiting her young friends, such as the princesses de Lamballe and Guéménée in their apartments—activities that caused much gossip.[8]

The queen's favorite haunt was the Petit Trianon, an elegant seven-room neoclassical building about a mile from the palace. There she felt comfortable and more serene among the wall hangings, her works of art, marble fireplaces, writing desks, and cabinets of exotic wood. Ubiquitous flowers, both inside and out, added to the beauty of the surroundings. She had had a lake excavated, little hills created, lawns laid down, a temple of love constructed, and groves of trees from exotic and distant places planted. In this quiet place she shed her cares, sometimes remaining for an entire month at a time.[9]

She also had created a little village there that became her own private fairyland. Eight thatched cottages were built with fractures in the plaster walls to make them appear old, their gardens filled with fruit trees and vegetables. There were barns for livestock, cows in a small field, a poultry yard, and a little mill. A farmer was hired to look after it all. To the cows, goats, sheep, rabbits, pigeons, and chickens Antoinette gave pet names, and derived contentment from the miniature farm and her imaginary world. She enjoyed dressing like a peasant and amused herself acting out the life of a rural woman in the mock village. All the queen's enormous expenses were met by the public purse, and the people knew it and resented it. Those who paid the bills through their toil and taxes were not so enamored of her little hamlet or with anything else she spent money on to gratify her desires. A real peasant girl working as a farm servant would have earned fewer than 30 livres per year. Many of the inhabitants of France were in a state of near-starvation in 1789 because of a bad harvest, and most of them by this time vehemently hated the queen. Some imagined that the shortage of bread and the soaring prices were deliberate—an aristocratic conspiracy to keep them down and in their place. "Let them eat cake!," a statement in circulation (wrongly attributed to the queen), increased the people's appetite for revenge on the foreigner from Vienna who was so indifferent to their plight.

The palace at Versailles was a microcosm of artificiality, conceit, jealousy, gossip, social climbing, stiffness of manners, cumbersome dress, flirtations, secret notes, and clandestine rendezvous, with little bearing on the reality of the ordinary people of France.

## COURTIERS

Daily life at court was often tedious. Courtiers had time on their hands to gossip, gamble, drink, and plot. They lived in cramped quarters with little light and fresh air; they jostled for space in the crowded, noisy salons and gala events and could never relax in public or appear uninterested. It was imperative to be alert, pleasant, tactful, and graceful and to smile even when the lice under the wig were nibbling relentlessly and the tight, pointed shoes incited rebellion among the toes.

The ambition of every courtier was to advance to higher office, gain more privileges, and grow wealthy. It could be a laboriously long road. Courtiers had to flatter superiors while keeping inferiors in their place. One might stand for hours each morning in the chamber next to the royal bedchambers waiting and hoping to be noticed and admitted into the king's presence to perform even the most insignificant task. Small recognition could lead to better circumstances at court.

Not yet privileged to dine with the king and queen or other notable personages, courtiers took their meals in the large communal dining hall, or *Grand Commun*. Here they ate with their fellows and conversed with writers, artists, scholars, lawyers, or judges who were visiting the palace on business or who were living there while performing some task or duty.

One recurrent theme in conversation was how to get away from palace life, even for a short time, and enjoy dining out and attending the theater in Paris. Most courtiers were always short of money, however, and many were in debt, especially to wigmakers, as theirs had to be the very best, made of human hair. Inferior horsehair wigs would be frowned on. The high prices of these and of hairdressers was a serious concern, as were the changing fashions—both required a substantial outlay of money. Nevertheless, to owe sizable amounts of money was expected of a person of taste and breeding. One who was known to economize was left in danger of gossip and lack of advancement on the palace merry-go-round.

The mythos of Versailles attracted many to its royal halls, but the substance was not for everyone. Taking part in special spectacles was always tiresome; for example, the courtiers had to learn and rehearse over and over intricate dances, such as one that formed the letters of the queen's name. In the struggle for advancement, little mattered except the positive attention of one's superior. Some—those who were ambitious, well connected, and sharp witted and who loved the game— could reach high office and become wealthy and famous; others would fall by the wayside and drop out of sight. But, in contrast to the squalid misery of the rural peasants and the urban poor, life at Versailles was paradise itself.

The queen chose her favorites to lavish money, offices, and gifts on; and they, along with their relatives and cronies, "clung to the ship of state with the tenacity of barnacles."[10] The queen's lavish display at the Paris theaters she frequented, in spite of her husband's objections, made for much prattle, but she cared not. Obedience and humility were not part of her vocabulary unless applied to others.

## ARISTOCRATS AT COURT

The court aristocrats numbered about 4,000, and, although they were not particularly endowed with morality or political astuteness, they nevertheless monopolized the lofty positions in the church (archbishops, bishops, and abbots), high judicial positions (judges), and the military (generals and admirals). Some were ministers of the crown or ambassadors to foreign countries. Many supplemented their income or inheritance with ventures into commerce and industry, using their prestige and influence at court. Some owned mining operations, some were grain speculators, and others were moneylenders or wholesale traders. The duke of Orléans, cousin of the king, owned vast properties in Paris and in the provinces and invested heavily in commercial and building enterprises in the 1780s. Retail activities, looked down upon by the aristocracy, would have meant loss of status.

There seems to have been no less hostility toward nobles at court than to the impecunious ones of the countryside. The latter were always too eager to collect their feudal dues and present their titles to the common people and felt no shame living in genteel idleness. They saw themselves as the true Nobility of the Sword and considered it their duty to serve the king as officers in his army; but the problem was that the army was run by plutocrats and all military commissions were subject to purchase with prices well beyond their means. At the royal court of Louis XVI, money opened every door.

## FOREIGN VISITORS

When Horace Walpole, fourth earl of Orford and writer, was first presented to the court at Versailles in 1765, he noticed that the duc de Berry, the future Louis XVI, then about 11 years old, looked frail and weak-eyed. Walpole was again at the court in 1771 and at this time observed that the country was in a sorry state, declaring, "Their next prospect is not better: it rests on an imbecile, both in mind and body."

The Spencer family visited Versailles in 1772, and Lady Harriet reported, among other things, that the dauphin looked stupid but was good natured and would be handsome if he were not so heavy.

In spite of hostilities between France and England during the American Revolution, some English visitors still came to France. The duchess of Northumberland was present at the wedding of the dauphin and Marie-Antoinette (the former 15 years of age and the latter 14). Of the future queen she wrote:

The dauphine was very fine in diamonds. She is very little & slender. I should not have taken her to be 12 Years Old. She is fair & a little mark'd with the Smallpox, the Corps of her Robe was too small & left quite a broad stripe of lacing & Shift quite visible, which had a bad effect between 2 broader stripes of Diamonds, She really had quite a Load of Jewells.

Other visitors spoke of Marie-Antoinette's liveliness, grace, and dignity, and some found the king more handsome than they had expected. Many were able to see the king and queen during the royal party's walks to and from Mass in the chapel. Sir Samuel Romilly, who, in 1781, attended a royal Mass, described it in a letter:

The service was very short, though it was on a Sunday; for kings are so highly respected in that country that even Religion appoints for them less tedious ceremonies than it imposes on the people. The moment his Majesty appeared, the drums beat and shook the temple, as if it had been intended to announce the approach of a conqueror. During the whole time of saying mass, the choristers sang, sometimes single parts, sometimes in chorus. In the front seats of the galleries were ranged the ladies of the court, glowing with rouge, and gorgeously apparelled, to enjoy and form a part of the showy spectacle. The King laughed and spied at the ladies; every eye was fixed on the personages of the court, every ear was attentive to the notes of the singers, while the priest, who in the mean time went on in the exercise of his office, was unheeded by all present. Even when the Host was lifted up, none observed it; and if the people knelt, it was because they were admonished by the ringing of the bell; and even in that attitude, all were endeavoring to get a glimpse of the King.

With the Treaty of Paris, signed September 3, 1783, at the end of the American War of Independence and the Franco-British conflict, a fresh wave of English travelers crossed the Channel. By this time, the king had grown rather corpulent, and visitors remarked on it. When he saw the king at Versailles, in 1784, in a procession through the Hall of Mirrors on Saint Louis' day, Adam Walker commented,

a short thick dumplin of a Monarch, the very picture of peace and plenty. He rolled along, with an air as perfectly disengaged from thought or care, and bore this great kingdom with so much ease upon his shoulders, that I could not but think him a jolly eating-and-drinking English 'Squire', perfectly at his ease, and without any other ideas coming across his thinking faculties than what must be next for his dinner!

Since the king was most often viewed at Mass, many of the comments about him were made there. Richard Garmston found it disconcerting to see Louis and his brother sit talking and laughing throughout most of the service. Not long before, Arthur Young had witnessed the investiture of the *cordon bleu* on the duc de Berry, younger son of the compte d'Artois. His notes were not flattering:

During the service the King was seated between his two brothers, and seemed by his carriage and inattention to wish himself a hunting. He would certainly have been as well employed, as in hearing afterwards from his throne a feudal oath of chivalry, I suppose, or some such nonsense, administered to a boy of ten years old.[11]

## ROYAL ENTERTAINMENT

Louis XVI was neither a strong nor a gifted ruler; having inherited a system that allowed ministers to pursue their own interests and policies, he permitted this state of affairs to continue, preferring not to involve himself too deeply in politics.

The royal hunting parties in which deer or boar were flushed out by retainers and then shot by their majesties seemed to be the king's preferred activity, while matters of state took second place. The king had a few other diversions, such as making locks or tinkering with them, for which he kept an expert locksmith in residence at his beck and call. He was also proud of his collection of clocks and the fact that he could make them all chime in unison at the same hour. At other times he liked to play the part of a construction laborer when some work was in progress on the palace. He often helped the workmen move paving stones and girders and labored with the masons and carpenters for hours on end before retiring exhausted but happy after the physical exertion.

Then, too, there were picnics at the palace, boating on the canal, coach rides around the grounds, gambling in the evenings (in which the king took small part), royal balls, masquerades, and fetes, theatrical plays, and sometimes a trip to the racetrack. In addition, there were always audiences to be given and time to be spent with friends, relatives, visitors, and foreign dignitaries.

An assortment of entertainers regularly came to Versailles to perform, including musicians and actors from the Paris theaters and animal acts, which generally appeared on the boulevards of the capital. Chain gangs, a form of entertainment for some, were marched through the town of Versailles on their way to the galleys at Brest. The route was changed, however, since Louis XVI, seeing their poor condition, pardoned too many of them.[12]

Of the banquets and parties that were held at the royal palace at Versailles, one particularly struck home in the minds of the people of Paris. On October 1, 1789, while the common people of France went hungry under near-famine conditions, the royal bodyguard at Versailles gave a banquet for the Flanders regiment, newly arrived in town. Such parties of welcome were traditional, but this one, in a time of great want, was ill timed. The best food was served in vast quantities, and the king and queen made an appearance. The queen showed off the four-year-old dauphin for the soldiers to admire, and a toast was drunk to the royal family, who then departed. More toasts followed, and men became more and more inebriated. As the party grew louder, court women handed out cockades—white for the king and black for the queen.

The following day the banquet was reported in the Paris papers and newssheets, depicted as an orgy conjuring up scenes of debauchery, gluttony, and treason against the revolutionary government. The patriotic republican red-white-and-blue cockade was said to have been trampled by the soldiers in their desire to show loyalty to the king. Disrespect for the revolutionary cockade was more than the Parisians could take, however, particularly as the papers reported that it happened with the queen's approval. Riots would soon begin again in the city.

To amuse the courtiers, there was a prodigious amount of pornography, which had evolved particularly in the last years of Louis XV, when stories of his private brothel at Versailles and the *Parc aux Cerf* (Stag Park) were circulating. Not only did Versailles have a number of bookshops where it was possible to buy just about anything, including erotica, but also the towns where the court habitually moved according to the season, Compiègne, Fontainebleau, and Saint-Cloud, had similar bookstores. The material was often of foreign origin. Noblemen and women were ideal to carry such merchandise, since they were normally immune from search and seizure.

Pornography at court would have distressed no one more than the queen, since she was the brunt of much of it. The salacious songs, drawings, and writings about her were circulated far and wide. By 1787, Marie-Antoinette was seldom seen outside court, and on the few occasions when she went to the theater now, she was met with silence or hisses.[13] The pornographers and the insulting songs in the Paris cafes made her shun the public. Speculation in the lowest form made the rounds concerning the size and potency of the king's penis, while the numbers and identification of the queen's lovers, male or female, were a constant subject of gossip. The king's brother, Artois, was the prime candidate for gossip related to her supposed sexual escapades as the two were often seen together. Whatever was in the fertile and fanciful minds of her enemies was put to pen and paper. Much of their inspiration came from the work *Essai historique sur la vie de Marie-Antoinette,* first published in 1781 and continually added to up to the time of her death. It took the form of an imaginary autobiographical confession and was widely circulated in Paris. In it the queen "confesses" to such crimes as learning new positions for copulation from Artois at the Petit Trianon, lesbianism with her ladies-in-waiting, sexually abusing her then 11-year-old son and being a sexual monster infected by sleeping with a diseased cardinal.

These "charges" and that of treason, including claims that she spied for the Austrian emperor, sent him money, and plotted against the National Assembly, contributed to the swift decline of royal prestige in the late 1780s. These same accusations were presented to her at her trial.

## CHILDREN, DOGS, AND OTHER DISTRACTIONS

Children of members of the court were uncontrolled and often underfoot, running through the corridors, up and down the stairs, playing games with each other as well as with the dogs. Marie-Antoinette had two curly-tailed pugs who were allowed the run of the rooms, chewing on or scratching holes in the curtains and tapestries. They gnawed on the gilded chair legs and romped on the damask-covered furniture, and they were allowed to relieve themselves wherever they pleased.

The royal children had tutors who took care of their education and their affairs. The dauphin had a priest who taught him, and the girls' education was looked after by Madame de Fréminville.[14]

Homeless barefoot children dressed in rags carried messages within the palace. They stole food when they could and slept in the stables and other outside buildings. Former servants of other households stood about the palace in groups, hoping to be noticed and given work.[15] With hundreds of staff hurrying through the great building, guards lounging about in their spare time gambling and boasting, tradesmen waited in the hallways for a chance to show the queen their latest creations in jewels or fashions. All the while, messengers scurried past, while attendants and visitors waited in outside rooms and antechambers for a word or message from the queen.[16]

The palace at Versailles was probably an unhealthy place where food was handled carelessly, people and animals fouled the dark corners, and courtiers were neither tidy nor clean. Pages, servants, and strangers trod in the dirt and mud from outside. Especially in the long winter months, when the rooms were cold and a fire might just take off the chill, the denizens of the palace were not inclined to worry about keeping themselves washed. But then, the rest of France was not given over to unrestrained bathing, either.

## NOTES

1. Erickson, 114.

2. Maxwell, *The English Traveler in France 1698–1815,* 109, cited in Erickson, 352.

3. The king also had dogs that he kept in a large kennel in the reception room at Fontainebleau. Each dog had three mattresses upholstered in red velvet in the capacious doghouse made of oak with gilt pilasters.

4. Young, 16.

5. Doyle, 41.

6. The notion underwent a shock when one of the greatest nobles to the court, the prince de Guéménée, declared himself bankrupt. He owed 33 million livres, and no one would give him further credit. His debt had been secured by the estimated future income of his high office, by his connections, and by his good name, and his creditors included tailors, wigmakers, jewelers, tradesmen, and financiers. Even the well-to-do peasants on his own estates, who had entrusted their money to his administrators, lost it all. About 3,000 creditors who now faced ruin had paid for his grand lifestyle and that of his extravagant wife, hostess to many gambling parties at which she usually lost heavily. The prince retired to his estates in Navarre, and Madame de Guéménée left court for their properties in Brittany, along with her dozens of little dogs. The king and queen maintained a discreet silence about

the entire affair. They, too, along with other members of the royal family, owed enormous debts. The king's brother, Artois, for instance, was said to have owed millions.

7. See Schama, 214ff. At the outbreak of the revolution, Elisabeth Vigée-Lebrun fled France. She was known for her portraits, including those of the English princesses Adelaide and Victoria, Lord Byron, Mme de Staël, and more than 20 of Marie-Antoinette.

8. For an account of Marie-Antoinette's daily routine, see Erickson, 100ff.

9. Campan, 189.

10. See Schama, 213–14, for this metaphor.

11. See Lough, 263–73, for more details.

12. Erickson, 116.

13. Schama, 221.

14. Erickson, 230.

15. Ibid., 117–18.

16. Ibid., 72ff.

# 5

# CLOTHES AND FASHION

In the eighteenth century, people dressed according to their social level. Aristocrats wore richly colored and extravagant clothes, setting themselves apart from the masses; clerics wore robes according to their place in the church hierarchy; and members of the upper middle class were identified by the good-quality cloth and discreet ornamentation of their apparel. Tradespeople, artisans, and market workers were identifiable by their aprons, and the readily recognizable urban poor were generally clad in rags. Black was the color worn by the less well-to-do as an economy measure, since not only did it not show the dirt so much but also it doubled as a mourning outfit.

On the death of a member of the royal family, a year of mourning was required by tradition; this period was reduced to three months just before the revolution. At such times, the entire palace staff was provided with new, black uniforms, and all the furnishings were draped in dark materials and the king's carriages in violet. The change in fashion could disrupt the entire luxury-trade industry, and when the court went into mourning, an abrupt end was put to the sale of colored silk and other material.[1]

As the century advanced, attire began to change as people started to dress above their station. Such behavior could invite police suspicion, and even arrest might follow. To dress below one's status was equally contemptible, as it suggested that the individual was on a downward social slide. Class distinction was one of the first casualties of the revolution; afterward, clothing was used to demonstrate not the wearer's class but his or her politics. A good republican had to be easily recognizable, and it could be dangerous not to conform.[2]

## THE UPPER CLASS

There was little change in men's apparel throughout most of the pre-revolutionary century. The *habit à la française,* with the coat opened wide in front to reveal a vest and breeches, continued to be worn at court. The preferred colors were apple green and light yellow with a white vest. Around 1780, the general trend changed as an English influence became noticeable; for example, the frock coat and the *redingote à la lévite* (riding coat) were introduced into France, the latter a double-breasted long coat with turned-down collar, worn along with several shoulder capes. The vests were generally white with silk embroidery in patterns of colored flowers. Breeches were skin tight, covering the thighs and ending just below the knees, fastened at the bottom with buckles or buttons. Stockings of silk or cotton, usually white, were pulled up over the bottom of the breeches and folded back over a concealed garter. Shoes had square toes and, for dressy occasions, red heels. Walking boots were of soft black leather. In bad weather, leather leggings buttoned up the sides were attached.

On either side of the vest, fob chains, charms, or tassels were displayed, and watches on chains, one of which might be false, were popular, They were often made (and carried) in pairs in case one failed to work. Buttons were enameled, often painted, or cut from steel.[3]

Silk and velvet were the preferred materials for men, and coats were heavily embroidered, with ruffles, ribbons, and laces, depending on the latest fads. Gentlemen spent an interminable amount of time on clothes fittings, which proved costly to individuals, many of whom were in debt to their tailors. Swords were usually worn at the side of the noble leg. Shirts of silk, linen, or cotton had a ruffled bib, as well as wrist ruffles, sometimes embroidered. Most men wore muffs in winter and carried canes with tasseled cords.

Members of the nobility who attended the Estates-General in 1789 were instructed to wear coats or cloaks of black with gold decoration, along with matching vest, black breeches, and white stockings. With this outfit went a lace cravat and a white-plumed hat. In contrast, regulations required that members of the Third Estate who attended the Estates-General wear a short, black coat, with black vest, breeches, and stockings, a cravat of muslin, and a hat turned up on three sides.[4] Later, when Convention members were sent as representatives on missions, they wore a blue coat and a red vest.[5]

European women tried to follow the fashions set by Marie-Antoinette and her *modiste,* Mlle Rose Bertin at Versailles. As a preview of what was going to be worn in French high society, large dolls, called fashion babies, dressed in the latest creations, were sent out to the European capitals to the eagerly waiting clientele.

At Versailles, wearing paniers (or hoops) beneath the petticoats and skirts of their stiff, formal gowns along with long trains that flowed from the waist, women had to be careful not to step either on their own skirts or on the trains of others. Tightly laced whalebone-lined corsets worn above the petticoats were drawn in to accentuate a small waist and curved out to show the line of the bosom; the neck and chest were bare, giving the body a long, slim look. Negotiating the corridors of the palace of Versailles, the women appeared to glide, but, as soon as they were able, they abandoned their constricting formal wear for something more comfortable.

The *à la française* robe, dating back to the previous reign, with its broad paniers and black pleats, ornamented with garlands of artificial flowers, pearls, and other gems, became the full dress for court, balls, and theater. Variations on this were the *polonaise* (with three paniers—one in back); the *circassienne,* with double sleeves; the *caraco,* a long gown with a ruffled peplum and sometimes a long train; and the *lévite,* a type of *redingote,* also with a train. Another *redingote,* adopted for horseback riding, had a double-breasted jacket and wide lapels.

Many exquisite and extravagant jewels were evident in necklaces, lockets, and crosses; even the little flat heelless slippers were encrusted with diamonds. A pair of handsome watches or charms often hung from under a vest in a style similar to that popular with men. Ivory writing tablets with tassels and fancy needle cases were sometimes carried, as well as eyeglasses mounted in gold and enamel. Buttons and buckles were of steel. Necklaces were finally supplanted by a simple velvet ribbon tied around the neck. Later, a pendant or miniature was suspended from the ribbon, and a *boutonnière* of fresh or artificial flowers was frequently worn by both sexes. Pale lavender, cream, light blue, green, and yellow were the preferred colors. Heavily embroidered materials were trimmed with lace and adorned with flowers, feathers, silk ribbons, fringes, and ruffles.

Women painted their faces red and white, and patches of black taffeta in various shapes were stuck on as beauty spots. The use of heavy perfumes declined because the queen preferred more delicate scents such as rose and violet.

The attire worn by the queen as she played on her fantasy farm at Le Trianon engendered a short-lived vogue for prints, aprons, and shawls, as well as large leghorn hats combined with feathers and jewels. Marie-Antoinette was also responsible for the popular *chemise à la reine,* a dress of sheer cotton or light silk with a ruffle at the low neck. A wide sash was tied around the waist. It was not an outfit for everyone, as prints and cottons, still imported from India, were expensive.

Wide side paniers were made from metal bands that were connected by tapes so that the hoops could be drawn up under the arms. In the 1780s, however, fashion went from wild extravagance to extreme simplicity, and paniers were replaced by bustles, although the hoops were still used for formal court wear. By 1783, skirts hung straight, and shoes had flat heels and sometimes were decorated with a tiny bow. The simpler, plain-colored satin *robe à l'anglaise* (in the English style), with its tight bodice, long full skirt, and long, slim sleeves, sometimes with an elbow puff, came into vogue, with a soft, full, shawl finishing off the neck.[6]

By 1789, people in Paris were still judged by their appearance. However, by that time, the lower classes, for example those in trade, who had the money could buy whatever they fancied, and they began to dress themselves in clothing normally worn by the nobility; thus, a tradesman's wife could wear the clothing of an aristocrat. The last sumptuary law of 1665, restricting people to certain forms of dress according to their level in society, was no longer enforced.[7]

Dress for children had also begun to change, and they no longer wore the tightly fitted clothes donned by their elders. A portrait of Marie-Antoinette with her two children, painted in 1785 by Wertmüller, portrays the dauphin in long trousers and a short, buttoned jacket. There is a frill at his open neck. The little girls wore simpler English-style dresses, and these, too, had frills at the low, round neck. A sash was worn around the waist.

Gentlemen continued to wear the tricorne hats, some with a rather flamboyant ostrich fringe. The most popular was a kind of Swiss army cocked hat that had two horns (bicorne), with a front and back flap. In the 1780s, a precursor of the top hat, with a high crown and a brim, also made its appearance, along with several other styles of headgear such as the Jockey hat, the Holland or Pennsylvania hat, and the Quaker hat.

Even as powdered wigs, once very common, began to disappear, they continued to be used by men in such positions as magistrates and lawyers, as well as by officials and courtiers at Versailles. In general, the hair at the back was worn in a very short pigtail or plait that was wound with a narrow ribbon. The cravat, wrapped around the neck and tied in a bow in front, endured well into the nineteenth century.

Early in the reign of Louis XVI, women's hair was worn high off the forehead with curls dressed over pads at the sides and at the back of the neck. The addition of false hair provided height and volume, and strings of pearls and flowers were added for full dress occasions.[8] When Marie-Antoinette became queen, coiffures became more and more fantastic as wool cushions were placed on top of the head, with both natural and false hair combed over them and held in place with steel pins. The hair and scalp were massaged with perfumed ointments; then, a paper bag covering the face, flour was thickly applied. Next, the hair was twisted into curls before being arrayed over the pads. Fastened on top was a fantastic variety of objects that could include flowers, ribbons, laces, bunches of fruit, jewels, feathers, blown glass, model ships, coaches, or windmills.

Behind, the hair was loosely curled into a chignon. These hairdos took so much time to prepare that attempts were made to keep them in place as long as possible. Scalps, however, suffering under the weight, itched and perspired. To alleviate this, pomade was used, but frequently it became malodorous within a few days, causing hair to fall out, with accompanying headaches and other problems. In addition, fleas and lice lived comfortably within the tresses, so that head-scratchers, long sticks with claws at the end, at times trimmed with diamonds, became the rage.

Sometimes the coiffure itself rose to two or three feet in height, making it difficult for the wearers to sit in a coach (they often had to kneel on the floor or ride with their heads sticking out of the window)[9] and even harder to sleep, since the hair had to be wrapped to keep everything in place. The story is told that one of Marie-Antoinette's most fantastic hair arrangements was so high that it had to be taken down so that she could enter the room for a soirée, then redone once she was inside.[10]

Hats for members of the court included circles of flowers, as well as more elaborate hats with cornucopias of fruit along with white feathers, worn with short veils.[11]

As the size of the coiffure increased, so did the bonnets. The *dormeuse*, or sleeping bonnet, so called because it was also worn at night, covered the cheeks and hugged the head tightly, being threaded with a ribbon that was tied in a bow on top. The daytime bonnet was worn higher, showing the ears and the back of the head. Others included the *thérèse*, of gauze or tulle or sometimes black taffeta, and the *calash*, with reed or whalebone hoops that could be raised or lowered by a ribbon to accommodate the height of the hairdo. Each of these was a kind of large cage that covered the huge coiffures.

There were many other styles, but two of the more unusual ones during the 1780s were the *coiffure à l'enfant*, in which the hair was cut short in a bob that became fashionable when the queen was ill and forced to cut her hair. Another, appearing about the same time, was the *coiffure à la hérissson*, or hedgehog hairstyle (not unlike that of men), which was cut fairly short in front, frizzed, and brushed up high off the face, with long, loose curls in back.

When the more simple styles became popular, bonnets became smaller, and all sizes and shapes of hats, made of felt or beaver, trimmed with plumes, ribbons, fruit and flowers, and worn at all angles, appeared. At this time, one of the most elegant was what is known as the Gainsborough hat, worn by the duchess of Marlborough in a portrait painted by Gainsborough.

In vogue for a while were straw hats with wide brims, a simple ribbon around the low crown. Their popularity was greatest during the queen's "milkmaid" period, and they were considered a rustic fashion.

The *pelisse*, a fur-trimmed wrap or cape with armholes, continued to be worn in winter, and women carried large fur muffs to protect their arms and hands. In the summer, small muffs made of silk and satin, beribboned and embroidered, were worn at balls. Long, soft gloves of light-colored kid were used throughout the century.

Slippers were made of satin, brocade, or kid, with moderately high heels; sometimes the back seams were encrusted with gems. Leather shoes were worn only by the middle or the lower class. Stockings of both silk and cotton were white.

## THE BOURGEOISIE

Some of the wealthier bourgeoisie dressed colorfully, but magistrates, lawyers, and officials kept to sedate and somber blacks, browns, or grays.[12] The materials they chose, however, were luxurious and included silk, wool, and velvet, and their wigs were elegant and expensive. Other professionals, like doctors, architects, and writers, did not spend much on their apparel and so, as a symbol of their sobriety, wore black in the main. Merchants were more richly attired and used jewelry and other adornments. In these groups, the wives and daughters were turned out with more magnificence than the men. Dressed for a special occasion, a lady might wear an outfit that included a lace cap decorated with a violet ribbon, a white dress, or perhaps a sheath dress with scarlet belt, and matching earrings, a pearl necklace, and a Madras bandana. Dull-colored frock coats of taffeta were generally worn. A young girl attending a festival at the Tuileries in 1793 wrote a letter to her father about her apparel:

I wore an overskirt of lawn [cotton or linen], a tricolor sash around my waist, and an embroidered fichu [shawl] of red cotton; on my head, a cambric fichu, arranged like the fillet round the brows of Grecian women, and my hair, dressed in nine small plaits, was upswept on to the crown of my head. Mama wore a cambric dress at whose hem there was a vastly pretty border and on her dear head a wide-brimmed straw hat with violet satin ribbons.[13]

A deputy from the Vendée, Goupilleau de Montaigu, made several trips to the south of the country between 1793 and 1795 and noted that "between Nevers and Roanne, all the women wore straw hats and between Roanne and Lyon the straw is black and the brims are wider." He went on to say that "at Nice imprudent beauties, grilled like toast, are coifed only with a light gauze scarf." At Marseille, women wore headdresses to protect their skin from the sun.[14]

## THE PEASANTS

Just before the revolution, many peasants wore homemade clothes of coarse black cloth, the dye coming from the bark of the oak tree. Others, who could afford it, wore wool. A contemporary writer commented:

A French peasant is badly dressed and the rags which cover his nudity are poor protection against the harshness of the seasons; however it appears that his state, in respect of clothing, is less deplorable than in the past. Dress for the poor is not an object of luxury but a necessary defence against the cold: coarse linen, the clothing of many peasants, does not protect them adequately … but for some years … a very much larger number of peasants have been wearing woollen clothes. The proof of this is simple, because it is certain that for some time a larger quantity of rough woollen cloth has been produced in the realm; and as it is not exported, it must necessarily be used to clothe a larger number of Frenchmen.[15]

The very poor often had only one miserable outfit for both summer and winter. A man's thin, cleated shoes, often procured at the time of marriage, had to last all his life. Peasant women wore short cloaks with hoods of coarse woolen material and often went barefoot.

Marie-Antoinette, showing some of the elaborate clothing and hairstyles of the age. Bibliothèque Nationale de France.

## THE REVOLUTION

After 1789, it became dangerous to display elegance and affluence in public, and hoops, paint, powder, beauty spots, artificial flowers and fruit, and all the trappings of the old regime in costume disappeared. By the time the court lost its influence, the social life of high society had ceased, and the privilege of wearing clothes made of fine materials, with feathers, red heels, and other such attire, now extended to all citizens, but such finery was scorned by most.

The fashion center now moved from Versailles to Paris, where political opinions (rather than social class) were expressed through dress: those loyal to the monarchy wore cockades that were white on one side (to represent the monarchy) and tricolor on the other (for the revolution)—presumably as insurance against the outcome whichever way it went!

Evidence of social distinction by means of dress was abolished by the National Assembly, and since fashion journals quickly disappeared, information concerning the mode in Paris had to come from contemporary English and German sources.

Although many of the bourgeois leaders continued to wear the old-style breeches and shirts with ruffles, the official costume for a "true patriot" required the substitution of trousers for breeches (or *culottes*), which created a new trade—the manufacture of suspenders and of hocks, that is, shortened stockings. The pants opened in front with a panel attached to the vest by three buttons. They were called *pantalons à pont* (bridge trousers) because the panel operated like a drawbridge. Previously, these had been used only by British sailors, but in late-eighteenth-century France, those who wore them—the sans-culottes (literally, without breeches)—were completely set apart from the aristocrats; they also wore the red bonnet or cap, with the cockade, one of the primary symbols of liberty. In addition, the patriot wore either a vest or a short, blue jacket called a *carmagnole* that was originally used by Piedmont peasant workers who came from the area of Carmagnola. Deputies from Marseille took the garment to Paris, where it was adopted and worn by the revolutionaries, sometimes accompanied by a brown *redingote* with collar and lapels faced with red and, as shoes, *sabots* (or clogs).[16]

Early in 1790, a "constitutional costume" was also prescribed for women. To be stylish now meant that patriotism had to be displayed, and militant women used badges and symbols to show their espousal of the revolution. Sometimes, especially at festivals, they wore only white, with tricolor cockades in their hair. Others appeared in the uniform of the National Guard, while some aggressive women armed themselves with pistols or sabers. The everyday clothing of working-class women would have included a striped skirt, an apron, and clogs.

The tricolor became obligatory in everything from gloves to shoes. For women, this meant red-white-and-blue cotton dresses (often printed with revolutionary symbols with the requisite colored stripes), sashes, shawls, shoes, hats, and even bouquets of flowers (daisies, cornflowers, and crimson poppies) placed to the left side above the heart. The tricolor was used by everyone of all ages, in all levels of society. The cockade in particular was worn all the time.

Like that of men, women's costume became simpler. The basic lines of the style of the last years of the Louis XVI period were retained, however, with the only noticeable change being the new raised waistline. The bodice was laced tightly from waist to breasts, and a full shawl of sheer white tulle or gauze was tucked into the neck of the bodice. Folds of satin reaching up to the chin were often added, making the wearer look like a puffed-up pigeon. Sleeves were long and tight; skirts were full and worn over many petticoats.

A ban against luxurious materials such as silk and velvet led to the increase of simple, figured cottons and linens. Satin, now used more rarely, was brownish green or dull blue. Later, ostrich plumes reappeared.

The peasant or milkmaid cap, called today the "Charlotte Corday cap," had a full crown with a ruffle around it and was decorated with the tricolor cockade. Hair was now cut low in front, sometimes parted in the middle, with soft puffs at the sides, the back hair hanging in ringlets or gathered in a chignon.

Embroidered handkerchiefs and fans continued to be carried, but, in place of the exquisite and costly works of art in ivory, tortoise shell, or mother-of-pearl, fans were now made of wood or paper and embellished with brilliant designs depicting, for instance, the National Guard, Lafayette, or the Estates-General.

Because they had operated under royal patronage, the lace factories were torn down and demolished. Some of the lacemakers were put to death and their patterns destroyed.[17]

The uniform of the sans-culottes did not meet with great success and lasted only a few years. It was cast aside after the fall of the Jacobins in July 1794, when the Convention, always looking toward uniformity, commissioned the artist Jacques-Louis David to create a national costume. Attempting to fill the requirements of an outfit suitable to the ideal of equality within the new social order, David produced a design that consisted of tight trousers with boots, a tunic, and a short coat, but this was never put into practice.

In 1797, the outcome of the search for a national dress was that all materials had to be made in France and the principal colors should be blue, white, and red. Eventually, all deputies were ordered to wear a coat of blue, a tricolor belt, a scarlet cloak, and a velvet hat with the tricolored plume.

Before the revolution, children were given traditional names such as Jacques, René, Antoine, Sophie, and Françoise. Saints' names, once so popular and widespread, were now out of favor, so others had to be found to replace them. Names of heroes of the revolution or taken from the

REFRAINS PATRIOTIQUES

Si vous aimez la danse,
Venez accourez tous,
Boire du Vin de France (bis)
Et danser avec nous.

Dansons la carmagnole
Vive le son vive le son,
Dansons la carmagnole
Vive le son du canon.

Ah! ça ira, ça ira ça ira,
Le Peuple en ce jour sans cesse répète
Ah! ça ira ça ira ça ira,
Réjouissons nous le bon temps viendra

A Paris Rue du Théâtre Français, No. 4.

Sans-culottes dancing around a Liberty Tree decorated with a cockade and the revolutionary red bonnet. The Bastille is shown on the right, and an Austrian army being routed is seen to the left. Bibliothèque Nationale de France.

much-admired Romans and Greeks now began to be used, and names like Brutus and Epaminondas (a Greek general who defeated the Spartans) were employed. One female infant was registered as Phytogynéantrope, which means "a woman who gives birth only to warrior sons." Other babies were given names containing Marat or August the Tenth, Fructidor, and even Constitution. One girl was called Civilization-Jemmapes-République. Her nickname has not been recorded.[18]

The red bonnet has a special place in French history. It was modeled on the ancient Phrygian cap adopted by freed slaves in Roman times as a symbol of liberty. Regardless of the material and whether it had a hanging pointed crown or was simply a skullcap with a pointed crown, it was always ornamented with the tricolor cockade. By the end of 1792, this cap represented the political power of the militant sans-culottes and served to identify them with the lower ranks of the Third Estate of the Old Regime. Although the revolutionary bourgeoisie rarely wore the red bonnet, many citizens did so spontaneously, wishing to demonstrate clearly their repudiation of all that had gone before. These bonnets were held high at ceremonies, sometimes placed on the top of poles or hung on liberty trees, and vividly symbolized the new freedom from the old absolute oppression. After the invasion of the Tuileries palace, on June 20, 1792, even the king put on one of these red caps, albeit reluctantly.

All streets and squares in Paris that had been named for the king, court, or someone who had served the monarchy were changed to honor the revolution: Place de Louis XV became the Place de la Révolution, rue Bourbon became rue de Lille, and rue Madame was changed to rue des Citoyennes. In addition, streets previously named for Saint Denis, Saint Foch, and Saint Antoine became simply rue Denis, rue Foch, and rue Antoine. The cathedral of Nôtre Dame became the Temple of Reason. Provincial towns with names of saints or royalty sometimes changed their name completely; for example, *Saint-Lô* became known as *Rocher de la Liberté*.

To conform to the egalitarian spirit of the times, the familiar second-person singular, *tu*, was used instead of the formal *vous* throughout much of the country. The idea of using *tu* in all circumstances was first proposed in an article in the *Mercure National* on December 14, 1790, but nothing more was said about it until three years later, when the article came to the attention of the Convention. No laws were passed registering the mandatory use of *tu*, but the debate stirred the public and that form of "you" began to spread. Now the baker's apprentice could address his master and clients in a familiar form, a practice that had been strictly forbidden. Within a short time, people in Paris were speaking to one another as if they were family or long-time, intimate friends. Anyone who continued to use *vous* was treated as suspect.

Similarly, the forms of address *Monsieur* and *Madame* were replaced by *Citoyen* and *Citoyenne* with the same objective of eliminating class distinction. All over the country, "Citizen" was the only recognized form of address. Plays already being staged and works in the offing had to have their wording changed to conform to the new usage. When a player at the *Opéra-Comique* inadvertently used the old forms in a speech, he was not excused for a lapse of memory and had to duck out of the way as the seats were thrown at him.[19]

## THE DIRECTORY

With the Directory came new trends based on the classical styles of ancient Greece and Rome. As fashion journals began to reappear, daily life returned to the trappings of normality. When *émigrés* returned to France, they were often seen wearing the blond wigs of the antirevolutionaries of the earlier time as well as a black collar as a sign of mourning for the fate of king, queen, and country and a green cravat signifying royal fidelity.

The revolutionary, on the other hand, wore a red collar on his coat, and the antagonisms between the blacks and reds led to numerous fierce street battles.

Instead of expensive necklaces and rings, women began wearing gilded copper wedding rings with the words "Nation," "Law," and "King" engraved on them and earrings made of glass and a variety of other trinkets, sometimes made out of bits of stone from the Bastille.

After the Terror and during the years of the Directory, the *Muscadins* and the *Merveilleuses*—children of the wealthy bourgeoisie—reacted against the austerity of the government. To demonstrate their independence and their repudiation of the republican state, they went to extremes in the way they dressed, openly showing contempt for what they considered to be Jacobin mediocrity. Very little attention was paid by this group to the principles of virtue and morality.

The *Muscadins*, also known as the *Incroyables, Impossibles,* or *Petits-Maîtres,* were rich and effeminate middle-class dandies who copied the clothes of the earlier court nobility, strutting about like peacocks. They were mainly young Parisians who had avoided conscription in the revolutionary wars.

They were seen in frock coats, sometimes with large pleats across the back and high, turndown collars and exaggerated lapels that sloped away from the waist when buttoned. Corsets helped show off small waistlines, since the coats fitted snugly. An elaborate vest with as many as three visible layers of different colors on the bottom edge would also have had a high collar that turned down to show the inside neck of the coat. Coats and vests were beribboned and had buttonholes of gold. A monocle, a sword, or even a hunting knife might be worn and a knotted, wooden, lead-weighted stick carried in the hand.

A large, muslin cravat, often fastened with a jeweled pin, had a padded silk cushion concealed underneath. It was wound loosely around the neck several times. Lace filled any remaining opening in the vest. Their breeches (or culottes), fastened with buttons or ribbons just below the knees, usually were worn with striped silk stockings and high black boots.

The *Muscadins'* felt hats were extreme in size and were decorated with red, white, and blue rosette,, although many appeared in the white, royalist cockade (in defiance of the law) and sometimes also a silk cord or a plume. Hoop earrings often dangled from their ears. They were thoroughly disliked, as their showy dress threatened the sedate and serious image being cultivated by the bourgeoisie. They were employed by the Thermidorians to terrorize former radicals but were repressed when their usefulness came to an end.[20]

Others chose to wear more dignified and refined styles, including frock coats with small lapels and stand-up collars in black or violet velvet, black satin vests, and very tight breeches of dull blue cloth. Other popular colors were canary yellow and bottle green with a brown coat, the latter with small lapels and a modest standing collar. The silk or muslin cravat came in green, bright red, or black. Boots of various heights were made of soft leather and had pointed toes; stockings were generally white or striped. Once again, two watches or charms hung from the vest, and the lorgnette was used. Hair was beginning to be cut short in the Roman style.

After the Terror, people began to enjoy themselves again. One of the best-known of the open-air dance pavilions was the *Bal des Victimes,* so-called because only those who had lost a relative to the guillotine could go there. Men who attended the dance pavilions generally kept their hair short, often in a ragged cut.[21]

The *Merveilleuses,* the female counterpart of the *Muscadins,* were often seen in gowns cut in the classical Greek tradition. In Paris, some of these women began to wear see-through or even topless diaphanous gowns or a transparent tunic over flesh-colored silk tights. The predominant color was white; this remained so throughout the period of the Empire. Neck-lines were very low, bodices short and tight, and skirts full and with trains that were carried over the arm. In addition, knee-length tunics were popu-lar, split up the sides, sometimes as far as the waist, to show a bare leg or flesh-colored tights.

Some gowns were sleeveless, the material held together with brooches at the shoulders, long gloves covering the bare arms. If there were sleeves, they were either long and tight or very short. Materials were sheer Indian muslin, sometimes embroidered, gauze, lace, or very light cotton. There were no pockets in the gowns, so small drawstring embroidered bags, often with fringes and tassels, were suspended from the belt to hold nec-essary articles.

Outdoors, long, narrow scarves of cashmere, serge, silk, or rabbit wool in colors such as orange, white, and black were worn over the light gowns. The scarves matched the wearers' bonnets. High-crowned straw bonnets were trimmed with lace, ribbons, feathers, or flowers. The meaning of the word "bonnet" (previously applied to men's toques) had changed by this time to designate a woman's hat that was tied under the chin. Other hats included turbans.

Blond wigs and switches of false hair again made their appearance. It was usual to change wigs frequently, and many women owned 10 or more. Wigs were curled and decorated with ribbons or jewels. Ancient hairstyles were copied, and in hairdressing salons, busts of goddesses and empresses were exhibited. When a woman chose not to wear a wig, her hair was plaited or curled in the manner of the ancients, brushed back, waved, curled, oiled, and knotted or twisted at the nape of the neck in a psyche knot. Some women cut their hair short, brushed it in all directions from the crown, with uneven ends hanging over the forehead and sides, occasionally with long, straggling pieces hanging down at the sides of the face, and shaved the back of their heads to create a style known as *coiffure à la Titus.* A short-lived fad was to appear with shaved heads and a ribbon of red velvet around the throat, a gruesome reminder of the victims of the guillotine.

Jewelry, such as necklaces, rings, and bracelets for bare ankles and toes, was extensively worn, along with strings of pearls in the hair and jeweled belts about two inches wide worn just under the breasts.

Apple green remained a favorite color, and the soft, flat, pointed sandals—sometimes just a sole strapped to the foot by ribbons—were often of this shade. The sandals could be laced up to and around the ankle with narrow, red straps decorated with jewels—but more often flat slippers of fabric or kid were worn with white silk stockings. A small bow or edging finished the slipper.[22]

## THE CONSULATE AND THE EMPIRE

At the turn of the nineteenth century, some men still wore breeches, but full-length trousers were becoming common. These were tight-fitting, and the most popular material for old and young for both formal and informal wear was buff or yellow nankeen cotton. During the Empire, trousers and gaiters appeared, combined as one garment. Suits were of dark blue, green, or brown cloth, while vests were usually made of cotton (percale) with a border of contrasting color and a row of buttons down the front. The starched points of the shirt collar showed above the (often two) cravats that together gave a thick look around the neck, a leftover from the style of the *muscadins* of the previous period.

For ceremonial or formal occasions, a colored velvet coat was worn with black satin breeches, an embroidered silk vest, a shirt with wrist ruffles, and a cravat. This ensemble was accompanied by a powdered wig, bicorne hat, and sword.

In winter, men generally used a double-breasted greatcoat of the fitted *redingote* style or a single-breasted coat with two or more capes. Hats had tall crowns and narrow brims and were made of felt or beaver. In summer, they were of straw. Boots of soft black leather, often imported from England, were worn with white stockings, and short gaiters came in about 1804. As trousers were used more and more, so was the short sock. Military boots, such as the Wellington, which came over the knee in front but below it in the back, caught on with the general public. Ironically, Napoleon was fond of wearing these. The Brutus haircut was popular, while powder and wigs for men disappeared altogether.

Women continued to wear the semitransparent chemise gown, sometimes of thin taffeta, over a slip and belted under the breasts. A variant was a tunic of colored silk or velvet over a white sheath gown. Embroidery in classical designs was favored, and muslin dresses were sometimes ornamented with gold and silver thread or spangles of copper or steel. Sleeves were long and divided into puffs by bands of ribbon. Petticoats were edged with lace frills to show beneath the hem of the sheer dresses, and sometimes flesh-colored ruffled bloomers were worn.

Originating in England, the spencer (or bolero), a very short jacket with tight sleeves and open in the front, had a standup collar and came usually in dark-colored velvet to contrast with the gown. It often had a border of fur or swansdown. A variation was the *canezou* or hussar vest, which was pulled on over the head, fitting tightly on the lower edge. In winter, fur coats of martin or sable were the rage.

The court dress of this period, established by the empress, Josephine, consisted of two ensembles: the little gown of embroidered blue satin with short puffed sleeves and a train that fell from the belt and the highly decorated grand costume, which comprised a gown of brocaded silver with long, tight sleeves and a train falling from the left shoulder. Both had necklines that were square in front and embroidered with pearls and spangles.

When Napoleon returned from his various campaigns, styles were influenced by where he had been fighting: Italian, Spanish, Turkish, and English fashions followed one another in succession. Cashmere shawls with embroidered borders continued in use. Others of silk, wool, chiffon, lace, or cotton became fashionable after the return of Napoleon's army from Egypt, where they were made on handlooms. It was said that Josephine had 300 to 400 shawls, each costing 15,000 to 20,000 francs.[23]

A popular coiffure of the times called for the hair to be drawn tightly to the back; this style was called *à la chinoise*. An increase in the popularity of luxurious turbans was a result of Napoleon's campaign in Egypt. Lace now returned to favor and was used in veils that hung from the front edge of bonnets and as edges for caps, aprons, and gowns. Fur bonnets were worn with fur coats.

Women carried handkerchiefs in the hand and hid coin purses in the bosom. Small painted or jeweled fans made of fine silk came back into style, and women used embellishments such as jeweled hairpins, hatpins, lockets, watches, and cameos. Artificial flowers were worn in the hair, on bonnets, and as corsages. Flat shoes made of fabric or kid were laced and tied around the ankle.

The use of powder and rouge all but disappeared under Napoleon, whose campaign of cleanliness discouraged it, and a pallid complexion became more popular. By 1800, soap was in general use in Paris, and men and women of the upper classes, now more conscious of personal hygiene, began their day with a bath. The emperor also changed his underclothes every day, and Josephine changed hers three times daily. A gift of the empress to a niece contained underclothes to the value of 25,000 francs.

Napoleon was devoted to pomp and pageantry as much as any king had ever been, and during his reign dress assumed a brilliance that had been abandoned only a few years before. Embroidery, lace, velvet, and silk came back into style, and their manufacturers, ruined during the Terror, made a vigorous recovery.

## NOTES

1. Garrioch, 53.
2. Hunt [1984], 75.
3. Wilcox, 207.
4. Cobb, 46.
5. Robiquet, 178.
6. For more details, see Wilcox, 209–11.
7. Garrioch, 286–89.
8. Erickson, 98–99.
9. Cobb, 46.
10. Erickson, 99.
11. Ibid., 98–99.
12. Hunt, 75.
13. Robiquet, 134.
14. Ibid., 180.
15. See Moheau, *Recherches et considérations sur la population de la France* (1778), 262, quoted in Braudel, 315.
16. The *carmagnole* was also an anonymous song and street dance popular during the Reign of Terror. Reportedly brought to Paris from Marseille, the song became well known after the storming of the Tuileries, on August 10, 1792. The *carmagnole* consisted originally of 13 two-line stanzas, each of which ended with a refrain praising the revolution. New stanzas were added from time to time, and a street dance was improvised. The dance itself was a form of *farandole*, the ancient chain dance of France. The *carmagnole* was sung and danced at revolutionary festivals as well as at executions.
17. Wilcox, 222–24.
18. Robiquet, 63–64.
19. For a discussion on this subject, see Robiquet, 56–61.
20. Cooke, 193, and Wrigley 265–66.
21. Wilcox, 228–31.
22. Ibid., 231–32; Robiquet, 224.
23. Wilcox, 240.

# 6

# Arts and Entertainment

## OLD REGIME

Not long before the revolution, popular theater had evolved from fairground spectacles to become a staple of city life. Boulevard audiences comprised a mixture of all classes and prices, for seats were regulated according to their location in the theater. The poor sat in the peanut gallery up high and in the far back, while the well-to-do had the option of the best seats or private loges.

Of the many theaters in operation at that time, the *Comédie Française,* the *Comédie-Italienne,* and the *Opéra* produced works written by some of Europe's finest writers. As major national theaters, they enjoyed a near-monopoly on the best dramatic material. They competed only with smaller establishments and had enough clout to have these competitors closed down by the police if they attracted large audiences. In addition, a complex set of rules restricted the activities of smaller theaters. For example, in some theaters, the characters could be wounded and faint or bleed, but they were not permitted to die on stage; in others, only acrobats or pantomime could be staged; in one theater, the number of acts put on was restricted, and in another, a gauze curtain was hung between the audience and the actors to reduce the effect of the production.[1]

The spectacle on the stage reinforced the status quo of daily life. Censorship was heavy on playwrights, who had to submit their manuscripts for approval, and the police were quick to suppress political material that did not reflect well on the royal government or the church. Nevertheless, theater in France had a fine reputation.

Beaumarchais was one of the first playwrights to ridicule the nobility and undermine the social system with his *Marriage of Figaro*, which was replete with references to contemporary issues such as the powers of the police, freedom of speech, and the privileges of the aristocracy. Written in a lighthearted manner in which the servants mocked their aristocratic master, the work itself was revolutionary in its theme, which treated the overthrow of the *droit de seigneur* (right of the lord to sleep first with a girl servant in his fief before turning her over to her new husband).

When Louis XVI heard the text of this play, he labeled it detestable, saying that it should not even be permitted to be performed in private.[2] Indeed, that is how it was first presented—in private. The queen and some of the courtiers were in favor of it, and when the king eventually allowed its performance, it was staged at court. Seven months later, on April 27, 1784, it was publicly performed in Paris.

## REVOLUTIONARY THEATER

Revolutionary Paris, as well as other large provincial towns against monopolies of any kind, forced the major theaters to be more egalitarian and to present a variety of works, plays, operas, and farces to appeal to the general public. More boulevard theaters sprang up, giving performances aimed at the tastes of average, working people.

As the revolution moved on, so did the theater. On January 13, 1791, the National Assembly abolished the restrictions that had previously limited the productions put on by smaller houses. At the same time, the office of censor was also done away with, and many of the new plays had themes of anticlericalism and antimonasticism. In one of the most successful, the villain, a licentious priest, is attracted to a young girl, whom he imprisons in his order. He tells her wealthy young man that she is dead and convinces him to enter the monastic life himself and leave all his possessions to the monastery. The two captives are placed in adjacent dungeons, but, to the delight of the audience, they are rescued by members of the National Guard, who have come to destroy the building.[3]

The productions put on between 1790 and 1795 were often banal, even idiotic. Passionate in its desire for spectacle and drama, the general public applauded everything equally. Identifying with the characters, the audiences would sometimes ask the actors to repeat their lines or omit references considered unfavorable to the revolution. If the audiences became angry, they sometimes rushed up onto the stage, and occasionally plays did not survive to the final act. Great works of the past era, such as those written by Molière, Voltaire, Racine, and Corneille were so mutilated that they were almost unrecognizable.

Sometimes there were as many as 4,000 persons in a theater singing loudly and dancing to the patriotic music. With the tradition of classical theater at a low ebb, subject matter became debased and vulgar. Performances took place not only in theaters but also in private houses, warehouses, markets, at fairs, and on the boulevards. Most of the new shows put on in Paris carried a political message.

One of the most successful plays was *Le Dernier Jugement des rois*, which features the kings of England and Prussia, Catherine the Great, of Russia, and the pope, all of whom are confined to a volcanic island. After a few scenes depicting the wickedness of such rulers, the madness of George III, and the nymphomaniac character of Catherine (who attempts to seduce the Pope), they are all finally engulfed by a volcanic eruption. The sans-culottes were ecstatic![4]

Under the Terror, artists of all genres suffered from political persecution and from the stifling atmosphere of fear and anxiety created by the reintroduction of censorship. Through art the government attempted to indoctrinate society to accept the new political culture. Art, architecture, painting, music, plays, and festivals were all used to pass the message. The Jacobins were concerned about projecting a good image: virtue was in, and vice, considered now to be an aristocratic disease, was out.

While refined audiences lauded the plays of the past, the majority patronized the small boulevard theaters and the fairs. Even in the presence of scaffolds, the theaters were filled, commented Madame de Staël.[5] In Paris, small theaters catered to popular taste. The *Gaité*, the largest, was known for its mix of acrobats, buffoons, and stories of unhappy lovers. It was packed every night.

Pantomimes were popular. *Harlequin*, for example, was continually played, since it was first written for the *Gaité* and generated great enthusiasm, especially when Pantalon, the old man, eager to marry off his daughter even to an unsuitable man, sets off an intrigue with all the elements of greed, lust, and unrequited love. The audience would wait impatiently for Harlequin's appearance, as he is the one loved by Columbine. He enters dressed in an animal skin so that he can court her in the kitchen undetected. Pantalon mistakes him for a real dog and tries to play with him. The dog spits in the old man's face and snatches his purse; in some versions, he sniffs Pantalon's clothes and lifts his leg, sending the crowd into peels of laughter.[6]

In 1793, there were about 250 new productions in Paris alone. Most dealt with such subjects as the virtues of the republican wife and honorable workers, the treachery of a priest or an aristocrat, or the lofty civic qualities of a son who would rather see his monarchist parents in prison than have the republic threatened. The highly rated cast of the *Comédie Française* was divided in its individual political convictions, and some members spent time in prison because of their antirevolutionary beliefs. Others, such as the great new actor Talma and a new group of entertainers, supported the Jacobins.

The revolutionary theaters had something for everyone: the *Saint-Antoine* had an orchestra of 22 musicians and seated 390 people; it also had three levels of loges. Prices there ranged from 24 sous for seats on the ground floor to much more for a box in the dress circle.[7] Madame Montansier's establishment at the Palais Royal offered gentlemen not only the latest in plays but also a choice of attractive young ladies to take home afterwards.

The melodramas of Guilbert de Pixérécourt represented the stage in its transition between classical and romantic. His plays were very popular with the general public, who liked his usual theme that evil must be punished and virtue rewarded. Born into an aristocratic family, in 1773, he was forced to hide out during the Terror. His *Les Petits Auvergnats* appeared in 1797 and dealt with the standard comic character of eighteenth-century literature—the country bumpkin in the big city.[8] But it was his colorful and exciting melodramas that thrilled the crowds; these were sometimes set in exotic places and often included a virtuous damsel in distress, a blaggard, and a hero who resolves a dangerous situation.

Audiences of all levels were demanding and, if not pleased, resorted to booing or hissing, and sometimes even to violence, tearing up the seats and benches in the galleries. A production that was late starting might provoke the audience to such unruly behavior. For these reasons, weapons were not permitted in the theater, and police were in attendance to control the spectators. Sometimes actors were jailed for failing to please the audience.

New plays significantly departed from past dramatic content: there were now no servants or masters. The stage became an avalanche of patriotic words, and dramatic interest was replaced by descending goddesses, conflagrations, combats, and the struggle of the republic, along with the iconic language of the revolution represented via liberty trees, flags, cockades, and sans-culotte costumes.

In 1793 and 1794, during the Terror, all plays that did not conform to the social and moral prescriptions of an egalitarian republic were purged through new rules of censorship. Buffooneries were now condemned and nobility banished from the stage. The most vapid plays that relied on social structures or comic conventions of the old regime were seen to undermine the revolution, and those who participated in these productions were regarded as preserving the degrading manners of enslaved men and women. Even the theater itself, with its seating segregated by price and therefore class, was considered by some to be counterrevolutionary.

By 1793, the aristocratic *Opéra* had devolved into republican opera both in repertoire and in audience. A particularly popular production, the *Siège de Thionville*, first performed on June 13, was demanded by Parisians even when it was not scheduled. The lyric patriotic opera in two acts was based on the failed two-month siege of the city by antirevolutionary *émigrés* and Austrians nearly a year before. The Paris commune ordered that the play be performed gratis for the entertainment of the sans-culottes.

In January 1794, the Surveillance Committee in Paris closed the *Gaité* and arrested the owner, Nicolet, and also his Harlequin, on a charge of corrupting the morals of the little-educated but respectable people who attended the theater. The actor was jailed for his crude gestures, the owner for tolerating them.

Paris and other large cities were not alone in the entertainment business. On Sundays and feast days, burlesque and puppet shows, acrobats, ballad singers, and magicians were all popular in small towns, where they were presented by itinerant actors.

With the fall of Robespierre and the Jacobins, reaction to the Terror set in, leading to the production of many new works. A series of anti-Jacobin plays were popular, including *Les Jacobins aux enfers* (The Jacobins in Hell), presented in March 1795. Here the devil is reluctant to accept the Jacobins until Harlequin, the assistant of Pluto (the devil), whose job is to escort them there, states:

> You surely cannot hesitate
> Whatever troubles you may fear.
> The Jacobins now at your gate
> Have earned the right to enter here,
> For all those left on earth agree
> That Hell is where they ought to be.[9]

While a handful of new plays had been produced annually before the revolution, at least 1,500 new plays, many topical, were produced between 1789 and 1799. In the last years of the Directory, a relative calm prevailed over the theaters of Paris. Censorship continued; with a few exceptions, dramatic plays were uninspiring, and the *Opéra* was producing nothing new of interest. Bankrupt, the *Opéra* was forced to close for a time, but it was revived with the aid of permanent government subsidies in 1803.

Theater productions were greatly curtailed by Napoleon, who permitted them only if they enhanced his own reputation in particular or the regime in general. His view of the theater was not unlike his view of the press: if it contributed to his reputation, fine, but it should not be allowed to pander to the tastes of the common multitudes. By 1807, only eight theaters enjoyed government sanction. Nevertheless, the average Frenchman was not about to give up the pleasures of the popular theater. In Paris one could still attend the reopened *Gaité* or the nearby *L'Ambigu comique* or be present at some of the scores of private performances staged in homes and even cellars. Plays were still produced in the provinces, and most major towns had several theaters. Bordeaux had four, and people waited in line for hours to see a performance by Talma in one of his tragic roles. Even the emperor himself was a follower of Mademoiselle Georges, one of the most celebrated actresses of the time.

By the last quarter of the eighteenth century, there had developed in major cities permanent attractions that gave the people more variety in their lives. Street performers with juggling acts were popular, as were fire and sword swallowers, puppet shows, acrobats, scientific exhibitions, animal shows, pantomime, and fireworks. Some theaters that specialized in pantomime kept prices low enough for almost anyone to be able to attend. There was entertainment, even for the destitute, who could see street performances and mingle with the crowds.[10]

## PUBLIC FESTIVALS

The majority of French people lived in rural surroundings and enjoyed their traditional festivals and pastimes at village fairs and popular balls; they enjoyed games of *boules*, dancing the *farandoles*, and celebrating the towns' saint days. These activities, if not in the local church, usually took place in a public field near the village. Some activities were secular and some religious; among the religious celebrations were Christmas, New Year's, Easter, All Saints Day, Saint John the Baptist Day, Mardi Gras, and the Assumption. Prior to the revolution, 35 holidays were recognized, not counting particular saints days, which were observed by parishes and guilds.

Secular festivals were frequent and involved feasting, dancing, and ribaldry at carnival time, which marked the beginning of Lent. Other days of celebration might mark a special occasion, such as a royal marriage or the birth of a royal child. More and more republican processions were held, taking on a moral-philosophical character, including the *Fête de la Fédération*, held on July 14, 1790, the anniversary of the storming of the Bastille, when thousands of National Guardsmen and soldiers from all quarters of France converged on Paris to take part in the events at the Champ de Mars, where a large open space was excavated in the middle with the dirt piled up on the sides, making it into a vast amphitheater. Many able-bodied men and women of Paris worked on the project along with 12,000 workmen already employed to complete it in time for the first event.

It was a prodigious ceremony. Everyone, rich and poor, old and young, clergy and secular, military bands and *fédérés*, marched to the sound of drums and often broke into song, especially the *ça ira*, a theme song of the revolution.[11] Some 300,000 people at the Champ de Mars witnessed the celebration in the rain. A bishop, attended by 300 priests, said Mass in the center of the amphitheater, and then, to the music of 1,200 musicians, the *Te Deum* was sung. The bishop blessed the 83 banners of the *fédérés*, after which cannon boomed and banners waved. The president of the Assembly rose and swore an oath to be faithful to the nation, and the deputies of the Convention did the same. All went silent when the king rose, and he too swore to uphold the constitution decreed by the National Assembly. The queen then stood, holding her son in her arms and affirming that they too joined in these sentiments. Thousands of voices greeted these pronouncements with *Vive le Roi! Vive la Reine!* and *Vive Monsieur le Dauphin!* The rain stopped, the sun appeared, and festivities continued for two more days, with parades, balls, fireworks, and banquets. The trees of the avenues were festooned with colored lights, and crowds danced and sang in the streets all night. Most people thought that the worst was behind them and that a free, unified France had burst forth. Far from home, many of the *fédérés* spent a good deal of time studying the pamphlets of the enterprising publisher that gave the names, addresses, and prices of potential Parisian playmates.

Life in France was profoundly affected by the new calendar that replaced the Gregorian one. Introduced by the Convention in October 1793, it reorganized the timeframe of the entire country, with the purpose of detaching republicans from what was perceived as religious superstition embodied in the old calendar. The 12 months were given new names in accordance with nature. For example, the first month began with the founding of the republic in late September and was called *Vendémiaire*, since this was the time for the gathering of the grape, the *vendange*, for wine making. Each month was divided into three 10-day periods or *décadis*. Days were renamed *primidi, duodi*, and so on up to *décadi*, the latter being a day of rest. This meant that there were nine working days before a day of rest instead of the six of the old calendar. The five days left over (sometimes six in a leap year) were designated as festival days (see Appendix 2). There were to be no more Sundays or religious feast days. The new calendar replaced the Christian holidays with metrically timed secular holidays commemorating Labor, Reason, Virtue, Genius, Rewards, and, finally, the revolution itself.

Many festivals were now held in Paris, and the provincial inhabitants wanted similar kinds of entertainment. These celebrations became such an integral part of daily life that the Convention created more national festival days celebrating the republic, youth, old age, marriage, agriculture, and liberty.

## MUSIC, SONG, AND DANCE

During the time of Louis XVI (and long before), music, and especially song, was popular in France. Songs of courtship, of seduction or rejection, as well as others less stereotyped in their content, such as those that spoke of freedom in America, of the king's impotence, or of the wicked queen, were sold in sheet copies by strolling vendors and were sung in the cafes of the cities. To the traditional and regional folksongs and ballads of the popular culture were added the new revolutionary songs.

No first-rate composers appeared during the decade of disquiet and strife after 1789, but revolutionary songs and chants were everywhere enjoyed by the people. Some singers were idolized by Parisians and

*La Marseillaise*. Contemporary text and music. Bibliothèque Nationale de France.

attracted large audiences. A few songs written at the time became famous. *Ça ira* was the most popular at the beginning of the revolution. The anti-monarchical *Marseillaise*, written by Rouget de Lisle, an army engineer, received its name after it was adopted by the troops from Marseille who took part in the storming of the Tuileries in Paris. It was designated the national anthem on July 14, 1792, and remains so to this day.

Even surpassing the enthusiasm for theater was the national passion for dancing. There was little to dance about during the Terror, but as it abated, hundreds of dance halls began to open all over Paris. Abandoned convents, seminaries, ruined chapels, any open garden, not to mention the hotels and restaurants, were places to dance and relish the moment.

Dance halls were for everyone. Some were luxurious and expensive, some so cheap that almost anyone could afford to go. Some attracted working-class couples, and others, adorned with the right kind of girls, brought in the soldiers. Musicians and dance instructors were making more money than ever before. Every evening about eight o'clock, the streets filled with women in white dresses on their way to the dance halls with their companions.[12] Among popular dances were the *bourrées* and *périgourdines* to which federal representatives from all 83 administrative regions danced.[13] One of the dances most enjoyed during the time of the Directory was la *folie du jour.* There were, of course, many thousands of people in Paris and in rural areas who were too poor to afford even the cheapest entertainment or to take part at all in the frenzied life of the capital and other large cities.

## PAINTERS, SCULPTORS, AND ARCHITECTS

Private exhibitions of the works of painters and sculptors were often held; in October 1790, Jean-Antoine Houdon exhibited at his own house a statue that later went to the *Académie des Beaux Arts*.[14]

The most famous artist of the time, Jacques-Louis David, whose work is austere, simple, and neoclassical in style, became the pageant-master of the republic. He presented paintings of all the great events of the period in a manner that combined art and virtue. Having studied in Rome, David was strongly influenced by Renaissance and classical art, and he transformed eighteenth-century French painting, rejecting its colorful frivolity in favor of somber representations—the death of Marat being perhaps his most famous work.

David stage-managed some enormous public occasions, including the celebration of the unity of the republic, on August 10, 1793, and the Festival of the Supreme Being.[15] After the fall of Robespierre, David survived and flourished under Napoleon. His major historical painting, *Intervention of the Sabine Women,* was a symbol of reconciliation and peace for France at the end of the Directory.

In architecture, the Paris *Bourse* (stock exchange) was designed by Théodore Brongniart, who also designed several hotels in the prevalent classical taste. The homes of the wealthy were decorated with Doric columns and nymphs, muses, olive leaves, lyres, and heavy gilded furniture. To show it had public interest in mind, the government promoted projects such as public baths, fountains, museums, and theaters. Furthermore, the revolutionaries wished to impress their ideals on the public by decorating buildings and statues with inscriptions proclaiming liberty and equality. While classicism dominated and much new construction was planned during the revolution, little was actually built. Money was not available for ambitious projects, and little was produced that was innovative, dynamic, or exciting. The environment inhibited creative innovation both during the revolution and under Napoleon, who preferred the artwork of the past.

## THE PALAIS ROYAL

Situated in the prosperous Faubourg Saint-Honoré, the Palais Royal, the Paris residence of the king's cousin, the duke of Orléans, was once a large park open to strollers and a favorite promenade for respectable people. In the 1780s, the duke enclosed the rectangular site with shops and galleries. Offering everything from freak shows to marionettes, magic lanterns, acrobats, shops, jewelers, watchmakers, restaurants, billiard rooms, ballad singers, magicians, and even a natural history display, the Palais Royal gardens soon became a favorite haunt for those seeking pleasure and amusement. Most important of all were the cafes, which attracted large numbers of people including politicians and prostitutes.

People of all classes enjoyed the atmosphere, and orators always found a ready audience in the cafes, which were to become centers of political agitation in 1788 and 1789. Since the Palais Royal was royal property, police were not permitted to enter without permission, and Orléans did nothing to suppress the excitement and disputes that arose when speakers expressed their views and seditious pamphlets were read out to the worked-up crowds. On July 13, 1789, the call to arms that began the insurrection in Paris was given from the Palais Royal. Here, Camille Desmoulins called on the people to march against the Bastille.

## OTHER AMUSEMENTS AND SPORTS

For working people, a walk through the city gates and past the custom houses into the country villages to drink wine in the local taverns was an agreeable pastime, especially since the country air was much fresher and everything in Paris was more heavily taxed. New and in demand among Parisians in the late eighteenth century were segregated public baths on boats on the river Seine. The puppeteer and the street musician were always popular and, prior to 1789, nonpolitical.[16] When the revolution came, the puppeteer's job was to represent allegories of the Third Estate, politicizing the old folk traditions.

The so-called sport of hunting occupied a lot of the time of the aristocracy before the revolution, while the common people were denied this activity. To assuage their gambling inclinations, the upper classes also attended horse races. They enjoyed fronton or pelota, too, a sport popular in the southwest; of Basque origin, the game required competitors to hurl a ball from a basket-like racket against a wall from a substantial distance.

Historically, kings and nobles played tennis (which seems to have originated in twelfth-century France as a game in which the ball was hit with the bare hand). The racket, first in the form of a glove, evolved over time. The first known indoor court was built in the fourteenth century, and the name "tennis" derived from the French word tenez (hold), a signal that the ball was coming. Gambling on tennis was widespread and sometimes fixed. In 1600, the Venetian ambassador reported that there were 1,800 courts in Paris. The revolution killed the sport for a time when the government banned the game as a symbol of the aristocracy, although, ironically, the revolution began on a tennis court.

Ascending in a hot-air balloon was a French innovation that began in 1782 and became very popular for a few. The following year, at Versailles, witnessed by the king, a balloon was sent up equipped with a gondola occupied by some farm animals. The animals landed safely after an eight-minute flight. Next came a two-man flight; the balloonists were a physicist, Pilâtre de Rosier, and a companion. Burning straw supplied the hot air to maintain the balloon aloft. The flight, on November 21, 1783, lasted 28 minutes, and the balloon rose to 1,000 meters. The hot-air balloon was replaced by one using hydrogen; this one went higher, and the race was on to produce the best. When the first man to go up was also the first to be killed in a ballooning accident, the incident more or less finished the sport for decades to come.

Fencing, usually an upper-class activity, was popular, and the French style of fencing became prominent in Europe. Its rules govern most modern competition, and the vocabulary of traditional fencing is composed largely of French words. The sport was imitated by children, even among the poor, with sticks or wooden swords.

## CHILDREN'S GAMES

Swimming, highly esteemed in ancient Greece and Rome, especially as a form of training for warriors, was mostly a sport of French schoolchildren, who were encouraged by revolutionaries to build strong young bodies, and competitions were sometimes held. The revolutionary government was also attentive to the young mind and believed that it could mold a new generation of ideal patriots if children could be taught the advantages of the glorious new age. By exposure to republican schooling accompanied by a deluge of images such as didactic plays, civic festivals, and revolutionary music, slogans, and printed matter, a new person would be created for the new society. There were, of course, numerous country children who would never see a play and seldom see a newspaper, even if they could read, and these needed to be instructed in other ways. One way was through the use of signs and symbols of cultural significance in place of words. As the cross symbolizes Christianity, a picture of the storming of the Bastille stood for liberty, and the red hat and cockade were symbols of revolutionary support, liberty, and equality. Rituals, too, such as civic events or dancing around the liberty tree, were important. The figure of the king, a symbol of absolute power in the old regime, had to be eradicated.

To attract children and the masses of illiterate adults to the new symbols and their meanings, few things could have been more important

Children's games: spinning a top in a Paris suburb. Bibliothèque Historique de la Ville de Paris. Photograph by Jean-Christophe Doerr.

than games, as Rousseau had once pointed out. Besides balls, dolls, spinning tops, and other amusements, children had board games designed to communicate to them the meaning of the struggle. The ancient *jeu de l'oie* (goose game) was changed to meet revolutionary criteria. Players rolled dice to see how far they could advance toward the goal by moving along squares placed in a circle around the board. Previously the object had been to move from squares showing Roman emperors through a series of squares with depictions of early French kings and finally to the prize square, which portrayed Louis XV. Updated versions appeared early in the revolution in which players progressed by squares from the siege of the Bastille through major revolutionary events or achievements to the National Assembly (or, in other versions, to the new constitution),

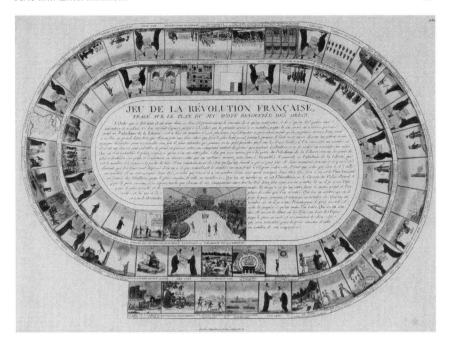

A board game used during the revolution in which participants moved pieces from square to square around the board. Bibliothèque Nationale de France.

thus providing a history of significant episodes in the struggle.[17] Players hoped not to be unlucky enough to land on squares depicting two geese in magisterial robes, since these were symbolic of the old, discredited parlements, which had been bastions of reactionaries. Some variations presented an extended view of history beginning before civilized societies and displaying a progression of abuses up to the Enlightenment and ending with the revolution. Republicans saw everything as having a moral purpose, even games.[18]

Playing cards were altered to represent republicanism. Cards that portrayed the king, queen, and jack, which implied despotism and inequality, were no longer acceptable. Publishers of playing cards replaced these images with images of human figures representing genius, liberty, rights, or some other republican attribute. Some produced cards with images of philosophers, republican soldiers, and sans-culottes.[19]

## BOOKS AND THE PRESS

Only books authorized by the royal government could be sold or read, and penalties could be imposed on those who disregarded the law. The regulation, lacking the support of the people was, however, unenforceable.

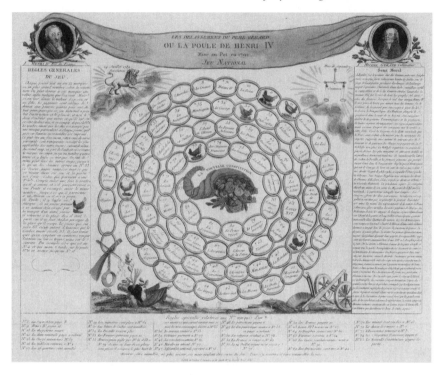

The pastimes of Père Gérard. Revolutionary Board Game. Bibliothèque Nationale de France.

Some famous writers who defied the law spent brief terms in the prison at Vincennes or in the Bastille but emerged more popular than ever. The more books were burned by public authorities, the more they were secretly printed, sold, and read. If a writer could be sentenced to imprisonment and his books condemned to the flames, he might regard his literary career as secure.

The writers of the age of Enlightenment laid the groundwork for change well before the revolution. Their theories and views, along with the momentous events in the North American colonies, were discussed, dissected, and judged in French salons and pamphlets. Voltaire had long been at the height of his fame, Rousseau had written his *Social Contract*, Holbach's *System of Nature* had appeared, and Diderot's *Encyclopedia* was finally finished and published. The popularity of these men and their works was unabated.

Novels written just before and during the revolutionary period were few in number, and most were insipid and mediocre, with the preferred themes being escapism from the realities of everyday life. With few exceptions, the literary market was filled with sentimental, anemic, and vapid romantic novels written for the most part by titled upper-class women. Historical novels, short on facts, were also in vogue.

LIBERTÉ DE LA PRESSE

Freedom of the press permitted news sheets to proliferate. Bibliothèque Nationale de France.

The best work of the period, far superior to the others, was *Les Liaisons dangereuses* (1782), written by Pierre-Ambroise-François Laclos, a French general and writer. Another exception to the run of undistinguished novels was *Delphine* (1802), written by Madame de Staël; this work was critically noted as a landmark in the history of the novel. The *Journal de Paris* stated that the streets of the city were empty the day following the book's publication; everyone was indoors reading *Delphine*.[20]

The poetry of the period was dominated by classical tradition and was generally uninspired. Many poets were alienated by the revolution. One of the most promising, André Chénier, enthusiastically greeted the revolution, but when he protested the excesses of the Terror, he was thrown into Saint Lazare prison. Four months later, in 1794, at age 28, he was condemned to the guillotine. Other poets, such as Abbé Delille, who among other things translated Virgil and Milton, left the country and did not return until Napoleon was in power. Dispirited by their social surroundings, poets spent the time translating Latin, Greek, and English poetry. The genre was to revive, however, as outstanding poets such as

A newspaper stand during the revolution. Bibliothèque Nationale de France.

Alphonse de Lamartine, Alfred de Vigny, and Victor Hugo appeared after the revolution.

## WRITERS AND GOVERNMENT

Before the mid-1770s, political news could be obtained only from abroad, from cities like as Geneva, London, Brussels, Amsterdam, and other places where Huguenots were often responsible for the publications.

Inside France itself, only two journals were officially licensed: the *Gazette de France* and the *Mercure de France*.[21] Both were dull and filled with articles and essays on uncontentious events. In 1778, the *Mercure* was drastically altered; its pages were enlarged and it began reporting news from European and American capitals, along with reviews of musical, theatrical, poetic, and literary works, and even puzzles and riddles. The *Mercure* spread throughout the country from the salons of the aristocracy to the unpretentious households of the bourgeoisie. On the eve of the revolution, the *Mercure* was read by people in many regions of the country, and Paris began to blossom with newspapers—some mocking the censors with such notices as "printed in Peking."

Initially, the revolutionaries abandoned all forms of censorship and control over publications, setting off a veritable explosion of printed matter. Journalists vied with one another to acquire readers and hold their attention. Hundreds of broadsheets and newspapers began to appear in the street stalls, reflecting the spectrum of opinion from the antirevolution-ary *Ami des Apôtres* to the scurrilous, coarse *Ami du Peuple*, published by Jean-Paul Marat, which encouraged revolutionary violence and advocated the execution of aristocrats. Marat's widely circulated paper preached the kind of justice that only the guillotine could give in order to rid France of so-called traitors. Using the language of the workers and the streets, Marat aided the political rise of the sans-culottes. Placards, which were posted and read out at building sites, markets, and street corners, were illustrated with symbols of liberty, equality, and justice and supplemented the news-papers for the illiterate portion of the population. The much-liked, vulgar *Père Duchesne,* was put out by Jacques-René Hébert after the demise of Marat. Hébert named the paper after a folk hero and printed anticlerical views.[22] The *Père Duchesne* and the *Feuille Villageoise* disseminated anti-church dogma and exposed conspiracies, imaginary or real, against the revolution, mostly in the countryside.

For leaders of the revolution, writers, pamphleteers, and journalists were crucial ingredients of inspiration and action, usurping the church's former role as the disseminator of values and symbols for the general soci-ety. Writers, confident of their own ability to guide the people along the true path of regeneration, believed that journalism would spread quickly the ideas of liberty and democracy while a plodding government lagged far behind.

Many revolutionary leaders had their own publications, which ranged from cartoons plastered on public walls to highly sophisticated and elegant journals that sometimes blended political and pornographic mate-rial. The source of the funding for much of this material is now obscure and its impact indeterminate but clearly powerful. The involvement of the press, which often created events based on half-truths, vague rumors, and images of abstract concepts, seems to have been a major revolutionary catalyst.

Not only were religious beliefs attacked by a storm of intellectual activity, but groups of people became interested in promoting the ideas of the philosphes and discussing the laws of government and the structure of the state. New conceptions of government, a willingness to finish with the institutions of the past, confidence in the promise of the future—all took possession of French literature and French society.

The newspaper *Révolutions de Paris*, published by Louis-Marie Prudhomme from July 1789 until February 1794, was one of the most influential papers, with an estimated 250,000 subscribers. It presented a factual narrative account of the previous week's events. Its orientation was radical but not inflammatory. Prudhomme chose to disband his paper under the Terror.

The revolutionary government usually conveyed its messages through public orators, and the press was given freedom never before dreamed of. However, when Robespierre came to power, the press fell mostly silent except for its fawning adoration of the regime. The guillotine awaited those who dissented from the new government's policies and the dictates of its controlling Committee of Public Safety.

## CARTOONISTS

Political caricaturists and cartoonists of the revolution were undeterred by tradition. The symbol of the wine press, a potent Christian image, was used to turn the public against the clergy by the dissemination of wood carvings and other art forms showing fat priests, whose girth represented their social and economic privileges, about to be squeezed flat under the press by partisans.[23]

The common people could readily identify with such (generally anonymous) drawings, which on one side might show an adult Frenchman of the old regime—an obese, babyish-looking man with his bonnet and chubby cheeks, pinwheels in one hand, a puppet in the other—stuffed into a child's playpen. His image is in contrast with that presented on the other side—a man of the new era, a mustachioed militiaman in the uniform of the National Guard with a battle ax in one hand, a lance in the other.[24]

The artist had to be careful, however. The symbolism and allegories could be misinterpreted or might offend powerful people. Jean-Louis Prieur, many of whose drawings recorded revolutionary events, was arrested on April 1, 1795, and sent to the guillotine on May 7 of the same year for the trivial offense of drawing the heads of those accused by the Revolutionary Tribunal (of which he was also a member).[25] The first 69 of 144 engravings depicting a record of the revolution, *Tableaux historiques de la révolution française*, were drawn by Prieur. His busts of the duke of Orléans and of Necker were destroyed.

## PORNOGRAPHY AND CENSORSHIP

In the political climate of the 1780s, many clandestine papers, generally circulated in manuscript form, arose that dealt with gossip, scandal, the sexual aberrations of the court, and anything that might be dug up to embarrass the church. Circulated throughout the country, these covert papers reached their destinations via back roads, rivers, and canal barges, thereby circumventing the custom houses en route. Most of the major cities were well supplied with this pernicious literature, and in Paris it was sold on the streets, in stalls, on the Pont Neuf, even in the lobbies of theaters. Vendors who specialized in satire, vilification, and violent libel against the queen seem to have had little fear of retaliation, for they had public opinion behind them, and city officials were not eager to become a target of the perpetrators.

Pornography was used first to degrade the church and clergy and later to attack the crown. An avalanche of lurid pamphlets appeared against

Marie-Antoinette and Louis XVI that excelled in depravity, their purpose to deny and discredit the dignity of the victim. Pornography was used as a deliberate and calculated act in the destruction of the royal family. Throughout the revolution, the French press pandered to the lowest instincts of its readers, while ironically extolling the virtues of honor and justice. French literature sank to depths unknown in Western history, even in the days of decadent Rome.

Under the Directory, censorship became stringent, more so when Napoleon rose to power and brought the press under his full control. Paris had perhaps 70 newspapers around 1799. This number was soon reduced to 13 and later, by the end of the empire, to 4, which were compelled to follow the official government line.[26] A department was created to censor letters, books, and newspapers that was more efficient than similar institutions under the old regime. After 1800, the most influential publication treating the arts and sciences was *La Décade*, edited by Pierre-Louis Guinquené. It was careful not to openly criticize the imperial government and so was tolerated.

In 1805, bulletins were published by the government that recorded the exploits of Napoleon's armies. These, along with the Bible, were found on church lecterns, to be disseminated to the masses by the reinstated priests. Under Napoleon, the press became the emperor's servant. It was thought wise to discontinue the bulletins in 1812, when Napoleon retreated in defeat from Russia.

## NOTES

1. Carlson, 12. For type of productions performed by the three major theaters see Root-Bernstein (1984), 17 ff.

2. Carlson, 2–6.

3. Ibid., 77.

4. Lewis (1972), 170.

5. Root-Bernstein, 26.

6. Ibid.

7. Lewis (1972), 170.

8. Ibid., 173.

9. Carlson, 231.

10. Garrioch, 244.

11. In June and July 1789, groups in the provinces formed patriotic organizations known as *fédérations*, which were joined by members of the various National Guards units.

12. Robiquet, 228.

13. Ibid., 110.

14. Jean-Antoine Houdon was the leading exponent of Rococo style. Noted as a perceptive portraitist, he made busts of George Washington, Diderot, Voltaire, Catherine II, Turgot, Moliére, Rousseau, Buffon d'Alembert, Franklin, Lafayette, Louis XVI, and Mirabeau. See Robiquet 34–35.

15. Germani/Swales, p. 43.

16. Ibid., 34.

17. This is in some ways similar to Monopoly, which teaches young people some of the basic tenets of capitalism.

18. See James Leith in Darnton/Roche, 288.

19. In Roman mythology, a genius was a guardian spirit, and every individual, family, and city had its own genius who received special worship because he was thought to bestow success and intellectual powers on his devotees.

20. Lewis (1972), 176.

21. Schama, 176.

22. Hébert (1757–1794) was a French journalist and politician who published radical Republican papers, especially *Le Père Duchesne* (from 1790). He helped plan the overthrow of the monarchy and was a leader of the sans-culottes. He was guillotined, along with many adherents.

23. Germani/Swales, 22ff.

24. Ibid., 31.

25. Ibid., 103ff.

26. Lewis (1972), 167.

# 7

# FAMILY, FOOD, AND EDUCATION

Family relationships and educational opportunities were transformed during the revolution in order to give a measure of equality to those oppressed by paternalistic and despotic heads of households as well as by a controlling religious educational system.

## THE OLD REGIME

Members of noble families did not engage in demeaning manual work or serve someone of inferior rank. Honor for the high-born meant keeping one's word and paying one's debts (usually from gambling) to one's peers or superiors, although money owed to subordinates such as shopkeepers was not a matter of concern.[1] Fidelity to the king, to the family name, and to one's calling—be it the military or the church—was what mattered.

Most men, noble or not, thought it reasonable that marriage, often a union of property and influence, should allow for a mistress, and it was normal for men of noble birth and money, from the king down, to have other women. Wealthy bourgeois agreed, as did the men of the lower classes, although the latter could not afford it. Similar privileges were not extended to their wives, whose infidelity could cause unwanted gossip and problems with the inheritance of property if she became pregnant.

Royal decrees and local laws and customs strengthened paternal control over marriage, defended its indissolubility, criminalized female adultery, and fostered the exclusion of illegitimate children from inheritance and civil status. An infamous weapon in the hands of the master of the household was access to *lettres de cachet* that facilitated the imprisonment of rebellious children or wives, or anyone else who crossed a superior by word, pen, or deed.

The ideals of an aristocratic woman were similar to those of her husband: while some women had personal ambitions such as writing, charity work, or creative art, the primary goal of most was to defend the honor of her family and to look after the interests of her husband and children. Such a woman often married early, sometimes as young as age 13, and she understood that her duty was to create the best social affiliations possible for her new family. She did not personally raise the children; a wealthy house might have as many as 40 servants—the more the better for prestigious enhancement.

Maintaining the right kind of friends was also expected of the wife, and this could be accomplished through establishing a salon or finding a high-placed position in the royal palace. Parents inculcated their children with their values of honor, duty, and opulence as a sign of distinction. Conspicuous consumption was the mark of a nobleman, although any overt reference to money was considered bourgeois.

## BOURGEOIS FAMILIES

Unlike the nobility, the bourgeoisie was without political power and was often considered grasping and greedy. The bourgeoisie was not a homogeneous group but existed on many levels: lawyers, physicians, surgeons, licensed dentists, architects, students from good families, engineers, writers, administrators, clerks, and teachers were distinguished by their education and training. Here, too, however, there were differences. Physicians, for example, looked down on surgeons, lawyers scorned clerks, and, indeed, most professionals felt superior to someone below them.

The commercial bourgeoisie included merchants and master artisans of many kinds (e.g., wigmakers, jewelers, furniture makers), heads of trade corporations, and industrialists and manufacturers.

They invested in real estate, from which they derived rental income, and those who owned their own homes usually passed them along to the next generation, but all were distinguished from their employees by station and income. Part of their daily lives was taken up by attending council meetings, organizing annual fairs, helping to provide relief for the poor, and other community projects. Unlike the aristocrats, they placed emphasis on thrift and hard work; retirement was practically unknown. Children were educated in the parish clergy schools or by private tutors. Male offspring of such families generally followed the occupation of the father, while girls were taught the social graces and how to run a household.

In a big city such as Paris, intermarriage was common among people in the same business or profession. Families established solid networks in the district where they lived and worked. Through such connections, their children found employment.

## WAGE EARNERS AND PEASANTS

Among the lower echelons of society, which generally lived in the poorer quarters of the cities or in country hamlets, laborers and poor peasants found it difficult to raise a family to the standards anywhere near the level of the bourgeoisie, but family connections were also important. In the city, a tanner might take on his nephews as apprentices, the shoemaker or mason his sons, son-in-law, or grandchildren. Booksellers or printers hired their relatives, and even the women of the markets had family members who lived nearby and worked shining shoes, cleaning sewers, or carrying coal or water. Parts of the city with close ties of kinship and occupation were not unlike villages in which one could find family support in rough times. Those in the low-income brackets often lacked the means to supply the essentials for a wife and children, and some children never saw the inside of a school. Country life often demanded the services of children on the farm, and education came second.

In all cases, noble, bourgeois, or worker, paternal absolutism ruled the family. The hierarchy of both state and household was thought to be ordained by nature and by God. Church sermons depicting women as seducers, beginning with Eve, emphasized the intrinsic superiority of man over woman, parent over child, and these assumptions formed the cultural framework of everyday life within the family.

## MARRIAGE

Marriage fell under the legal jurisdiction of the church, and divorce was prohibited. When a wedding took place, the local church was decorated, bells tolled, and everyone attended the festivities. The bride wore a white dress and a wreath of orange blossoms and brought a dowry that might consist of money or a piece of land if her family was well off; for a peasant girl it might just be some bed sheets, towels, perhaps some furniture or cooking utensils. The dowry she brought to the marriage was controlled by the husband.

While the aristocracy could marry off their children at a tender age, or at least promise them to a suitable partner, the children of the commoner or peasant married relatively late in life—men when they were about 28, women at about 25. Peasants and the poor working class had to wait until the man had established himself in some manner so that he could support a wife and family. A peasant couple might have to wait for a death in the village to marry, since good land was limited.

The father exercised full authority in the home, and the wife was expected to be docile and submissive. She was not allowed to own property in her own right unless so defined in the marriage agreement or to enter into private contracts without her husband's consent. He could discipline her by corporal punishment or verbal abuse without fear of rebuke from the authorities or the church. Children who remained under their father's roof could be forbidden to marry and forced to work. Some observers compared them to slaves.

## WIDOWS AND DEATH

If young men or women managed to remain in good health until about age 25, they had a good chance of living on into old age, or about 60. Accidents on the job and fatal epidemic illnesses were frequent enough, but the greatest killer of men of all classes was war. As a result, widows were common and represented about 1 person in 10 of the population. About all a poor widow could count on was the return of her dowry (if it had not been squandered), and a roof over her head. Some widows had small children, which made their lives a constant struggle. Their options might come down to accepting charity from the parish church or from neighbors. If they had adult children, help might come from them. In the country, they could supplement their meals by collecting scraps missed in the harvest or by gathering wild fruit and berries. A last resort for the aged country widow was to move to a large city and live and beg on the streets; such a woman would probably soon die in a charity hospital. If she was lucky and owned a piece of property or something else of value, she might exchange it, when she was too old to work, for a room in a nunnery where she could live out her remaining years.

Class and family lineage were clearly visible at funerals and at burial sites. Commoners were interred in the churchyard, for a price, or else in the communal cemetery in or near the city, with neither a coffin nor a monument. Those people with noble status or wealth were interred in stone coffins within a niche in the wall or the floor of the church itself.

## REVOLUTIONARY CHANGES IN THE FAMILY

Household politics and the broader political system of absolutism were mutually reinforcing. Critics of the old regime, such as litigating wives, philosophers of the Enlightenment, reform-minded lawyers, and bourgeois feminist novelists, condemned both domestic and state despotism.

Since the principles of justice and equality applied to the state after 1789, many believed that the same precepts should apply to the family. The revolutionaries recognized the central position of the family as the elemental building block, the basis for social order, and argued that children raised with republican ideals were likely to become good patriots.

The Constituent and Legislative Assemblies often deliberated the nature of marriage and the secularization of civil recordkeeping. A law passed on September 20, 1792, replaced the sacrament of marriage with a civil contract that dispensed with the services of a priest and the church. It was necessary only to post an announcement outside the Town Hall, and the marriage could take place. The couple then appeared before a functionary in a tricolor sash who muttered a few legal words, finishing with "You are married." Unlike earlier wedded couples, the newlyweds were told that if things did not work out, they had the alternative of divorce. Within the space of a few weeks, the representatives had moved swiftly to curtail arranged marriages, reduce parental authority, and legalize divorce. In large cities, 20 or 30 marriages would often take place at one time in a group ceremony.

Under the old regime, marriage as an indissoluble union had not been questioned. The abrupt change in custom demonstrated the antireligious nature of the revolutionary movement and its belief in personal freedom. Married couples who desired to break their marriage bonds for any reason could do so and just as easily remarry. Causes for divorce usually revolved around incompatibility, abandonment, and cruelty, and more women than

A republican marriage, after the enactment of the law of September 20, 1792. Bibliothèque Nationale de France.

men seem to have initiated the process. Citizenness Van Houten, anxious to extricate herself from an unhappy situation, decried her arranged marriage to a "quick-tempered, vexatious, stupid, dirty, and lazy husband … with the most absolute inability in business matters."[2] Large notices in the rooms where the vows of fidelity were exchanged bore the title "Laws of Marriage and Divorce." Both the poison and the antidote were clearly stated and dispensed by the same office.[3]

Primogeniture (the right of the eldest son to inherit all land and titles) prevailed under the old regime, but this was abolished early in 1790 so that all children should inherit equally. In November 1793, illegitimate children were granted the same rights of inheritance if they could provide proof of their father's identity. The law was made retroactive to July 1789, but by 1796 the retroactive condition was removed, although the principle of equality for all children regardless of sex, legitimacy, or age was kept intact.[4]

For those offspring who, for lack of money were not able to marry and begin a family until parents were too old and feeble to continue working, parents could sign over their property to the heir with the written stipulation that the parents would be taken care of for the rest of their lives. If a woman inherited the property and then married, her husband was expected to take her family name, and she retained legal rights over the inheritance.

In 1790, the National Assembly established a new institution to deal with family disputes, setting up temporary, local arbitration courts known as family tribunals *(tribunaux de famille)*. Family members in conflict each chose two arbitrators (often other members of the family or friends) to adjudicate their disagreements and make rulings on matters such as divorce, division of inheritance, and parent-child disputes. Appointed by the litigants themselves, these temporary family courts made justice accessible, affordable, and intimate. In 1796, these councils were suppressed, however. Further edicts lowered the age of adulthood to 21, established the principle of compulsory education throughout the country, and abolished *lettres de cachet*.

The laws on divorce, egalitarian inheritance, and parental authority also raised questions about the subordination of wives and daughters. It was difficult for the revolutionaries to rid themselves of long-held views that women belonged at home, and they continued to maintain that women could best show their republicanism by being good mothers. They should strive to please their men and introduce republican morality in their children, while husbands displayed their patriotism as soldiers and public citizens. Almost everyone envisioned distinct but complementary roles for men and women in the new state. This view was not without its detractors, however. Long-established ideas on docile republican mothers and wives were opposed by advocates for equality between married couples, who supported greater independence, power, and control over property for women.

It was also a fact that France needed to increase its population, since the number of young men in particular was declining as they marched off to become cannon fodder. Banners carried by processions of patriotic women through the streets of Paris declared: "Citizens, give children to the *Patrie!* Their happiness is assured!"[5]

In the late 1790s and early 1800s, as the political mood shifted toward the right, the courts once again tightened the boundaries around families, curtailing, for example, revolutionary promises to illegitimate children, who now lost the right of inheritance. Under Napoleon, divorce was more difficult to obtain, especially for women. A husband could sue for divorce from an adulterous wife, but a wife could seek divorce against the husband's wishes only if he maintained a mistress in the family house. In 1816, under the restoration monarchy, divorce was abolished altogether.

## FOOD

Comparing English food to French, Arthur Young found to his surprise the best roast beef not at home in England but in Paris.[6] He also spoke about the astonishing variety given to any dish by French cooks through their rich sauces, which gave vegetables a flavor lacking in boiled English greens. In France, at least four dishes were presented at meals (for every one dish in England), and a modest or small French table was incomparably better than its English equivalent. In addition, in France, every dinner included dessert, large or small, even if it consisted only of an apple or a bunch of grapes. No meal was complete without it.

Describing the dining process in high society, Young said that a servant stood beside the chair when the wine was served and added to it the desired amount of water. A separate glass was set out for each variety of drink. As for table linen, he considered the French linen cleaner than the English. To dine without a napkin (serviette) would be bizarre to a Frenchman, but in England, at an upper-class table, this item would often be missing.[7]

By the mid-eighteenth century, a small meal, the *déjeuner*, consisting of at least *café au lait* or plain milk and bread or rolls and butter had spread across all classes. Workers and others whose days began early had their *déjeuner* (breaking the overnight fast) about nine in the morning. More substantial meals at this hour included cheese and fruit and, on occasion, meat. It seems likely that they took something lighter and earlier, and this became known as the "little breakfast" or *le petit déjeuner.*

In 1799, Madame de Genlis wrote a phrasebook for upper-class travelers in which she gave the names for quite a large variety of foods consumed at breakfast, including drinks (tea, chocolate, coffee), butter, breads (wheat, milk, black rye), eggs, cream, sugar (powdered, lump, sugar candy), salt (coarse or fine), pepper, nutmeg, cinnamon, mustard, anchovies, capers, chopped herbs, radishes, cheese (soft, cream, gruyère, gloucester, dutch, or parmesan), artichokes, sausages, ham, bacon, cold meats (veal, mutton) for sandwiches, fruits (lemons, oranges), biscuits, cakes, jams, almond milk, oysters, wine, beer, pastries, and so on.

Chocolate had been introduced into France in the previous century, brought to Europe from the Americas by the Spaniards. By the beginning of the eighteenth century, it was being regularly served at Versailles, and courtiers might be invited to *chocolat du régent* (breakfast of chocolate with the king). Marie-Antoinette usually had a light breakfast consisting of *café au lait* or chocolate, along with a special kind of Viennese bread. Another drink taken at breakfast was *bavaroise,* a mixture of tea and maidenhair syrup; however, tea (introduced in France in the mid-seventeenth century) was never popular and was generally considered a remedy for indigestion.

By far the most popular drink for all classes and in all households was coffee, after 1750 almost always taken to start the day. It was to be found not only in coffee shops but also in markets, and it was sold on the streets. Cafes sprang up in Paris and became the place for fashionable men to meet, as well as refuges for poor people, who used them as shelters. In 1782, Mercier wrote:

There are men, who arrive at the café at ten in the morning and do not leave until eleven at night [the compulsory closing time, supervised by the police]; they dine on a cup of coffee with milk, and sup on Bavarian cream [a mixture of syrup, sugar, milk, and sometimes tea].[8]

In the provinces, coffee was not so welcome. In Limoges, for example, coffee was drunk as a medicine. Equivalent to coffee houses were chocolate houses that served chocolate with vanilla, sugar, and cinnamon. By midcentury, this drink was added to the breakfast, although wine and brandy were still consumed at the same time by many workers.

**The Aristocracy**    In 1788, as cookbooks began to appear, a gourmet made a list of France's best gastronomic foods. It included turkey with truffles from the Périgord, *pâté de foie gras* from Toulouse, partridge pâtés from Nérac, fresh tunny *pâtés* from Toulon, skylarks from Pézénas, woodcock from the Dombes, capons from the Cux, hams from Bayonne, and cooked tongue from Vierzon.[9]

A typical dinner for members of the royal family and the elite class before the revolution comprised a first course (*entrée*) of one or more soups and plates of roasted or stewed meat, served along with similar dishes of poultry or seafood. The second (main) course contained the largest dishes of meat and poultry, accompanied by various vegetables and salad, and this was followed by the third course, comprising cheese, fruit, pastries, and often *pâtés*.

When the royal family was confined in Paris under guard, members were permitted to take with them 12 servants, including a head cook and his assistant, a scullion, a turnspit, a steward and his assistant, a boy, a keeper of the plate, and 3 waiters.[10] While imprisoned, the royals enjoyed a breakfast that included coffee, chocolate, thick cream, cold syrup, barley water, butter, fruit, rolls, loaves, powdered and lump sugar, and salt.

For dinner there were three soups and three courses consisting (on nonfast days) of four entrees of meat, two roasts, and one side dish. For dessert there were pears, other fruit, jam, butter, sugar, oil, champagne, rolls, and wines from Bordeaux, Malvoise, and Madeira. Whatever they left was eaten by the servants. Supper again comprised three soups and three courses consisting of two roasts and four or five side dishes. On fast days, supper was composed of four nonmeat entrées.[11] Dessert was the same as for dinner except that there was also coffee.

By 1793, affluent Parisians were eating dinner around three or four o'clock. It included soup, lamb or cold beef, beet salad, fish (such as sole or skate), turnips, potatoes, and, on occasion, a ham omelet. Dessert included fruit (such as apples or pears) or cherries in brandy, cheese, and jam.

The diet of the peasants had little in common with that of the wealthy. Even though many people raised animals, these were used mostly for milk, cheese, and wool; the peasants and farmers could not afford to eat them, and they **Rural Practices** were not permitted to kill any game animals as these were reserved for the aristocrats. Hence, before the revolution, the poor ate practically no meat. Instead, a kind of gruel made from boiled grain formed the center of their diet, especially in winter. Some eggs, fruit, or vegetables were consumed at home, but the best produce was taken to be sold in the markets. Encouraged by the government, people began eating more potatoes, one of the principal healthy food items of the rural population. Whereas grain was threatened with destruction in wartime and from natural causes such as hail, causing great hardship, the potato, growing below ground, was not exposed to such devastation, and by 1787 it had become a staple food for country people.[12]

A bourgeois wife of a future deputy to the Convention from the Drôme area kept an account book. For a dinner in honor of Robespierre in early 1793, she recorded her **Prices** purchases, along with the prices for that day.[13] A laborer's daily wage at the time would barely pay for two loaves of bread.

| | |
|---|---|
| milk and cream | 14 sous |
| 2 loaves | 24 sous |
| vegetables | 6 sous |

| | |
|---|---|
| salad | 10 sous |
| oil | 2 sous |
| vinegar | 12 sous |
| pepper | 5 sous |
| cheese | 1 sou |
| cider | 18 sous |
| a fat pullet | 8 livres 10 sous |

During the five years between 1790 and 1795, rampant inflation left many people begging, seeking charity, and starving.

After 1795, prices continued to rise at a rapid rate doubling, tripling, and more.[14]

**Bread**
Parisians believed they had the right to cheap, good bread, and throughout the eighteenth century the greatest concern of wage earners, small businessmen, artisans, and housewives was the availability of bread at a reasonable cost. Concerns about bread appeared in all correspondence of the period and whenever prices threatened to rise, there was much disquiet and agitation, sometimes leading to violence.

To a large extent, farmers' fields determined the diet of the rural population, since the staple, bread, had to be made from whatever grains were grown locally. If it was wheat, then whether the wheat was hard or soft, large- or small-grained, gray or yellowish in color, and even if it had begun to sprout just before the harvest, locals simply worked with whatever they had. And if instead they grew rye, or rye and wheat

| | 1790 | 1795 | |
|---|---|---|---|
| | Livres | Sols | Livres |
| 1 bushel of flour | 2 | | 225 |
| 1 bushel of barley | | 10 | 50 |
| 1 bushel of oats | | 18 | 50 |
| 1 liter of olive oil | 1 | 16 | 62 |
| 1 pound of sugar | | 18 | 62 |
| 1 pound of coffee | | 18 | 54 |
| 1 pound of butter | | 18 | 30 |
| 1 bushel of peas | 4 | | 130 |
| 1 bunch of turnips | | 2 | 4 |
| 1 cabbage | | 8 | 8 |
| 1/2 barrel of Orléans wine | 80 | | 2,400 |
| 25 eggs | 1 | 4 | 25 |

mixed (a common combination), or barley, that was what they used to make their bread.

Once the wheat and rye were harvested, they were sent to the miller, who returned it in the form of white grain flour. Breads were divided into categories based on the degree to which the bran and the germ had been sifted out of the flour. The coarser the bread, the bigger the loaf; the whiter the bread, the smaller the loaf. Wafers and pastries were made with the finest white flour, created in a labor-intensive process.

In some places, such as Brittany and Normandy, flour ground from buckwheat, known as *blé noir* (black wheat), was also made into a cheaper and inferior bread that was usually eaten by the poor. Another source of flour was the chestnut; this was used to make biscuits.

Watkin Tench, a British naval prisoner of war, in a letter sent from Quimper, Brittany, on April 4, 1795, describes the local bread as being gritty and of poor quality. It tasted of small sandy particles, a result of both the softness of the grindstones and the grain's being insufficiently washed after being trodden out by the oxen. (Thrashing was not employed in this region.)[15]

A poor man's bread was also made of barley and rye and, sometimes, of oats and millet. Rice did not perform as well in France as in other countries. It was eaten by the wealthy on occasion, cooked in milk, and sometimes it was imported from places such as Egypt to feed the poor. Hospitals often supplied rice to their inmates, and the military found rye useful at times to feed the troops. In Paris, food distributed to the poor by the church often contained rice mixed with mashed-up carrots, pumpkin, and turnips boiled in water. Cheap bread made of rice and mixed with millet was also distributed to the needy.

After the great hailstorm that destroyed much of the harvest around the Paris basin in July 1788 and the concomitant bad weather in large areas of the country that resulted in bad harvests, most of the population of France would have been happy with a crust of bread. In this period of brutal and widespread famine, the marquis de Ferrières-Marsay mentions in a letter to his wife a light repast he had on April 26, 1789 as: "six courses, more like hors d'oeuvres than anything, and including black puddings, sausages, pâtés, a couple of joints of meat, two roast fowls, four kinds of sweet, two mixed salads."[16] Not everyone went hungry!

During the periodic shortages of bread, French women had an alternate source of nutritious food in the mushroom. They grew them in cellars with a little sand and horse manure and in abandoned quarries around the cities. Asparagus also was a food of value and vitamins—the tips mixed with egg yolks and truffles were a delicacy. Some people believed in the aphrodisiac properties of asparagus.

The diet of the peasant was generally poor in vitamins and protein. Travelers reported that farm families in the high Pyrenees lived almost exclusively on a thin porridge of milk, barley, or oats. Sheep were too precious to eat, as in other regions. In Brittany, cider, rye bread, hard cheese, curds, and whey were staples of the diet. In Anjou, white bread, fresh butter and jam, wine, and even liqueurs were a daily source of nourishment.

**Drink**
The sources of water were rivers, streams, and wells. In Paris, water from the Seine, supposed to be healthy, was distributed and sold by about 20,000 water carriers throughout the city. The carriers delivered two buckets of water, even to the top floors of buildings, for two sous a load. It was a miserable wage and very hard work. Most Parisians, it can be assumed, drank unclean water, and foreigners loathed its taste. It was said that it was still better than that from the wells found along the left bank. There was also celery water, fennel water, divine water, coffee water, and a bewildering host of others. The various flavored waters came mostly from Montpellier.[17] By the time of the revolution, however, for those who could pay the price, purified water was available thanks to a process established by the Perrier brothers.

Although the practice of distilling spirits goes back a long way, the making of alcohol from grain and the production of brandy, discovered in the sixteenth century, were well entrenched in French drinking habits by the eighteenth. For many years, brandy was used as medicine to treat plague, gout, and other ailments, but eighteenth-century Paris imbibed an array of alcoholic concoctions—some fruit based, some composed of sugar, and rum called "Barbados" waters. Brandy was made from plums, pears, apples, and cherries and was produced wherever these could be grown.

Much brandy was made in the south, as was cognac, which came from the area around the town of that name. What had been once a luxury and a medicine became an everyday amenity. Liqueurs such as anisette (from anis) and absinthe were popular. Calvados, made in Normandy from apples, was enjoyed as a regional drink. Beer was not as popular as wine, which was the favored drink and was often watered down.

**Eating Out**
With the coming of the revolution, chefs who had previously worked in aristocratic houses now found themselves unemployed, and, while some of them chose to go into exile, some entered the service of the Parisian bourgeoisie; others opened restaurants. The redeployment of these master chefs contributed to the spread of *grande cuisine.*

Up to the eighteenth century, the word "restaurant" had signified a curative bouillon "restorant," or something that would strengthen and restore a person. Before that time, the only choice had been between the not-very-pleasant taverns (where more was drunk than eaten) and the purchase of food that had been prepared by a professional caterer.

The first person to actually use the name "restaurant" as we know it was a M. Boulanger, among whose clients was Diderot. From this time on, restaurants began to multiply; establishments included the *Frères Provençaux* (who introduced regional cuisine to Paris in 1782), *le Grand Véfour,* in 1788, and *Véry,* in 1790. For the client, the introduction of restaurants was advantageous: the menu was at a fixed price, the food was good, and you could eat at your own pace in company of your choosing. At that time it was possible to dine in a fairly good restaurant for less than 30 sous. Less expensive places served soup, boiled beef, an *entrée,* and a small glass of wine for about 10 sous.

Inns might offer a *table d'hôte,* cramming together a lot of hungry people at the same table, When the meal was ready, the guests dug in, arguing and grabbing the choicest bits of food. Such crowded and low-quality places were frequented mainly by impecunious students, artists, and traveling merchants.

When Napoleon came to power, in spite of not being a *gourmand,* he kept at his table all the splendor necessary to affirm his power in the eyes of French or foreign dignitaries. In fact, eating for him was an **The Napoleonic Eras** obligation, to be accomplished with utmost haste. Talleyrand, who was responsible for diplomacy under Napoleon, employed one of the most talented chefs of the period, Antonin Carêm, a perfectionist who codified French cuisine and even studied architecture and engraving in order to improve his layer cakes.

To meet the nation's military needs, France under Napoleon saw the development of new industries. For instance, because of the English continental blockade, cane sugar from the Caribbean was replaced by beet sugar that could be processed at home. Also, wishing to give his soldiers food that would last and remain edible in faraway battlefields, Napoleon organized a competition in 1795 to find a solution to this problem; the winner was Nicolas Appert, who invented the process of conserving food by heating it in a sealed jar. Subsequently named official supplier to the army and benefactor of humanity, Appert saw his canning invention copied with great commercial success in England and America.

Up to this time, those involved in cuisine were considered practitioners—professionals who gave recipes and technical counsel, be it doctors who treated dietary problems or writers who celebrated the pleasure of eating well. As a result, some special literature was produced, and two major figures—Grimod de la Reynière and Brillat-Savarin—began what was to be known as the art of gastronomy. In 1803, Grimod published *l'Almanach des gourmands,* which contained the latest culinary creations, selected by juries, making it the ancestor of today's food guides and cookbooks.

## SAMPLE RECIPES

---

### ECONOMICAL SOUP FOR THE POOR

Cook 2 bushels of potatoes, peel and purée them, then put in a pot.
Add 12 pounds of bread, cut in slices
1 quarter of a bushel of onions
1/2 pound salt
1/2 pound of lard cut in small pieces (or grease, or butter)
30 pints water*
Frozen potatoes can be used if reduced in powder before putting them into the pot
with the other ingredients
*Affiches au Dauphiné. Almanach de 1789.*

*In the recipe, this is written as 30 pints. The French old measure *pinte* is .93 liter,
or roughly a quart. Today, the pint is half a quart.

---

### SAVOY CAKE

4 eggs, separated
1 tablespoon minced crystallized orange blossom (or other flowers) (optional)
1 tablespoon flaked almonds
100 g crystallized sugar
1 tablespoon minced pistachios
1 tablespoon crystallized lemon peel, finely chopped
200 g sieved flour
zest of a lime

Put the eggs on one of the scales, and on the other (scale) put the powdered sugar;
the weight of the eggs should equal that of the sugar. Next, remove the sugar leaving half the eggs which should equal the weight of the flour to be used.

Separate the whites and yolks and beat the whites as hard as possible. Then put in
the yolks and continue beating.

Add the sugar, followed by the flour, lime zest and a few leaves of chopped, can-
died orange blossom, if available.

Butter a mold or casserole and empty the mixture into it, sprinkling over it a few lightly
caramelized finely chopped almonds and pistachios and the glazed lemon peel.

Cook in a moderate oven for an hour and a half. Remove from the oven and take
it out of the mold and if it is a good color, serve it. Alternatively you can cover it
with a white icing, or glaze it with a little syrup and sprinkle small pellets of multi-
colored decorating sugar over.

Serve for dessert.
*Vincent La Chapelle, Le Cuisinier moderne (1742), 2. 186–87.*

---

## EDUCATION

The church was paramount in education, especially in elementary
schools, where the stated goal was above all to produce good Catholics,
with reading, writing, and arithmetic taking second place. Indeed, once

they had mastered the alphabet, children were normally put straight to the task of reading the catechism. Chiefly responsible for this indoctrination were the Brothers of Christian Schools, who made certain that prayers were said every morning and afternoon.

Up to the time of the revolution, priests—especially the Oratorians—taught in both private and church-run schools.[18] At this time, the church had about 500 primary schools in Paris, many of which were free to their students, who lived in a world controlled by priests, nuns, and monks. By the 1780s, the Latin language had largely been replaced by French as a medium of instruction.

During the course of their preparatory education, young men were carefully imbued with moral, political, and religious precepts that would, it was hoped, stay with them the rest of their lives. Daily attendance at chapel and weekly sermons, combined with spiritual exercises and political indoctrination of the values of the establishment, led humanities students to come away with the belief that righteousness meant obedience to the church, to parents, and to the divinely constituted monarchy. The reward for following these principles was salvation.

By 1789, some 48,000 students attended colleges (the equivalent of an American junior and senior high school) run by the church, with about one in 52 boys between the ages of 8 and 18 being admitted. Some of these came from noble or rich bourgeois families. All members of the professional elite began in a similar way, most spending a large part of their adolescence preparing for the humanities or science in a *collège de plein exercise*. Some students chose to pursue their studies in a seminary, and those who had set their hearts on a bishopric moved to Paris with the hope of eventual access to the highest positions in the church. After about six years of study in the humanities, including four hours every day spent in the study of the Latin language and literature, students emerged to take up duties or go on to higher education.

Rousseau, who did not spend his impressionable years in one of the sterile institutions of higher education, expounded a theory of learning that appealed to the revolutionaries. It emphasized the importance of expression rather than repression as a means of producing a well-balanced, free-thinking child. The church and universities, however, were not interested in freethinkers.

One of the first changes to come from the revolution was the elimination of the prominent role played by the church in the educational system. With a shortage of trained teachers, and with priests and nuns now considered unacceptable to teach the youth of the republic, chaos reigned on the educational scene. By 1799, the number of students attending colleges had dropped significantly.

The constitution of 1793 declared education to be one of the basic human rights open to everybody; but little was done to ensure that this was actually the case. The constitution of 1795 ignored the problem and made no such commitment. Under the Directory, each department established a central school, and a few schools of higher learning were established in Paris. No public funding was offered by the government for primary education.

**Student Life**     A student's social position was determined by the rank of his immediate superior and by the characteristic dress of the seminary, college, or university he attended. The local academic establishment, with high legal and social standing within the urban hierarchy, maintained a prominent position among the dignitaries at ceremonies and festivals, and its members were exempt from most municipal and royal taxation.

University recruits, especially those who wished to study the law, were mostly the sons of professional families. These represented some 65 percent of the students entering the University of Douai in the mid-1770s and 77 percent of those at the University of Nancy between 1782 and 1789. There were 22 faculties of law throughout the country, and these graduated some 1,000 lawyers each year.[19] Church prelates also began attending university, and many of these had taken a baccalaureate in theology by 1789.

Within the institutions, there was an accepted order: theology, law, and medicine ranked as the higher faculties, followed by the arts. This hierarchy was evident everywhere, from the order followed in processions to the selection of speakers for official assemblies. Just as in corporate groups, the professor was the master and the student the apprentice. A major difference was that the student had a good deal of relative freedom and was under the professors' controls only during the time he spent in the classroom. While some students lived in seminaries or colleges, where discipline was as strict as that for any apprentice, the majority lived at home or took private rooms with no supervision outside the institution where they studied.

Collegiate studies usually began at the age of 10 or 12, and, by the time they reached their early 20s, the students were ready to start their career. An exception was those studying for the degree of doctor of theology at the University of Paris, which required a minimum of 16 years.[20] Preparatory studies in philosophy and the humanities were done in secondary schools so that pupils would be prepared to attend university in their late teens.

University classrooms were simple, furnished with rows of benches equipped with candleholders and facing a raised lectern. A student was expected to provide his own candles, paper, pens, and writing table or desk. Walls were of bare stone covered with whitewash, and it was customary to hang a map of the world on one of them. Students spent about three to four hours a day in the classroom. At Paris, according to the regulations of 1765, students had to attend two classes a day, each lasting about one and a half hours.

In general, life in a classroom, especially in science, was far from stimulating. After reading from one of his papers, the professor would spend the next half hour or so discussing and explaining it before he ended the class, perhaps with a question-and-answer period, after which came the roll call. It seems that senior academics spent more time censoring heresy than stimulating intellectual exchange. There were not many possibilities for the students to do experiments or procedures discussed in the classroom unless they could find a practicing scientist or surgeon to work with.

In the humanities, the diet was a little more varied: less time was spent listening to the professor read from a text and more emphasis was placed on literature, with exercises involving written work as well as writing essays outside the classroom. Both oral and written examinations were given. After the new subjects of history and geography were added to the curriculum, more time was given to student participation and weekly debates.

Sometimes professors, who were required to teach one class a day, were overwhelmed by the number of students, so helpers or assistants were used fairly commonly. The class would attend the professor's lecture, after which it would be divided into smaller groups led by the brightest among them, whose job it was to make sure the others had understood the lesson, done their homework, and corrected their written work, assigned by the professor.

In both the arts and the sciences, students were expected to be in class on time and to leave only at the sound of the bell. They had to dress in a gown of the color appropriate to the faculty, and they were not permitted to carry a sword or any other offensive weapon.

What was expected of them and what they actually did were often rather different. In the eighteenth century, there were many complaints about young men who registered each term, then paid another person to attend the class and take notes for them. Law students, in particular, were notorious for missing classes. Like the rest, they were forbidden to wear swords in class, but they often defied the rule, and little was done about it. Professors had no means of dealing with rowdy or impolite behavior, unlike professors in the colleges, where discipline could be instilled by the whip or by other measures for minor infractions (e.g., students could be forced to perform extra work).

On average, students lived in idleness and boredom and enjoyed long summer vacations. The older ones spiced up their lives dueling, brawling, and generally making nuisances of themselves in public by intimidating and harassing people. They were a fairly large force and as such were considered formidable and rather frightening.[21] A victim of their pranks had no recourse but to appeal to the local criminal courts—a long, arduous, and costly process. By the end of the old regime, students were still swaggering around Paris disturbing the peace, and sometimes bodies were found on the paving stones after they left. By 1789, many provincial capitals had theaters where students could amuse themselves in their free time; they could also attend lectures by itinerant experimental scientists, take fencing, riding, or dancing lessons, join a lending library, or attend town-sponsored events or even a public séance at the local academy of arts and sciences. Those old enough could enroll in the rapidly spreading order of Freemasonry. Both secular and theology students amply employed the services of prostitutes.

Since most students were studying theology or law, science education was provided primarily for future candidates for the upper levels of the church and the bar. During the course of the century, the number of those interested in medicine grew, but even on the eve of the revolution, they formed fewer than 10 percent of the total number of students. There were relatively few doctors in the cities of France at this time compared to the number of lawyers, judges, canons, and curates. Near the end of the century, the town of Angers, with a population of 27,000, recorded a dozen physicians but 70 canons and 17 curates.[22]

Medical students in Paris usually attended the Jardin du Roi and the Collège Royal. On the national stage, only three universities were notable for medicine—Paris, Montpellier, and Toulouse.

Professors within the colleges or universities took care not to let new ideas disturb the established prejudices and order. The thoughts of the eighteenth-century philosophers, who worked and created their ideas outside the universities, were generally dismissed. The teaching profession's support for the monarchy and professors' espousal of the concept of the divine right of kings predisposed many of their students to become supporters of absolutism. Higher education thus played a role in preserving such ideals. In addition, professors were unwilling to remove God from their views and theories.[23] By the beginning of the revolution, study of the humanities generally remained unrewarding, as teachers did little more than provide the same old commentaries on the same old texts they had been using for years. New philosophical ideas were considered a nuisance to be ignored if at all possible. In 1789, the sciences, physics, and medicine were advancing from simple explanation to a more empirical approach but offered no threat to church or state.

**State Education**

Once the revolutionary government was in place, control of schools and education was transferred from the church to the state, whose proclaimed goals were the promotion of intelligence, morality, and patriotism. On May 4, 1793, Condorcet, the chairman of the Public Instruction Committee, renewed an earlier proposal that claimed that the nation had the right to bring up its children and could not concede this trust solely to families and their individual prejudices. Education was now to be common and equal for all the people. Thus, indoctrination by the Catholic Church was replaced by indoctrination by the state, with nationalism becoming the religion.

In the same year, the Convention ordained that no ecclesiastic could teach in state-run schools, which henceforth would be free of charge, with attendance compulsory for all boys. Girls were to have private governesses or tutors if the family could afford it. This practice was taken up primarily by the bourgeoisie and might consist of instruction in music (piano), art, reading, and reciting of the classics; otherwise, girls had to rely on their mothers for instruction in needlework, care of the household, and the art of being a good wife and mother. The revolutionary government always kept in mind young men and the particular concern that their education prepare them for future roles in the new society.

Sometimes the application of theories bordered on the absurd: consider the following dialogue in which the mother of a patriot family takes it upon herself to inflict upon her young child the questionnaire included by Citizenness Desmarest in her *Elements of Republican Instruction.*

"Who are you?"
"I am a child of the *Patrie.*"
"What are your riches?"
"Liberty and equality."
"What do you bring to society?"
"A heart that loves my country and arms to defend it with."[24]

For most members of the Convention, a new regime required a new kind of education. Robespierre and Saint-Just were obsessed by this idea, maintaining that, as a citizen, the child belonged to the state, and communal instruction was essential. Until the age of five, they were their mother's concern (but only if she clothed and fed them). After that, they belonged to the republic until their death. Pupils were to sleep on mats, dress in linen in all seasons and weathers, and eat only roots, fruit, vegetables, milk foods, bread, and water. According to Saint-Just, no one was permitted to either beat or caress a child, who, in turn, was not allowed to play games that encouraged pride or self-interest. Emphasis was placed on training students to express themselves well and succinctly in the French language.

Schools were to be set up in the country, away from the towns. Saint-Just wanted two kinds: primary schools, where children ages 5 to 10 would learn to read, write, and swim. Secondary schools were to serve students ages 10 to 16 and deal with both theoretical and practical agricultural sciences (whereby farmers would be helped during the harvest) and military sciences, including infantry maneuvers and cavalry exercises. As part of the military curriculum, the young men were to be divided into companies and battalions each month, and the teachers would pick a promising student to lead them. After reaching the age of 16 and passing the difficult endurance test of swimming across a river before an audience on the day of the Festival of Youth, a boy would be permitted to choose a trade and leave school, but he was not allowed to see his parents before he reached the age of 21, at which time he would be considered an adult. This program was not followed, however, and the teaching and the educational system adopted by the Convention was, in fact, not so radical. It was governed by three successive laws. The first, enacted in December 1793, announced that all compulsory primary schools were to be free for children ages 6 to 13, with the curriculum to emphasize politics and patriotism (for example, study of the constitution, the decrees of the National Assembly, the Declaration of the Rights of Man, and Common Law). Schoolchildren were also to concentrate on physical education, among other subjects, and were to take part in civic festivals. This program was difficult to implement due to lack of money and time, so, in November 1794, a second law was passed that made education no longer compulsory and that permitted nonstate-run schools to operate.

As more attention was paid to reforming the educational system, teacher training became one of the top priorities. Salary scales were established, and committees of teachers were set up to run the schools and to meet every 10 days. Educational policy became extremely centralized, and the Committee for Public Instruction was to be responsible for the composition of textbooks used in the central schools. Unfortunately, as money became harder to find, teacher salaries soon became the responsibility of local governments, to be paid by the parents.

A third law, passed in October 1795, required that students pay a small fee to help pay for education in state schools; by then the government under the Directory was in a state of financial collapse. The parents were once again given the choice as to whether their children would attend official institutions or be educated privately, and this meant that many members of the clergy were able to maintain themselves by again opening schools or becoming private tutors. To strengthen attendance at state schools as opposed to religion-based institutions, and to gain a competitive advantage over private schools, the government announced that anyone who wished to work with the government must have evidence that he had attended one of the republican schools.

In October of that year, the idea of schools for girls only was conceived, but emphasis was placed on piety and morality, rather than on academic subjects. By the late eighteenth century, in the south of France, about two-thirds of boys were given some education, but only 1 girl in 50 was schooled.[25]

Schools in many areas were in run-down, inadequate buildings. They were short-staffed with mediocre teachers, there was a lack of books, and undisciplined children ran wild. Truancy, a major problem, was often encouraged by parents who had no confidence in schools that were not run by priests. In one town, mothers burned the few republican schoolbooks available. In Puy de Dôme, the Ecole d'Ambert listed an inventory comprising "wretched furniture, rickety tables, empty bookshelves, and dilapidated floors."[26] Finding competent teachers was difficult. Some of the candidates who applied to teach spelling, for example, could not themselves spell; some who applied to teach mathematics could not add up half a dozen figures correctly. With few qualified candidates available, the selection boards gave teaching certificates to many whose own educational level went barely beyond that of the pupils.

The current uniform, highly centralized, secularly controlled French educational system that was begun during the Terror was completed by Napoleon, under whom teaching appointments based on the results of competitive examinations were opened to all citizens regardless of birth or wealth.

## NOTES

1. The archbishop of Narbonne, for example, had a princely income of 400,000 francs, but when he fled the country for safer ground, he left a debt of 1.8 million francs. See Madame de la Tour du Pin, 315.

2. Quoted from Desan, 102.

3. Robiquet, 78.

4. Hunt (1992), 40; McPhee, 200.

5. Robiquet, 81.

6. Young, 306.

7. Even "a journeyman carpenter in France has his napkin as regularly as his fork; and at an inn, the *fille* [waitress] always lays a clean one to every cover that is spread in the kitchen, for the lowest order of pedestrian travellers." Ibid., 307.

8. L.-S. Mercier, *Tableau de Paris* (1782), vol. I, 228–29, in Braudel, 260.

9. L.-S. Mercier, *Tableau de Paris* (1782), vol. XI, 345–46, in Braudel, 187–88.

10. Dr. John Moore, "Journal during Residence in France" (1793), in Tannahill, 6, where he gives an account of the last few months of 1792—a time when there were few foreigners remaining in Paris.

11. Louis XVI fasted; his family did not.

12. Braudel, 169–70.

13. See Robiquet, 112, for more detail.

14. Ibid., 202–4.

15. Tench, 82.

16. Robiquet, 19.

17. Braudel, 246.

18. The Jesuits dominated French higher learning from the sixteenth century until 1764, when they were expelled, leaving the educational system in France in turmoil. Out of about 400 colleges in all of France, the Jesuits had run 113, and these were subsequently taken over by other religious orders or by secular priests. The original Congregation of the Oratory was founded in Rome in 1575; shortly thereafter, it became a distinct institution in France. It was suppressed during the revolution and reconstituted in 1852 as the Oratory of Jesus and Mary.

19. Lewis (2004), 160.

20. Brockliss, 55.

21. Ibid.,100 ff. for more detail.

22. Ibid.,105.

23. Ibid., 45.

24. Robiquet, 81.

25. Wiesner, 123.

26. Quoted in Robiquet, 84–85.

# 8

# HEALTH, MEDICINE, AND CHARITY

In large part because of the lack of hygiene and the poor living conditions, the population in France in the early eighteenth century was faced with epidemic diseases as a common occurrence. In large cities such as Paris, drains and drinking water intermingled, animal and human dung in the streets filtered through the soil into the groundwater with every rainstorm, and flies in summer contaminated the food in the markets. Even those affluent enough to order water brought by the bucketful to their doors were not safe, because the water came from the river Seine. Daily living in Paris was not a healthy experience, and smallpox and scarlet fever struck often and spread rapidly. Typhoid fever was never far off, and malaria was a curse for those living near stagnant water and its breeding mosquitoes. Further, dysentery was a major problem, and shortages of fresh food often led to outbreaks of scurvy.

Among the poor, illness routinely cut a swath through the young and old, sometimes leaving entire communities devastated. Such was the case about 20 years before the revolution, when typhus raged through Brittany, decimating the local population.

The health of workers in industry was affected by employment conditions. Thread flax workers, for example, labored in damp circumstances to safeguard the thread. Many of them not only developed debilitating arthritis but also, often fatally, contracted pneumonia. Weavers and lace-makers, who performed precise and intricate labor, often worked in poor light that rendered them prone to serious eye problems, even blindness. Tuberculosis took its toll of girls doing menial work in silk and paper manufacturing, while those working with glass and metal were subject to lung diseases. Tailors and shoemakers, after years of hunching over their work, were sometimes left crippled.

At this time, people, especially the poor, had little use for doctors. When they became ill, most took the matter into their own hands, trying to improve their diet, drinking more red wine for its health benefits, and putting their faith in the saints. The poor suffered great agonies before going to a doctor or a hospital—the former was expensive, the latter usually a place to die.

Common problems encountered by the poor included cataracts, sprains, burns, and broken bones. Many men developed hernias from performing heavy work, but unless the condition brought their ability to earn their livelihood to a halt, they generally did not consult a doctor, who, to diagnose the problem, would examine the patient's stools, vomit, and spittle, prescribe various powders and pills and then perform a bloodletting, the panacea for nearly everything from recovery after childbirth to smallpox. Although ideas about medicine were undergoing change, the practice, especially in rural areas, was still medieval.

In the countryside, faith in physicians was rare, and when an epidemic struck, a fatalistic apathy took hold. There were no effective pain relievers and no antiseptics available, and for country people, care from itinerant healers or quacks, with their plasters and ointments, a visit to the village blacksmith, who set bones, or the drinking of mineral waters or potions concocted by the local wise woman all were preferable to seeking outside treatment. A tanner from the Perché region, for example, sold an eyewash containing alum, green vitriol, and dog excrement in the 1780s.[1] If outside treatment was sought, it was more likely to be from a surgeon than a physician, even though the surgeon might be barely literate and know only how to bleed, purge, or shave the patient.[2]

## PHYSICIANS AND SURGEONS

The best doctors were almost always to be found in cities, and, with their superior university background, physicians were considered much more distinguished than surgeons. Medical courses were still based on centuries-old classical Latin texts and were far from arduous in any empirical sense. It was entirely possible for a doctor to complete his medical studies without ever visiting the bedside of an ill person. It cost some 7,000 livres to be registered, but the majority of doctors were middle- or upper-level bourgeois who were able to start fashionable practices and soon recoup their expenses by charging high fees.

For common people, doctors were not only feared; they were also economically out of reach. Doctors were traditionally represented as a rapacious group whose few minutes of advice cost a worker several days' pay. The complaint was that all a doctor cared about was prestige and wealth. A government survey, conducted as late as 1817 to assess the geographical distribution of medical personnel, reported that there were still many rural areas without doctors, who continued to be distrusted and avoided by the local populace.[3]

Surgeons, on the other hand, were respected by the poor because they worked with their hands. Before 1743, their training rarely involved attendance at university. Instead, they were required to do an apprenticeship under a tutor. Previously known as barber-surgeons, these men once cut hair, shaved clients, pulled teeth, stitched up or cauterized wounds, treated dislocated bones, and handled a host of other maladies for which the lofty physician would not dirty his hands. For many years, surgeons strove to combat their perceived association with barbers. A small percentage of those living and working in the capital earned good money, but most surgeons lived on much less. In the provinces, the average income of a surgeon was only around 1,000 livres. While the poor preferred to go to the quack, they might consult the surgeon on occasion for some kind of treatment.

## HOSPITALS

Of the 2,000 or so hospitals in France under the old regime, some consisted of only one room staffed by a couple of nuns in a rural village. Others were large public institutions like the *Hôtel-Dieu* in Paris. By 1789, most major cities were equipped with a general hospital that could attend to routine illnesses, as well as care for the elderly. Bordeaux had seven hospitals of varying size and efficiency, and the facility in Paris comprised a number of buildings.[4] For many people, with no resources, these disease-infested places, dreaded as the ultimate refuge, amounted to a dingy and pathetic place to die.

Poor hygienic conditions and the failure to segregate those with contagious diseases from people suffering from broken bones (although the wealthy could obtain a separate room, since their good treatment augured well for charitable donations) were the result of both lack of financial resources and power struggles within the institutions.

Poor sanitary conditions were often aggravated by the fact that many hospitals were situated on the edge of town next to cemeteries, refuse dumps, and the municipal abattoir or close to fetid rivers and streams, giving rise to humid and overpowering odors.[5]

Daily life in the hospital often involved stormy sessions between doctors and the nursing sisters. For instance, in 1785, at the *Hôtel-Dieu* in Montpellier, the royal inspector of hospitals and prisons, Jean Colombier, insisted on the subordination of the sisters to the medical staff, who accused the sisters, among other things, of overfeeding the patients. The Mother Superior

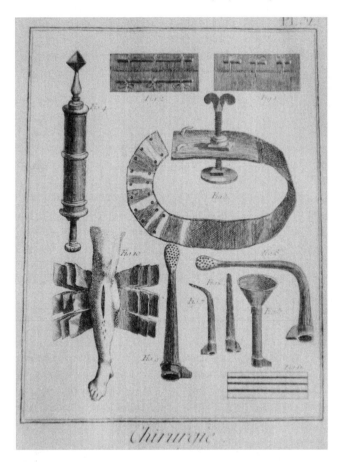

Surgical equipment ca. 1770, showing a wound compress comprising a hooked leather strap, leg binding, and several other items.

resigned because the doctors were given more sway than the sisters in the internal affairs of the hospital. Championing better hygiene, the doctors clashed with the sisters, and the struggle for supremacy became one of traditional sympathy and consolation versus scientific and therapeutic treatment. The management and the sisters both insisted that the hospital should be a charitable institution, rather than a medical one. The administration (made up of the city's elite) preferred to see medical care administered in the home and believed that the emphasis in the hospital should be put on the spiritual and material wellbeing of the patients.

The buildings themselves were often in a sorry state of disrepair. Frequently, the walls were crumbling, the roofs leaked, and broken windows precariously adhered to rotting frames. The money for upkeep was not always there, and the shortage grew worse throughout the eighteenth century. The straw beds were breeding places for lice, fleas, and germs, and in summer months, beds crawling with vermin became unbearable. Further, ventilation was often poor, and the stench of urine and excretion was sometimes overwhelming. Lack of hygiene in overcrowded rooms constituted an extreme health hazard in many hospitals. Sometimes two or three people, each with different diseases, might occupy the same bed, and straw was distributed around the floor for those without a mattress to lie on. On occasion, a patient entered a hospital with one ailment and contracted another there, one that could be fatal. Smallpox ran through the children's wards and led to many deaths. Tinea and scabies were often endemic, typhus and dysentery were sometimes introduced, often by sick soldiers, and gangrene, too, was a problem.

In winter, heat was precious, and lack of hot-water bottles, foot warmers, and braziers meant that elderly patients developed hypothermia and pneumonia. For young children and the elderly, the hospital was too often the gateway to the grave.

As some progress was made in the understanding and control of disease, most doctors became aware that good food and hygienic conditions, as well as the isolation of patients with contagious diseases, played a part in health. Such measures, however, were often sporadic, incomplete, and not economically viable.

Conflict arose over the use of corpses for anatomical research on the workings of the human body. This, along with teaching, was firmly opposed by the sisters and the administration. When teaching was allowed, procedural regulations were strict so as not to offend the sensitivity of the nurses, who also felt that the sick and poor should not be molested by students asking questions and trying to examine them.

The medical profession's demands eventually convinced hospital staff to allow some dissection of bodies, but, apart from executed criminals, few bodies were procurable. In some instances, doctors, surgeons, and medical students in private schools took liberties such as raiding graveyards, often treating the remains in a cavalier manner once they had finished their dissection. Body parts were dumped outside the cities in heaps or thrown into a river, where bits might wind up at a public washing site.

As a result of the contentious situation, doctors vied with one another to acquire posts in military garrisons, prisons, and the new Protestant hospital in Montpellier, where they had direct access to the sick without the obstructive influence of nursing sisters and administrators.

Whenever possible, people, even of modest means, avoided hospitals; hospital admissions were usually not confidential, and the experience was humiliating. Those who were desperate enough to enter the General Hospital in Montpellier, for example, had to appear before the full administration board of the institution, headed by the bishop, and a committee of the city's prestigious nobles. There, as often as not in rags, they pleaded their case for acceptance. If they were admitted, their effects were confiscated,

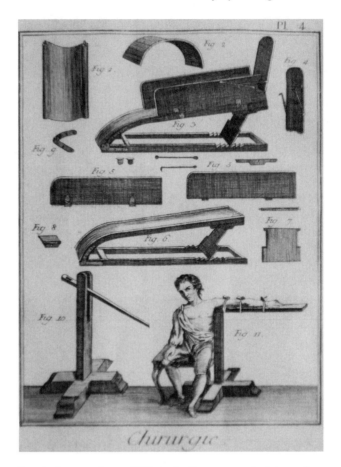

Surgical supports ca. 1770, including arm restraints and an
adjustable reclining seat, with diagrams of its various parts.

their clothes taken to be washed and rid of fleas, while the patient was
examined by a student surgeon to ascertain if the illness was genuine and
that the patient was not suffering from any of the diseases that were barred
from the institution. If all was in order, the patient received a kind of uniform from the nursing sister and was then sent to the hospital chaplain
for confession. Finally, the patient was ushered to a bed.[6] With thousands
of dying old men and old women, babies, orphans, and handicapped and
deformed people, the hospitals gave an impression of a scene from hell.

By 1789, Paris was being cleaned up, and in the process the establishment began to realize that mortality in cities was greater than that in the
country because the urban environment was so deleterious for its inhabitants. Doctors agreed that a serious health risk was present because people
were forced to breathe air infected with the odor of bodies decaying in the

cemeteries, where they were often not properly buried, and by the open sewers in the streets. Many houses still had chamber pots for toilets, and these were emptied into the streets at night, giving the neighborhood an insalubrious and disagreeable ambiance.

New graveyards were created outside the walls of the city, but this met with opposition from those who wanted their loved ones buried close by, and, in the end, burials continued in town for some time to come.

During the late eighteenth century, proper nourishing food began to be a subject of discussion, along with the quality of the air. At least for the wealthy, wholesome food and clean air were becoming priorities. Concern was also expressed over the *Hôtel-Dieu* in Paris, whose humid and airless interior gave rise to perpetual pestilence.[7] Enlightened campaigns advocated opening windows both in hospitals and in private homes to let fresh air circulate.

Preoccupation with cleanliness within the city slowly began to extend to concern for the cleanliness of the body; doctors started encouraging people to wash themselves more frequently. Up to this time, little or no attention had been paid to washing even excrement off the body.

Since the nuns were also in the business of making good Christians out of the patients, many hospitals had chapels of their own or altars in the rooms. Salaried priests kept track of death records and led the sick in prayer, helped draw up wills, buried the dead, administered the sacraments, catechized children, confessed new entrants, and said Masses for benefactors. Sisters also watched over the patients at mealtimes to ensure that there was no trafficking in food, no blasphemy, boasting, or inappropriate conversation that reflected poorly on the hospital and the Catholic religion. Sisters could impose rebukes and mild punishments, such as reducing rations or short imprisonment. Serious matters of insubordination or discipline were taken up by the administration board, and retribution could include corporal punishment or banishment from the hospital.

Up to the middle of the eighteenth century, if a patient under a doctor's care died (as frequently happened), the cause was put down to God's will. Once the doctors were put in charge, however, they increasingly saw disease as part of nature, unrelated to sin and God, and insisted on a secular medical program set apart from the spiritual explanations of the church.

## QUACKS AND CHARLATANS

The common people, superstitious and with a faith in panaceas, were often beguiled by medical charlatans. The elixirs these itinerant vendors offered might have been made of harmless vegetable juices and herbs, but all were touted as a cure for most ailments.

Peddlers gathered crowds on street corners, extolling the virtues of their product. Some, to attract people's attention, supplied entertainment:

acrobats, jugglers, firework displays, dancers, musicians, and tightrope walkers beckoned the curious. Markets, festivals, and fairs drew the dissembling healer to put on his show and sell his concoctions. In one case, Alexandre Cosne, son of a Parisian building worker, appeared with a huge pool complete with mermaid, who answered questions from the crowd. Cosne would turn up in cities claiming to be a magical healer whose potion would cure eye ailments, skin disease, stomach problems, halitosis, and syphilis. It was also touted as particularly effective for dyeing hair![8]

In Paris, the Pont Neuf, which spans the river Seine, was a primary gathering point for swindlers, thieves, beggars, entertainers, and other sundry people. Here there was someone to pull a rotten tooth, make eyeglasses, or fit an ex-soldier with a wooden leg. There were those who sold powdered gems guaranteed to beautify the face, drive away wrinkles, and add to longevity.

## MIDWIVES

An integral component in the lives of the French were the midwives who assisted in the delivery of children. They generally lacked any formal education, especially in rural areas, but as good Catholics they could be relied on by the state and the church under the old regime to record the births and to report those to unmarried mothers. Midwives were usually middle-aged and often widowed women who used their skills in childbirth to help make ends meet by charging a small fee. In the 1780s, they began to receive a little technical training at state expense in a number of dioceses, and they could receive a diploma of competence from their local guild of surgeons after a six-month course at the *Hospice de la Maternité* in Paris. Few attended these classes, however. After the revolution, the government attempted to extend its control over midwives when the medical establishment complained that they were very ignorant and illiterate and in many cases did not understand the French language. Government agents weeded out the most incompetent but realized that to ban all who were unqualified would essentially eliminate their function. Those who had won the confidence of local inhabitants were allowed to carry on.

## BABIES AND WET-NURSES

Special care was taken of abandoned children, the future hope of the revolution. These *enfants trouvés* (foundlings) increased in number as the wars took many fathers. Government grants were dispersed to operate the foundling centers, but soon funds dried up and the children's living situations reverted to the terrible conditions that had prevailed before the revolution, with a 2 or 3 percent survival rate.

There was generally no shortage of babies and children in the medical institutions. Foundling children abandoned on the steps added to the inventory of unwanted infants brought in by the parents and of orphans. Overcrowded conditions were generally the rule. After spending a little time in a children's ward, where the majority died while waiting for arrangements to be made, the surviving infants usually spent their early years of life with a wet-nurse.

Wet nursing was common in villages, especially those close to large towns, from which thousands of babies of all classes were sent each year to foster mothers who performed the service of breastfeeding. Even poor working mothers sometimes put a child born out of wedlock into the hands of a wet-nurse, maintaining contact with it if it survived. The trade was regulated, and, at a special office in Paris, police kept dossiers on women engaged in this business, supervising the agents whose job it was to connect the mothers with the nurses. The government feared a drop in population, and breastfeeding was felt to be the natural and healthy way to nourish a baby.

Montpellier's General Hospital and that of Nîmes recruited women in the impoverished villages of the Cévennes and paid them about four livres a month to act as wet-nurses. Local wet-nurses were generally not available since they could make more money from private families; but the destitute women of the mountain villages were willing to take their chances with contracting venereal diseases, which were sometimes carried by foundlings.[9] On occasion, the women would lie about their ability to feed the babies, instead feeding them animal milk or water with boiled, old, and even moldy bread in it. The journey to distribute the babies from the hospitals to the villages, a distance of more than 60 miles, was slow and difficult. The children were placed four at a time into a basket stuffed with straw and cushions and hitched to a mule for the miserable ride to the Cévennes. Forty percent of those who reached their destination alive died within the first three months, and more than 70 percent died within the first year.[10] Many deaths were caused by malnutrition, neglect, and dysentery. Those sent to the villages often sat in animal and human excrement, their mouths stuffed with rotting rags, or were slung from the rafters in makeshift hammocks, their swaddling clothes seldom changed. Similar baby-farming was carried out in other major cities, including Paris, and often the agents failed to report the death of a child to the authorities, pocketing the money for the child's nurse instead.[11]

At five, the children returned to the hospital (although in a few cases they were adopted by the wet-nurse). Here they continued to be exposed to unhealthy conditions, and, again, survival was at stake. For those who managed to grow to adulthood, attempts were made to integrate them into society, but all carried the melancholy scars of their past; most were sickly and tended to become misfits in society at large.

## CHARITY AND THE WELFARE STATE

One of the most serious problems in eighteenth-century France was poverty. The poor and sick, the crippled, the old, the widows, the orphans—all were of concern and were eligible for charity. Relief was administered through the Catholic Church, and, although it did little more than preserve the poor and afflicted at the most elemental level of existence, this aid saved lives. Parish priests, as well as cathedral chapters and abbeys, took on the role of distributing funds that came from donors abiding by their religious obligation to give alms.

The desperate financial problems of the 1780s reduced royal patronage for the poor. The number of destitute people reached staggering proportions, and their suffering rose to unprecedented levels, with about one in five people poverty-stricken.

Besides the sisters of various Catholic organizations, many women were dedicated to charity. They lived mostly in small towns or villages and were often widows, spinsters, or young single ladies. Most were of modest means, but they saw charity as a way of enhancing the social life of the town. Sometimes they gave their time to help the illiterate learn to read or gave a few coins regularly to a destitute family. The abolition of the *dîme* or church tithes curtailed the ability of the church to administer charity to the poor.

The revolutionaries explored the issues and extent of charity and poverty through the *Comité de Mendicité* (Committee for Charity), hoping to find solutions that would benefit the recipients. They stressed the role of the state in combating this blight on the nation. As under the old regime, the poor were feared because they lived outside the established modes of society, often begging or involved in crime. Nevertheless, it was agreed that one function of the state was to help those who could not help themselves. Old age, sickness, the premature death of the family breadwinner, injury, and unemployment—all were common reasons for being poor. Vagaries of climate and weather conditions, fires or flooding that destroyed crops, or outbreaks of disease could reduce entire towns and countryside to a state of virtual starvation.

In the early years of the revolution, poor relief was no longer considered a form of charity; the right to receive necessary assistance was seen as a basic human right. Every man had the right to feed and clothe himself and his family. Relief was to be paid for by taxation, which went to hospitals, state pensions, public work projects for the unemployed, and care for abandoned children.

The government was heading toward a welfare state from about 1789 to 1795. The reports of the *Comité de Mendicité* were thorough, and the results indicated that the old regime and the church had failed to give aid to the poor when and where it was needed. The committee believed that poverty could be alleviated only by concentrating all relief efforts in a centralized state authority. Only then could a rational program be devised and better administered, on the basis of population densities and fairly assessed taxes. It was felt that every community should have a charity office to provide home relief for the aged and the ill. Workshops would also be made available for those who were able-bodied but unemployed. Prisons were to be established for those beggars who refused state relief measures.[12] It was also suggested the property of the church be split up in small lots and distributed to the poor, since property and employment were the best safeguards against increasing poverty. The committee recommended that hospitals (badly administered, secretive, unhygienic money-wasters) be restricted to taking care of orphans and foundlings waiting for foster homes and the homeless aged. The sick could be better cared for at home.

The *Comité de Mendicité* proposed that able-bodied men receive relief only in return for labor; the infirm would receive free food and money financed by the government. State work schemes were arduous, the tasks often menial, and unwilling workers were sent to 1 of the 34 poorhouses, called *Dépôts de Mendicité*. The plan to register everyone needing help failed. High prices, the rapidly declining assignat, price controls during the Terror, industrial stagnation, the costs of the revolutionary wars—all conspired to thwart the plans of the government.

State workshops to alleviate unemployment were introduced in 1790 but were not well received by the general public and were discontinued by the Directory. The proposals that might have created a welfare state and lifted the nation out of poverty were soon in full retreat as the government, lacking the money, experience, and bureaucracy needed to match the ideals with the practice, reneged on its relief efforts and rejected financial responsibility for the poor.

The beginning of the nineteenth century brought the recovery of poor-relief institutions, which in part owed their salvation to the rehabilitation of the Catholic Church under Napoleon.

## REPORTS OF ENGLISH TRAVELERS

In the eighteenth century, charitable institutions, prisons, and hospitals were as much on the agenda of tourists as Nôtre Dame and the Tuileries gardens.[13] Some English travelers reported their observations. On the whole, the institutions in the provinces seemed more humane and less offensive than those in Paris.

Harry Peckham, a barrister, traveled in France and published an account of his tour in 1772. In it, he states:

the whole kingdom swarms with beggars, an evidence of poverty, as well as defect in the laws. The observation was confirmed at every inn I came to, by crowds of wretches, whose whole appearance spoke of their misery. I have often passed from the inn door to my chaise through a file of twenty or thirty of them; even the churches are infested with them.

George Smollett visited the *Hôpital des Enfants Trouvés* and remarked:

When I first saw the infants at the *enfants trouvés* in Paris, so swathed with bandages, that the very sight of them made my eyes water....

Thomas Pennant left his account of a visit, stating that nearly 6,000 foundlings were admitted annually and taken care of by the nuns, the *Filles de Charité*. "Their names &ca are kept in a little linnen purse and pinned to their Caps that their parents may know them if inclined to take them." It is not clear how the sisters would know their names if they had been abandoned on the steps of a church or left in a ditch.

In October 1775, Mrs. Thrale and her companion, Admiral John Jervis, visited a hospital as part of their sightseeing tour, and she described it as "cleaner than any I have seen in France." She also wrote, "and the poor Infants at least die peaceably cleanly and in Bed—I saw whole Rows of swathed Babies pining away to perfect Skeletons, & expiring in very neat Cribs with each a Bottle hung on its Neck filled with some Milk Mess, which if they can suck they may live, & if they cannot they must die."

In 1776, Mrs. Montagu reported that she saw about 200 infants in their little beds, none above seven or eight days old: "if some had not cried I should have taken them for dolls. After keeping them at most 8 days they are sent to be nursed in the country."

The *Hôtel-Dieu* in Paris also attracted many travelers and foreign doctors who have left various comments. Thicknesse wrote that the hospital was a noble charity and worthy of the name if it was well regulated:

But alas! it is no uncommon thing to see four, five, six, nay sometimes eight sick persons in one bed, heads and tails, ill of different disorders, some dying, some actually dead. Last winter a gentleman informed me that he heard one of the patients there complain bitterly of the cold, and particularly of that which he felt from the dead corpse which lay next to him in the bed!

Dr. James St. John, a London practitioner, was appalled by what he saw at the *Hôtel-Dieu*, commenting (besides remarking on the number of patients in one bed):

The corrupt air and effluvia in some parts of the hospital are more loathsome and abominable than can be conceived. It is amazing, that there are men of constitutions sufficiently vigorous, to recover in such a place of vermin, filth, and horror.

Other visitors and writers of the period reported similar conditions. Adam Walker, a science lecturer, who was there in 1785, remarked on the size of the hospital as larger than any in London and on the number of patients as more than would be found in all the hospitals in London, adding:

It seems an assemblage of all human miseries! ... In one bed ... you may see two or three wretches in all the stages of approach to death!

He goes on to describe more favorable features—clean, high-ceilinged rooms and constant ventilation.

The following year, the Reverend Townsend confirmed seeing many patients in one bed but stated that "The practice of stowing so many miserable creatures in one bed is to be abolished."

Edward Rigby, who practiced medicine in England, was in Paris in 1789 and found the hospital that he visited in July to be "very dirty and crowded, containing 8,000 patients."

Visitors went to other hospitals in and around the capital, such as the *Hôpital Général*, established primarily to meet the problem of poverty, and two other multipurpose establishments—the *Salpêtrière* and *Bicêtre*. Pennant recorded his visit:

Went to the Hospital de Salpetriere, a little way out of Paris, a sort of workhouse for girls and women, of which there are in the house 7500. I saw 400 at work in one room: 500 in another. They embroider, make lace and shirts, and weave coarse linen, also cloth; all which is sold for the benefit of the hospital.... It is also an Asylum to such poor families whose head is dead, or has deserted them; in short, it is the asylum of the miserable, tho' each is obliged to work to support the whole.

*Bicêtre*, an even larger hospital, was farther from the center of Paris and had fewer curious visitors. According to Dr. John Andrews, it was a place for "defrauders, cheats, pickpockets ... convicts for petty larceny ... vagrants, idlers, mendicants." He went on to speak of the mentally ill and the unemployed. Discipline was severe. Andrews considered *Bicêtre* a humane and useful institution, but opinions differed. In the autumn of 1788, Sir Samuel Romilly, a lawyer and reformer, traveled to Paris and visited the hospital in the company of others, including the antiroyalist Mirabeau. Both were horrified at what they saw.

Romilly followed Mirabeau's suggestion that he write down what he had seen, and Mirabeau later translated his notes into French and had them published. The publication was suppressed by the police, but Romilly published the English text in London. The tenor of the essay was expressed in the first paragraph:

I knew, indeed, as every one does, that it [*Bicêtre*] consisted of an hospital and a prison, but I did not know that, at Bicêtre an hospital means a place calculated to generate disease and a prison, a nursery of crime.

There were boys under the age of 12 incarcerated there, and men who were often kept for years in underground dungeons. In the common room were boys and men who had simply argued with or insulted the police on the streets of Paris. Every vice was practiced; the author fel1t obliged to describe these in Latin.

## DENTISTS

Joseph Daniel, who called himself a surgeon dentist, fitted crowns of a new design that would function like natural teeth. He claimed that they would always keep their color.[14] One of his advertisements read as follows:

**DENTAL SURGEON**

M. Daniel, dental surgeon, Fossés-St. Germain l'Auxerrois Street, no. 15, has acquired, by long experience, much dexterity in removing the most difficult teeth and roots when they cannot be preserved. He cleans, whitens and dries them and destroys the nerve, fills them successfully, takes out **geminates, puts back the good ones and inserts artificial teeth, **on spring-loaded posts of a new invention, stable and unbreakable. He has also discovered a metallic thread for teeth and false teeth much cheaper than gold. He blends a toothpaste for tooth and gum care; 3 livres and 6 livres per jar.

CP—13 April 1792

In addition to cleaning and extracting teeth, dental practitioners sold a variety of painkillers. They were also interested in the repair of decayed teeth and the replacement of lost ones. By the 1790s, complex restorative and prosthetic techniques and specialist dental practice was well established.[15]

To have a tooth extracted, the patient was normally seated in a low chair or on the ground, while the dentist stood over him, tongs in hand. As the patient held on to the dentist's legs for support, the toothpuller could certainly tell how much pain he was causing by the intensity of the grasp, but conducting the procedure in this manner benefited the dentist, for it allowed him to get a good grip on the tooth and jerk it out.

One of the most flamboyant mid-eighteenth-century tooth extractors was a huge man called Le Grand Thomas, who could usually be found on the Pont Neuf in Paris. Accompanied by his magnificent horse, adorned with an immense number of teeth strung like pearls around its neck, assistants would examine the teeth of any willing passerby to see what might need to come out. Thomas stood by in his hat of solid silver, which balanced a globe on top and a cockerel above that. His scarlet coat was ornamented with teeth, jawbones, and shiny stones, a dazzling breastplate represented the sun, and his heavy saber was six feet long. A drummer, a trumpet

The itinerant dentist, his patient, and interested onlookers. National Institute of Medicine.

player, and a standard-bearer made up the balance of his retinue. Grand Thomas did not live to see the revolution, but there were thousands of such rogues around the country who seem to have had little trouble finding patients. Most people of the time neglected their teeth until something drastic had to be done. Only the rich could afford a qualified dentist.

By 1768, to become a dentist, a practitioner was obliged to present himself for examination by the community of surgeons of the town in which he wished to practice and to have previously served either two complete and consecutive years' apprenticeship with a master surgeon or an expert who was established in or around Paris or three years' apprenticeship with several master surgeons or experts in other towns. Dentists in Paris and other large cities were trained at the *Collège Royal de Chirurgie* (Royal College of Surgery), which opened in 1776. They had to pass examinations in both

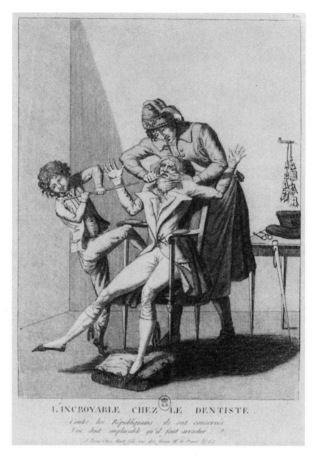

L'INCROYABLE CHEZ LE DENTISTE

The extraction of teeth was very painful! Bibliothèque
Nationale de France.

dental theory and practice and, by the second half of the century, were
obliged to take two separate examinations during the same week—the
first one theoretical, the second practical.[16]

Laws to suppress those who practiced without a license were poorly
enforced up to and during the revolution. Charlatans would set up their
signs, a stage, and other paraphernalia in the square on market day or
operate from an inn or from private premises and advocate a variety of
techniques to remedy toothache, gum disease, and other ailments of the
mouth. To ease the pain of a teething child, magnetized bars were used,
as were various concoctions of herbs and roots. Rattles made of ivory or
coral were often hung around the child's neck to be chewed on, thus helping to reduce the pain of the inflamed gums. If necessary, the gum over the
emerging tooth was lanced.[17] Sometimes a blistering ointment was rubbed
into the area to make saliva flow.

Other curative measures for toothache included bleeding or placing leeches behind the ears; the most frequently used remedy was a special elixir made up of various ingredients to cure decayed and painful teeth. Gondrain's elixir was advertised as "dissipating toothache in a trice."[18] Other potions eliminated swelling of the gums, nourishing and firming them at the same time.

One method of stopping toothache was by destroying the dental nerve by using a file, cauterization, vinegar, essences, and elixirs. All were mentioned in a booklet put out in 1788. Transplants were also attempted, but human teeth were scarce and expensive, and most failed to take root. Taken from a living donor or a corpse, the teeth also had the potential to transmit disease. Artificial teeth, made from ivory or bone, were also unsatisfactory because they absorbed odors and soon became discolored. With the discovery of porcelain for replacement teeth, prosthetic dentistry took a large step forward at the beginning of the revolution.

Not a great deal is known about the fees charged by dentists, but there is a document from 1785 that lists a fee of four livres four sols for an extraction and a filling. Costs for elixirs were usually 5 and 10 livres a bottle, and toothpaste cost 3 to 6 livres. For a small brush mounted in ivory, the cost was 3 livres. By the end of the eighteenth century, a number of dentists practiced from a fixed location, especially in large cities; when they worked in other towns, they rented premises for a few days.[19]

## NOTES

1. Lewis (2004), 156.
2. Colin Jones (1982), 119.
3. Ibid., 236.
4. Forrest, 60.
5. Jones (1982), 99.
6. Ibid.
7. Lewis (2004), 158.
8. Jones (1982), 118.
9. Hufton, 65.
10. Jones (1982), 105.
11. Schama, 146.
12. Jones (1982), 160.
13. For additional reports of English travelers and other observations, see Lough, 121–34.
14. Hillam, 58.
15. Ibid., 15.
16. Ibid., 42–44.
17. Ibid., 113.
18. Ibid., 79.
19. Ibid., 58–60.

# 9

# RELIGION

With some 170,000 secular and regular priests, the church in France represented the first order of society, comprising about 26,000 monks and friars, 56,000 nuns, 60,000 curates, 15,000 canons, and 13,000 clerics with no permanent office or regular duties.[1]

Besides caring for the soul, the church held the monopoly on primary and secondary education, as well as being a major source of charity. It maintained registers of births, marriages, and deaths and ran the hospital system, such as it was, under the old regime.

In rural areas, not only was the village church the center for the spiritual care of the locals but also it served as the hub of administrative affairs. The church put order into every aspect of country life: the tolling of the church bells ordained the rhythm of the daily cycle, resounding throughout the village when it was time to rise, at noon when it was the hour for a break, and at vespers, in the evening, when it was appropriate to pause and say a prayer. The sound of the bell was also the alarm alerting the populace of a fire or warning of mischief in the village.

The kingdom was divided into 18 archiepiscopal provinces and 136 dioceses. Many bishops held jurisdiction in more than one: the noble bishop of Dol, in Brittany, for example, had 33 posts.[2]

## LIFE OF A NOBLE CLERIC

A rural abbot, Emmanuel Barbotin, financially well off as a tithe holder and director of an agricultural business in the north of the country, was elected representative from Hainaut to the Estates-General. He wrote letters back to his parish about his day-to-day thoughts and experiences. In one letter, penned while he was in Paris, he wrote to a fellow priest who was looking after his farm at Prouvy in the north, with a number of instructions about selling the oats, wheat, flax, and bundles of faggots in good time; he informed his caretaker when to plant colza, when to bleach linen, to whitewash the barns, the bake house, and the pigeon-cote. The abbot also wondered if there was enough butter for the month of October and asked about the amount and the quality of the harvest, insisting that the different grains be sorted as cleanly as possible. Not least important was the condition of the wine cellar. For this, his instructions were as follows:

If the red wine is ready to be tapped, it must not be allowed to stand and spoil. If you haven't already changed the cask, the wine must be clarified. In order to do this, you must first broach the cask and put in the cock, draw out the bung, and, if the cask is full, draw off at least one bottle, beat the whites of six eggs with a pint of wine, pour it all back into the cask, stir it in with a stick for five to ten minutes, bung it up well again, let it stand seven or eight days and then tap.

The abbot also made inquiries about his flock and asked Father Baratte to try to find the time to teach the children of the village the catechism:

It is in childhood that the eternal truths of our religion are engraved most readily on the spirit, when they can act freely upon hearts devoid of lustful passions; and we are living in a time when religion needs to be upheld by our preaching and even more by our practice.

From these instructions it is evident that the abbot lived a comfortable life on his farm, as did all churchmen of rank in their abbeys, palaces, and manor houses. Half of the revenues of the large abbeys went into the pockets of the abbots, whose only qualifications for their positions were noble birth and the amount of influence they exercised at the royal court.

Barbotin also wrote that after long hours in heat and dust, he and his colleagues arrived at Versailles on May 8, 1789. After a good dinner that cost one louis for the four of them, they looked for lodging, eventually finding clean and convenient but somewhat cramped quarters near the palace at a cost of 60 livres a month. As food was expensive, they ate lightly in the evenings and drank a few glasses of beer. The luncheon meals were huge, however, more than they could eat, but the worst wine at home was much better than what they had to drink at Versailles. He complained that bedbugs prevented him from enjoying sound sleep, and the incessant rain confined him indoors. When the sun did briefly appear, they went sightseeing. He remarked that everything was going smoothly there as long as one had plenty of money.

The transfer to Paris of the Assembly found the abbot less cheerful. Not only was the move bothersome, but the noise and din of the immense city annoyed him. His lodgings were surrounded by streets on all sides in which vehicles (presumably wagons and carts with iron wheels) did not stop clattering over cobblestones from six in the morning until three the following morning. Sleep was difficult for a man accustomed to the quiet countryside.[3]

## CHURCH INCOME AND THE PARISH PRIEST

In spite of its wealth (much of it in land), the church, like the nobility, was not required to pay taxes. It did, however, under coercion, make "voluntary" payments of about 5 percent of its income. The archbishop of Strasbourg made about 400,000 livres per annum and the archbishop of Paris more than half a million.[4] A village priest was lucky if he made 750 livres a year. Many bishops, once having secured their diocese, seldom visited it, preferring to spend their time at court or in their mansions.

The *dîme* (or tithe) was a tax collected by the church in cash or kind (crops or animals). Amounts varied throughout the country, from practically nothing in some regions to 25 percent of income in others. The church was the largest land-owning corporation, counting among its rich possessions about one-fifth of Paris, as well as properties in towns and villages, from all of which it collected rents. Rural church land, which was farmed by peasants, has been estimated to have brought into church coffers some 100 million livres annually. By 1789, there were 1,700 monastic houses that operated schools and hospitals (the latter mostly homes for the poor).

Within the church hierarchy there was an enormous gap between the generally noble archbishops, bishops, abbots, and other high-placed functionaries and the lowly, poor, sometimes barely literate village priests. Living in cottages beside the church, priests often relied on a small vegetable patch to help supply their alimentary needs. The poorer the parish, the poorer the curate, since donations for his welfare were meager. Some parish priests resented this financial discrepancy; despite the enormous wealth of the church, they, the vast majority, lived no better than their peasant parishioners.

The relationship between the church and the rural communities was intimate and complex. The power of the priest's blessing, religious rituals, and sacraments was of great importance to ward off evil, bad weather, and poor harvests. Generally considered the indispensable member of the village or locality, the priest heard confessions and absolved the sinner, performed baptisms and marriages, and gave the last sacraments to the dying. From the pulpit he was also the conduit for government decrees, which he read and explained, being, in many cases, the only literate person in the village. The priest also worked in collaboration with the village inhabitants on communal business, with Sundays, after Mass,

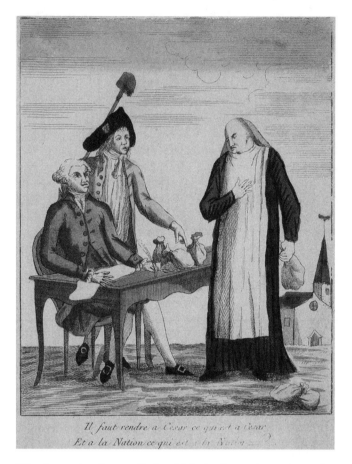

*Il faut rendre a Cesar ce qui est a Cesar
Et a la Nation ce qui est à la Nation*

"Render unto Caesar that which is Caesar's, and to the Nation, that which is the Nation's." The priest is reluctant to give his bag of money to the tax collector. Behind is a man from the Third Estate who is insisting that the cleric part with his money. In the background is a church. Courtesy Library of Congress.

the traditional time for meetings that took place, usually in the church. In larger communities, the meeting of townsmen in taverns was often seen by the clergy as a threat to church influence, taverns being the gathering site for those least prepared to accept priestly authority and places where alcohol brought out anticlericalism. Sometimes priests attempted to have the taverns closed or at least restricted in their hours of opening. Furthermore, there was competition for the attention of the people when itinerant healers and soothsayers appeared with love potions, prophecies, and cures for sick people or animals, which the rural population took with great seriousness.

## SUPERSTITION

From the southwestern town of Agen, in 1791, a report noted that country priests had once been heard demanding that sorcerers and sorceresses leave the church before Mass.[5] Many areas abounded in tales of bogeymen, werewolves, and vampires. Peasants walking home on dark nights were constantly alert to the idea that they might meet some supernatural being on the dark, lonely road. Some enlightened priests tried to disabuse their parishioners of such superstitions, but to little avail. The pagan past was still present, and communities lived in fear of the mysterious and impenetrable. To offset the unnatural forces of this shrouded world, they relied on the priest's blessings, prayer, and religious rituals such as Communion. Only the holy church had power over the dark world of the devil. Crops and livestock were blessed on a regular basis; prayers went out for a good harvest; church bells, themselves holy objects, were rung to ward off storms, rain, and hail, especially around the time of harvest; and the Host might be brought to a fire to prevent it from spreading. If the supplications were of no avail, then the unwelcome event was accepted as God's will.

The tithe on the land collected by the church was reputedly used for upkeep of the ecclesiastical buildings, the priest's living expenses, and charity to the needy. The right to collect the tithe was owned by religious institutions often far removed from the parish where it was paid. Thus, it became simply another burden on the peasants, with no direct connection to the performance of the priest. If he was good, bad, or indifferent, the tithe was still collected, and the money disappeared into church coffers. The parish priest still charged fees for weddings, baptisms, and funerals. There were further complexities when the church was the landowner as well as the seigneur, collecting rents and feudal dues; although the church responded to complaints with a network of charities, often there was resentment over its economic interests and prosperity. To some, the church seemed less interested in saving souls than in maintaining its property and privileges. In spite of this, the majority of the peasants were closely attached to their local priests.

## THE REVOLUTION

The dissatisfaction of the lower clergy had dramatic results when the Estates-General began meeting in Versailles. On June 13, 1789, during the debates and the formation of the National Assembly, a number of the elected parish priests defected from the First Estate and joined the Third Estate. They, like others in their position, wanted a more democratic church—one in which talent and work would be more important to advancement than the accident of noble birth. Along with a few noblemen, they broke ranks, and the Third Estate declared itself the National Assembly on June 17. On June 27, by the king's order, the three estates united. Their first task was to nullify all feudal rights and privileges, and on August 11, the church was deprived of its rights to the *dîme*. In the last weeks of that month, the men who drafted the Declaration of the Rights of Man and Citizen refused to make Catholicism the state religion, opening the door for Protestants, who had enjoyed few civil rights for more than a century, and for Jews, who had been oppressed much longer than that.[6]

There was much more in store for the ecclesiastic community than anyone thought possible, however. On November 2, the government nationalized church property, and in December the first 400 million livres worth of these lands were placed for sale on the open market. Desperate for money, the government paid off its creditors with the new paper currency—assignats—with which church property could be purchased. Ownership of these vast lands then changed from the hands of the church to mostly those of bourgeois or wealthy peasants, the general practice being to sell the land by auction, which benefited the more wealthy buyers.

On February 13, 1790, all monasteries and convents not dedicated to charitable or educational work were closed and new religious vows were forbidden. This policy reflected the view of many deputies, even some clerics, that contemplative orders of monks and nuns were parasites on society. It seemed that this niche in the daily life of the nation was on the verge of extinction.

## CIVIL CONSTITUTION OF THE CLERGY

The church was now no longer an independent order in France, and the loss of the tithe, the sale of its lands, and the assault on the monastic orders were followed by the Assembly's publication, on July 12, 1790, of the Civil Constitution of the Clergy.[7] Salaries were to be paid by the state, and residence requirements were strict at every level: there were to be only 83 bishops, instead of the previous 136, one for each department, and only one parish in all towns of fewer than 6,000 inhabitants. The clergy existed to minister to the faithful and had no other justification for being tolerated as far as many deputies were concerned. Chapters not involved in the caring for souls were abolished. Many of the lower priesthood found they would be better off financially under the new rules and felt the provisions so far satisfactory.[8] However, a major problem arose with the matter of appointment, as all clerics were now to be elected by the people in the same manner as other public officials—bishops by departmental assemblies and parish priests by district voters. Among the voters, it could be argued, might be Protestants, Jews, and even atheists, which displeased many. The pope, who had hitherto sanctioned episcopal appointments, would now simply be informed that they had been made.

Many prelates sought the advice of Rome on this matter, but the pope procrastinated, and no word came. The debate in the Assembly and among the populace turned acrimonious. The deputies were annoyed by the lack of response from Rome, and the religious situation grew worse as pious country people blamed the government and the city dwellers (especially in Paris) for wanting to eliminate God from their lives. Catholics and Protestants renewed hostilities with bloody battles, especially in the south, where Protestants were more numerous. Rumors were started whenever possible to implicate the few Jews living in the country. Opinions became polarized, and the conservative press denounced the Civil Constitution as an attack on the Catholic Church. Naturally, the patriotic press responded with anticlerical vehemence.

The situation seemed to be heading toward religious chaos as all but a few of the bishops refused to accept the Civil Constitution; tired of waiting for a response from the pope, the deputies decided to have the clergy take an oath of allegiance to the new constitution. Those who refused (it was thought) would be dismissed. The king reluctantly sanctioned the decree at the end of 1790, and on January 2, 1791, priests were told to swear their oath before their parishioners to be faithful to the nation, the king, and the constitution. Unexpectedly, about 40 percent of the clergy and the vast majority of bishops refused. It was not practicable to dismiss the thousands, especially in the west of the country, who denounced the Civil Constitution. Those who refused were referred to as nonjuring or refractory priests. The country was now split along religious lines in support of or against refractory priests, some of whom were murdered while others fled.

On April 13, 1791, the pope finally condemned the Civil Constitution of the Clergy, and many priests renounced their oath. Opinion in the church and among the people was about evenly divided. During the summer, some departments took it into their own hands to exile or imprison refractory priests. In September, the government annexed Avignon, a papal enclave in southern France. On November 29, the Assembly decreed that all refractory priests were antirevolutionary suspects.

Meanwhile, in regions such as the Vendée and much of Brittany, where there was widespread refusal to take the oath, the departments took it upon themselves to keep a close eye on rebellious priests, introducing their own policy of exiling or imprisoning them.

On May 27, 1792, a new law was issued according to which any nonjuring priest could be deported if denounced by 20 active citizens (later reduced to 6). By August, all refractory priests were ordered to leave the country within two weeks or be deported to French Guiana. After August 11, sans-culotte vigilantes were arresting them in Paris. Flight was difficult as no one could leave Paris without a passport issued by city hall, and to obtain a passport one was required to show a certificate of civic responsibility from the section Surveillance Committee.

The prison massacres of September 2–6, 1792, during which most of the prisons in Paris were broken into and the prisoners butchered by sans-culottes, resulted in about 1,200 deaths. More than 200 priests were among the victims.[9] Nevertheless, in the countryside, in spite of government efforts to disestablish the church, many thousands of village inhabitants encouraged their priests to resist the government and to refuse to take the oath.

## DE-CHRISTIANIZATION AND REACTION

Anticlericalism had gained momentum since the outbreak of the revolution and the downfall of the monarchy. Many patriots assumed that if the revolution was to survive and flourish, Catholicism must be eradicated. A campaign against the church began in the spring of 1793 and was taken up by the Paris Commune under the leadership of Chaumette and Hébert, whose anticlerical paper *Le Père Duchesne* had laid the groundwork.

In May 1793, the Commune terminated all clerical salaries, closed churches in Paris, and forced some 400 priests to resign. The revolutionaries demanded that the metropolitan church of Nôtre-Dame be reconsecrated as the Cult of Reason. The Convention complied, and on November 10, a civic festival was held in the new temple, which displayed the inscription "to philosophy" over the facade. Although the various factions of the revolution had begun splintering into subsects, anti–Roman Catholic religious activity continued to rise in both volume and severity, and eventually this started to reflect badly on the Revolutionary Council.

By autumn 1793, there were few refractory priests left in France. Those who had remained or returned secretly to their parishes from exile led the life of fugitives. The clergymen who had taken the oath fared little better. They were blamed for royalist revolts in the countryside on the assumption that they had not taught their flocks proper obedience to the new state.

Equally avid in shaping the new religion for France were the *représentants-en-mission,* members of government who administered the provinces. Local sans-culottes supported their endeavors and did much of the work, destroying shrines along the roads and stripping the village churches of their statues, ornaments, bells, and crosses, after which they turned the buildings into stables, barns, and storehouses.

The Revolutionary Army, a product of the Terror, in September 1793, set off from Paris for the departments of the south. About 3,000 men in all, they took the route through Auxerre, southeast of Paris. Along the way they indulged in ferocious atrocities against church properties. As recorded by a local official, they smashed church doors, hurled altars, statues, and images to the ground, and took anything of value.[10] Around Auxerre they spread out in smaller detachments along the back roads to pillage the chapels and churches, even climbing onto the roofs with ropes to throw down any sacred object. Joined by the young men of Auxerre, the marauders ensured that little in the town or the surrounding country, including beautiful and ancient religious objects, escaped them. Within a week, nothing of the Catholic faith remained visible in the region except the battered shells of religious buildings.

Constitutional priests were mocked and forced to renounce the priesthood, and, in some areas to marry, by officials who denounced clerical celibacy. Those too old to marry were compelled to take in an orphan or an elderly person and care for the person. Sundays and Christian feast days were abolished by the new revolutionary calendar adopted on September 22, 1793.

In spite of the efforts to destroy the Catholic faith in France, there remained a deep and widespread substratum in the provinces that would never abandon its cherished beliefs. A vague, undefined Deism had no place in their intimacy with the highly organized Christian world in which they had participated all their lives, knowing what to expect in this life and the next.

The deputies of the Convention agreed with the process of de-Christianization for a time, but the excesses multiplied, and many were not enthralled with the events taking place. Voices were beginning to be raised in strong protest as the disturbances created financial instability. Some, like Danton, believed that the campaign alienated France's neighbors and encouraged them to join the allied coalition against the revolution. Robespierre ardently disliked priests but also opposed the excesses of the sans-culottes on moral and practical grounds. He felt that the unbridled attacks on the church were driving people into the ranks of the counter-revolutionaries. As the Committee of Public Safety exerted more and more power over the sans-culotte movement, de-Christianization began to weaken until it was finally brought under control in 1793 and 1794.

On February 21, 1795, the state renounced all financial support for or ties to the constitutional church or any other kind of worship. Formal freedom of religion was proclaimed, as a result of which many new cults sprang up, such as that of Marat, of Atheism, of Reason, of Rationalism, and of the Supreme Being, which regarded Rousseau as the high priest.

Popular demand that churches be reopened could no longer be ignored by the government. On Palm Sunday, March 29, 1795, for example, a massive demonstration marched to the cathedral of Saint-Etienne in Auxerre, opened it up, cleaned out the clutter and the classical pagan images that had been used there, and burned them. The Assembly passed another decree, in October 1795, penalizing nonjuring priests, many of whom were in prison, but it was withdrawn in December 1796. Uncertainty and confusion prevailed among the people and the church. What was next? All legislation against refractory priests was repealed on August 24, 1797, and then reinvoked on September 4. Some 1,500 priests were deported the following year, and the authorities made a concerted effort to reintroduce national festivals and make the *décadi* again the day of worship.[11] Not until the Concordat of 1801 was the matter resolved in favor of the church.

## RELIGION AND POVERTY

Under pressure from the Paris authorities, the Constituent Assembly turned its attention to relief for the poor and added to its bureaucracy the *Comité de Mendicité*, whose object it was to formulate a new public-assistance policy. The members began with preconceived ideas about poverty, grounded in Enlightenment literature, that included an abhorrence of religious clerics. Not only did the ready availability of Catholic charity, it was thought, deceive the donor into thinking that his chances of going to heaven would be greater because of his philanthropy, but also, it was argued, donations to the poor created a large and growing class of social parasites. The donor was locked into superstition, while the recipient, generally considered indolent, passed on his unsavory habits to his children. Often using God's name to solicit alms, the poor employed a kind of spiritual blackmail, knowing that if little or no alms were forthcoming, they still had Catholic charity to fall back on. With this in mind they saved nothing for the future for themselves or their families.[12] *"J'irai à l'hospice"* (I'll go to the hospital) if other methods fail was considered to be the philosophy of the beggar. In addition, the government viewed with consternation the hold that the Catholic Church established on society through poor relief. The committee thought that hospitals were uneconomical and mismanaged their task of coping with the poor; its members were convinced that the state could do a better job once the truly poor had been identified among the lazy and shiftless.

## CULT OF REASON

A rationalist religious philosophy known as Deism flourished in the seventeenth and eighteenth centuries. Deists held that a certain kind of religious knowledge or natural religion is either inherent in each person or accessible through the exercise of reason, but they denied the validity of religious claims based on revelation or on the specific teachings of any church. Deists advocated rationalism and criticized the supernatural or nonrational elements in the Judeo-Christian tradition.

Practitioners of reason opposed fanaticism and intolerance and viewed the church, especially the Roman Catholic Church, as the principal agency that enslaved the mind.[13] Many intellectuals believed that knowledge comes only from experience, observation, reason, and proper education, and through these methods humanity itself could be altered for the better. This approach was considered more beneficial than the study of dubious sources, such as the Bible. Advocates of reason further believed that human endeavors should be centered on the means of making this life more agreeable, rather than concentrating on an afterlife. The church, with its wealth and suppression of reason, was ferociously attacked.

James St. John, who practiced medicine in Ireland, visited France several times and sent his last letter home on October 20, 1787, perhaps foreseeing some of the difficulties soon to come:

There is not, nor never was a nation in the world, who have less religion than the modern French. The lower class of people, and also the clergy, may keep up the shew (*sic*) of religion, but the generality of their genteel people make a scoff of the faith, and think it ridiculous to be a Christian. The Deistical works of Rousseau and Voltaire, are every where distributed through the kingdom, are universally read, and studied, and in my opinion have been the cause of undermining the whole structure of Christianity in France; and in the course of half a century more, in all human probability will totally erase all vestiges of revealed religion in the French nation.[14]

In April 1794, Robespierre proposed a new state religion, the Cult of the Supreme Being, based around the worship of a Deist-style creator god. It had few distinguishing characteristics other than being opposed to priests and monarchs and in favor of liberty.

The festival of the Supreme Being was set for June 8, 1794, and Robespierre laid out an elaborate series of somber, mandatory observances, which largely involved everyone dressing in uniforms with the colors of the new French flag and marching around in formation. He made a speech that included the following:

French Republicans, it is for you to purify the earth that has been soiled and to recall to the earth Justice which has been banished from it. Liberty and virtue spring together from the breast of the divinity—neither one can live without the other.[15]

Other cities and villages staged similar fêtes and added a few twists of their own. The only tenets of the cult were that the Supreme Being existed and that man had an immortal soul. Despite the blessing of the Supreme Being, Robespierre did not survive two months after the first celebration of the feast. The process stands as an example of a religion manufactured by government officials. When Robespierre went to the guillotine, the cult went with him.

## RESULTS OF THE REVOLUTION FOR THE CHURCH

All in all, the church fared badly during the revolution. It went from being the First Estate of the land and the most powerful corporation to being a nonentity. The sale of church land, its main source of wealth, was the worst blow, one from which it never fully recovered, but the churches and monasteries were rebuilt, and the priesthood revived under Napoleon, who set about restoring ecclesiastical authority, believing that it was an effective tool for keeping the people in line. He struck a deal with Rome that allowed him to keep the church property seized by the revolution, while reestablishing Catholicism as the primary religion of the country.

## NOTES

1. Lewis (2004), 44.
2. Doyle, 4.
3. See Robiquet, chapter 2, for this account.
4. Lewis (1972), 37.
5. Andress (2004), 22.

6. Louis XIV persecuted Protestants mercilessly, and on October 18, 1685, he revoked the Edict of Nantes, which had given them religious freedom. Although Louis XV issued an edict in 1752 that declared marriages and baptisms by Protestant clergymen null and void, the edict was recalled in 1787, under Louis XVI. King Charles VI of France had expelled the Jews from the country in 1394, ending Jewish history in France until modern times.

7. Gallicanism, a position of the French royal courts, or parlements, advocated the complete subordination of the French church to the state and, if necessary, the intervention of the government in the financial and disciplinary affairs of the clergy. The pope became somewhat irrelevant in France, except in strictly spiritual matters.

8. Doyle, 140.
9. Ibid., 192.
10. See Cobb/Jones, 206.
11. Andress (2004), 252.
12. Hufton, 62.

13. Deism was also influential in late-eighteenth-century America; Benjamin Franklin, Thomas Jefferson, and George Washington were among those who held such views. The most outspoken American Deist was Thomas Paine. Elements of the Deists' ideas have been absorbed by philosophies such as Unitarianism. Lough, 151.

14. Ibid.
15. Schama, 834.

# 10

# WOMEN

## WOMEN AND POLITICS

In pamphlets and in delegations to the Revolutionary Assembly, women activists unsuccessfully demanded universal suffrage, but Sieyès spoke for the majority of deputies when he said that women contributed little to the public establishment and hence should have no direct influence on government.[1] He also claimed that women were too emotional and easily misled, and because of this weakness it was imperative that they be kept at home and devote themselves to their natural maternal roles.

While formally excluded from politics, women were involved in local causes that included religious rights and food issues. They also formed auxiliaries to local political clubs and actively participated in civic festivals and relief work.

In the critical issue of suffrage in the new France, three categories of people were immediately excluded: the very poor (that is, those who did not pay tax equivalent to the proceeds of three days' labor); servants (because they would vote as instructed by their masters); and women. The first two exclusions were debated; the last was taken for granted. For the bourgeois revolutionary leaders, a woman's place in society was not equal to that of a man. This point of view existed in France up until 1944, when women finally got the vote.

For many women during the revolution, the terms "liberty" and "equality" must have had a hollow ring. The Declaration of the Rights of Man and Citizen, approved by the Constituent Assembly on August 26, 1789, disenfranchised well over half the population. Denied their rights, women were judged equal only in the defining moment of the guillotine. The Constituent Assembly also rejected the premise that women were citizens, adopting a patriarchal attitude that made women chattels and, as such, the property of men. When a husband left home, either to join the army or to simply abandon his family, the wife was left to bring up their children alone, generally with means that were far from adequate.

## GRAIN RIOTS AND THE MARCH ON VERSAILLES

There was little new about grain riots in France. They had taken place long before the revolution and had not been deemed a threat to the aristocracy. When there were shortages, the uprisings were generally instigated by women, who blamed the producers and distributors for causing the shortfall in order to raise the price. This was the case in the spring of 1789, after the preceding harvest had been severely damaged by bad weather. The price of bread shot up 60 percent, and riots broke out around the country. There were attacks on granaries and bakeries in all major cities.[2] At Virally, between Versailles and Paris, women set up a blockade, checking convoys of wagons before allowing them to pass. If grain or flour was found, the women helped themselves to it.

Much of the recently harvested grain, what there was of it, had not yet reached Paris, again due to poor weather. Hence, bread was in short supply, and prices were rising. About the only thing the city was not short of were rumors. The king was not cooperating with the National Assembly and was slowing down the pace of political change, it was said; he was strengthening his bodyguard in order to attack Paris and destroy the recently established Commune and the people's bid for liberty. Bread shortages were a conspiracy of the nobility to starve the people into submission. The king was controlled by his evil and dissolute wife, as well as by the sycophantic aristocrats who wanted to halt the advance of freedom. Many people demanded that the king come to Paris to escape the grasp of the greedy nobility. They feared the aristocrats would take him away to some unknown place and that they would then run the country in his place—the first item on their agenda being to crush the insurrection in the capital.

On October 5, 1789, excited by rousing orators speaking in the cafes of the Palais Royal and in the public squares of the city, throngs of women, outraged by the bread prices and shortages, gathered at the Hôtel de Ville, from where they set out for Versailles to take their complaints directly to the king. Organized mainly by workers from the central market and the faubourg St. Antoine, they came from all over the city, united in their anger. They were joined by hundreds more, including about 15,000 National Guardsmen (and even their reluctant general, Lafayette). Taking

*Un Sans-culotte instrument de crimes dansant au milieu des horreurs, Vient outrager l'humanité pleurante auprès d'un cenotaphe. Il croit voir l'ombre de l'une des victimes de la revolution qui le saisit a la gorge. Cette effrayante apparition le suffoque et le renverse*

Satire on the death of Louis XVI. A sans-culotte waves a banner labeled "Fête du 21 Janvier" at a female figure "Humanité"; in the background is a scene of murder and mayhem. Courtesy Library of Congress.

matters into their own hands, they marched along the road to Versailles, chanting their demands that they be given bread and that the king come to Paris, where he would be more accessible to the people. Brandishing kitchen knives, brooms, skewers, and a variety of other implements, the women led the march, shouting invectives directed mostly at the queen. It was raining heavily as they walked the 12 miles, but their spirits were not dampened.

Late in the afternoon, the horde massed in front of the palace gate, and some of the demonstrators pushed their way into the nearby meeting hall of the National Assembly, then in session. Shouting for bread and mocking the deputies, the mud-spattered women sang, danced, and shrieked their demands, creating an uproar in the hall.

In the meantime, the king returned from hunting and, although tired and wet, agreed to see a delegation of the protesters. This decision may have been inspired by the fact that the Versailles National Guard had joined the protest and the Paris National Guard was approaching the palace, which was protected by only a few hundred of the king's body-guard. The women met with the king, along with the president of the National Assembly, Jean-Joseph Mounier. Demanding bread, whose shortage the king blamed on the deputies of the Constituent Assembly, the women were determined not to leave Versailles until they had a promise of lower prices and reform. The king pledged to look into the matter the following day.

By now, some demonstrators who had penetrated the palace court-yard were shouting abuse and obscenities at the royal family. Frightened advisers and military officers pleaded with the king to call out the Flanders regiment, recently moved to Versailles and stationed nearby, or to set up cannon to intimidate the crowds, but the king refused, hoping no blood would be shed in spite of the fact that a few of the palace guard had already been killed. Besides, the soldiers could not be counted on to fire on their own people, even if so ordered.

A little before midnight, the Paris National Guard arrived, and Lafayette, apologizing to the king for his inability to control his troops, guaranteed the safety of the royal family by leaving 2,000 of his guardsmen in the palace. It was reported that Marie-Antoinette went to bed about two o'clock in the morning, protected by bodyguards outside her room, as well as by four maids inside, sitting with their backs against the door. One of these women later told the queen's biographer that about 4:30 that morning, they heard loud shouts and the sound of firearms discharging. The mob had invaded the palace, and the National Guard had capitulated. Lafayette soon arrived, however, and, with more soldiers, emptied the building of intruders. Outside, the crowd demanded that the queen come out.

Marie-Antoinette bravely appeared on a balcony, which quieted the throng. Lafayette joined her there for a moment and then led her back inside while the crowd again let it be known that the royal family must come to Paris. The king acquiesced, and eventually the royals began the two-hour-long journey, flanked by the howling Parisian mob. Accompanying the procession were bodyguards, National Guardsmen, the Flanders regiment, servants, palace staff, members of the National Assembly, wagons full of courtiers, and many wagonloads of bread and grain taken from the palace. The king, the little dauphin, and especially the queen were subjected to verbal insults and rude gestures throughout the journey. Despite having had little or no sleep, the immense crowd was highly charged, but the presence of Lafayette, riding beside the royal carriage, may have deterred any attempt to harm the royal family, who, on arrival in Paris, were deposited at the rundown Tuileries palace, which had just been emptied of its aging retainers and retired officials to make room for the 700 or so members of the royal staff. Bringing the king back to Paris, it was thought, would guarantee that something would be done about the women's grievances.

Urban lower-class women in general caused the government much distress during the revolution by their demands, rioting, and disruptions of meetings of the National Assembly, now in Paris. They were seldom physically violent but generally caused havoc by heckling and resisting removal from the Convention meetings. Some were able to force issues onto the agendas; however, women who intervened in a traditionally male activity were not welcome, and their militant stance infuriated the men of the Assembly. Even more upsetting was that no one seemed to be able to control them. Numerous drawings and cartoons of the time of lower-class women show them as decidedly unfeminine, with ugly, twisted features.[3]

## COUNTERREVOLUTIONARY WOMEN

Most women who disagreed with revolutionary politics and values were less strident. They boycotted Masses given by constitutional priests, and in the difficult times of 1793–1794 they organized clandestine Masses. They continued to put a cross on the forehead of the newborn, repeated the rosary, taught their children prayers, and named their children not after revolutionary heroes but after saints, to whom they still paid homage. All of these were counterrevolutionary offenses, and records were kept by the police. In addition, these women rejected the idea of the Supreme Being and resented the new calendar, which destroyed the traditional Christian day of the Sabbath. They did not send their children to state schools, and many buried their relatives at night with a Christian service.

Most of these women lived in small villages or towns, and, unlike their compatriots in the big cities who were the products of the early revolutionary days and who were committed to the overthrow of the old regime, they were traditional in outlook and opposed to change.

The many thousands of women who supported the church in the 1790s and who objected to the intrusion of the revolution in religious matters were forced to live with the scorn and opposition of officials of the government, as well as of their revolutionary neighbors. Such women were often involved in defending the Catholic Church and their priests. On May 10, 1790, in Montauban, about 5,000 women, some of whom were armed, massed to stop revolutionary officials from making an inventory of church property.[4]

In February 1795, in the small town of Montpigié, Haute-Loire, a government representative ordered (in his words) "a large assembly of stupid little women" to bear witness as the local *béates* (quasi-nuns, who lived under simple vows) took a revolutionary oath. The *béates*, however, showed willingness to face the guillotine for their faith. The other women supported them with loud cheers, and the official's attempt to exert his authority by arresting some of them led to a general free-for-all that grew into a full-scale uprising. The "stupid little women" then emptied the local prison and incarcerated the city officials, their collective defiance rendering the official authority powerless.[5]

At the height of the Terror, in June 1794, in the community of Saint-Vincent, also in the Haute-Loire, everyone gathered in the church to hear a talk on the Supreme Being. When the address began, the women stood up all together, turned around, and displayed their bare buttocks to the speaker. Word soon spread, and the performance was repeated in other villages.[6]

Staunchly religious women sheltered nonjuroring priests from arrest and persecution and heard secret Masses in houses, wine cellars, barns, and other safe places. They scrubbed churches that had been used for profane purposes until they were spotless and removed irreverent posters and notices from the premises.

They were not often prosecuted for participating in riots and religious activities, but they had to live with the scorn and arrogance of the men in power, who considered them to be irrational, unfocused, naive, and slow witted, hence best suited for tending babies, doing housework and cooking, performing menial tasks such as sewing and washing, or working as servants. They were considered by their government to have about as much intelligence as their farm animals.

## TWO CASUALTIES OF THE REVOLUTION

Among the upper-class women who were victims of the guillotine were Madame Roland and Charlotte Corday. Daughter of a well-to-do Parisian engraver, Manon Roland was well educated, widely read in classical literature, and greatly influenced by Rousseau. In 1780, she married the wealthy Jean-Marie Roland, 20 years her senior and a functionary of the city of Lyon. They moved to Paris, where he was associated with the Jacobin club and was twice minister of the interior, the last time under the revolutionary government, in March 1792. His tenure was short lived, for he was among those who denounced Robespierre for the September 1792 prison massacres, transferring his allegiance to the Girondins. His wife, meanwhile, opened a salon, which soon became a place where the Girondist leaders congregated. Here, twice a week, she held dinners for the members. She also published newspaper articles and supported her husband in all his political endeavors. When the Girondins came under attack, in December 1792, from the Jacobins, she, as well as her husband, was accused of subversive activity. She defended herself so well before the National Convention that the deputies voted her the honor of the day. Manon helped her husband escape from Paris and was arrested by the Paris commune in May 1793. Again she brilliantly defended herself and was set free—but not for long. Her courage in thwarting Robespierre and other Jacobins led to their deep hatred of her, and, on May 31, 1793, she was arrested again and thrown into prison. She was tried for treason, although her trial focused as much on her relations with the Girondins as anything else. Accused of influencing her husband when he was minister, she was insulted by the prosecutor when she tried to defend herself (she had refused to allow her lawyer, Chauvieu, to defend her, saying he would only endanger himself without being able to save her).

Madame Roland, often considered one of the most remarkable women of the revolution for her vitality and courage, was cruelly and callously condemned to death by the Jacobins. As she bravely walked past a statue of Liberty erected near the scaffold, she cried, "Oh Liberty! How many crimes are committed in thy name!" Her husband, having escaped to Normandy, committed suicide on hearing of his wife's execution.

Charlotte Corday, an entirely different type of woman, came from an ancient titled family and spent her early years in a convent. Her sympathies lay with the Girondins, some of whom had fled to her town of Caen in open opposition against the Jacobins, The 25-year-old woman made the decision that she would save France from misfortune by committing the heroic act of eliminating the bloodthirsty Marat, who every day demanded more and more heads in his paper *L'Ami du Peuple* to satisfy what he considered his patriotic duty.

On July 13, 1793, she left her home in Normandy and went to Paris, where she wrote Marat a letter saying she had some vital information about the Girondins in the town of Rouen to pass on to him if he would see her. The ruse worked. He was ill and at home, and, after talking with him for a few minutes while he was in his bath, she took out a knife and stabbed him. Arrested immediately, she was taken to prison. At her trial, she freely admitted the murder of Marat, saying that she did it so that peace would return to France. On July 17, 1793, she was guillotined.[7]

## POLITICAL CLUBS AND POPULAR SOCIETIES

Popular societies, mainly bourgeois clubs, gave Parisian women a limited chance to participate in contemporary politics, but there were various rules: the Luxembourg Society permitted daughters (age 14 and up) of members, and other women over the age of 22 to attend meetings, provided that their numbers did not exceed one-fifth of the total number of members present. The society of Sainte-Geneviève permitted women if there was room and if they sat apart. The Cordeliers Club allowed women from the beginning, but in July 1791 it restricted their share of the membership to 60 women, preferring that they be primarily symbolic. Earlier, in February 1790, it had even allowed a woman, Théroigne de Méricourt, to address the assembly and put forth a motion. Her request to take part

A sans-culotte woman, 1792, ready to play her part in the revolution. Bibliothèque Nationale de France.

in further sessions was turned down by the lawyer, Paré, who nevertheless conceded that the council of Mâcon recognized that women, like men, possessed a soul and reason.[8]

Some clubs, less stringent about membership, freely admitted women. These included the Indigens and the Minimes, among others. Women also attended the original meetings of the Société Fraternelle at the Jacobin club. The rules adopted June 2, 1792, allowed both sexes to seek admission and to take part in discussions and elections. An attempt was made to reserve a share of the club's offices for women and to ensure they were represented on delegations, but this was not successful. A fairly high percentage of members of these various societies were from the artisan and shopkeeper class. With the exception of the Indigens, very few of the desperately poor enrolled in them. Madame Moittre, of the *Académie de Peinture,* organized a deputation of women artists as well as wives of artists to visit the National Assembly in September 1789, where they presented their jewels to the nation as a contribution toward the national debt. Etta

Palm, in December 1790, became very busy lobbying the committees of the National Assembly for equal rights for women but failed to organize a network of women's clubs in Paris.

Pauline Léon, 21 years old at the outbreak of the revolution, in February 1791 led a group of female rioters to a house, looking for the Abbé Royou, editor of the paper *Ami du Roi,* who was staying there at the time. They demolished the house and threw a bust of Lafayette out of the window.[9] About this time, Léon began to appear at both the Cordeliers Club and the Société Fraternelle. On July 17, 1791, she narrowly escaped injury in the massacre of the Champ de Mars, where she, her mother, and a friend had gone to sign a republican petition sponsored by the two societies. She later associated with the Luxembourg Society and served as a committee member with responsibility for admissions.[10] In February 1792, with the support of the Minimes Popular Society, Léon, along with 300 other women, signed a petition to the National Assembly to organize a women's armed fighting force. The proposal seems to have been rejected on the basis that this kind of agitation was distracting women from their proper household duties. In May 1793, Léon made another attempt, announcing at the Jacobin club the beginnings of an organization to recruit women volunteers to fight in the Vendée against royalist insurgents. This was the beginning of the Revolutionary Republic Women's Society, a club whose membership was limited to women. In two years, she had moved from the Cordeliers (where women were patronized), to the Fraternelle and the Luxembourg (where they were given a measure of equality), to the Revolutionary Republic Women's Society, which excluded men.

While women attempted to start their own clubs, by 1793 the Convention had severely repressed them and excluded them from formal political activity, putting a ban on women's membership in political organizations of any kind. Most politicians were firmly against women's political rights, and there were often strong verbal attacks on women. A Jacobin had tried to justify the banning of the militant women's organizations at the Convention on October 30, 1773, by describing men as

strong, robust, born with great energy, audacity and courage … destined for agriculture, commerce, navigation, travel, war … he alone seems suited for serious, deep thought … and women as being, unsuited for advanced thinking and serious reflection … more exposed to error and an exultation which would be disastrous in public life.[11]

The idea of rights was universal, however, and the discrepancies between principle and practice were sharply pointed out by many courageous women.[12] On September 1791, a butcher's daughter and part-time actress, Olympe de Gouges, published *Déclaration des droits de la femme et de la citoyenne* (Declaration of the Rights of Women and Citizens). It was a bold move, but to no avail. Once women's clubs were banned altogether, women began to frequent the cafes and bars instead, where they made their views known.

## SALONS

Salons were historically aristocratic institutions where one could mix with privilege and rank. Here, opinions were shared by both men and women in private houses. These gatherings were hosted by women and date back to the seventeenth century; the first salon is attributed to Madame Rambouillet.[13] Many more soon followed, organized by influential women who set the agenda for discussion, selected the guests, and decided whether or not additional activities, such as poetry readings or the presentation of a dramatic piece from an up-and-coming playwright, would be included. There was no official or academic status involved, but to be invited enhanced a person's prestige and opened doors. Participants were generally philosophers, scientists, novelists, politicians, playwrights, and wealthy entrepreneurs. Some politically oriented women found their way into society through their salons, such as Louise Robert, a journalist whose salons were attended by Danton and Chabot. The discussions that took place often served as a source of material for the newspapers.

For many of these people, discussion was not only a diversion but an occupation. They might meet at two in the afternoon, talk until about seven, dine, and then meet again later in the evening to exchange views on subjects from Plato to Benjamin Franklin, from agriculture to politics, although literary topics and current events were high on the agenda. Ideas of the Enlightenment were freely discussed away from the eyes of censors or the royal court. Some salons engaged in special subjects; for example, the elite of the artistic world met at the house of Julie Talma, and paintings and sculpture exhibitions might also take place at a salon where the artist displayed his latest work.[14] Patriots attended sessions at the home of Madame Bailly, wife of the mayor of Paris, and at Madame Necker's on Thursdays, where such luminaries as Sieyès, Condorcet (whose wife held her own salon), Parmy, and Talleyrand gathered. After 1791, more radical salons began to appear, such as those of Madame Desmoulins and Madame Roland.

## MADAME GERMAINE DE STAËL

Germaine Necker was born into a wealthy Protestant bourgeois family on April 22, 1766. Her father, Jacques Necker, a Swiss banker, became the minister of finance under Louis XVI. Her mother gathered the finest minds in France and from abroad at her salon, and she permitted Germaine to attend, where she impressed many with her quick wit. Her mother became her primary tutor as she learned history, philosophy, and literature, especially studying the books of the exponents of the Enlightenment. At age 25, Germaine married the bankrupt Magnus Staël von Holstein, the Swedish ambassador to France, for the independence this would give her, and in 1786 she took up residence in the Swedish embassy in Paris, where she

Madame de Staël. Courtesy Library of Congress.

presided over her ailing mother's salon. Later, she established her own salon, where writers, artists, and critics spent much time in discourse on good manners, good taste, and literary trends.

Her father was dismissed from office and recalled several times, and Germaine fully supported him with tongue and pen as she became more deeply involved in politics. When he was ordered out of the country, he left, accompanied by his wife and angry daughter and with ambassador Magnus, who, it seems, preferred to stay closer to the money than to his job.

Germaine encouraged the Girondins and supported the government, but she pleaded for a bicameral legislature under a constitutional monarchy that would assure representative government, civil liberties, and protection of property.

She soon lost respect for her incompetent and insolvent husband and did not object to his taking as his mistress a 70-year-old actress on whom he spent his official income as ambassador—a position he neglected as he spent much time gambling and losing while the Neckers reluctantly paid his debts.

A free spirit, Germaine was known for her sparkling wit and strong will; although she was not pretty, any bed she chose was generally available to her. In one of her many influential books, *Delphine,* she wrote, "Between God and love I recognize no mediator but my conscience." The first of her many affairs was with Talleyrand.[15] Later, there were other lovers, including Louis de Narbonne-Lara, to whom she formed a deep attachment. As a member of the aristocracy, he was against the bourgeois regime, but the persuasive views of Germaine brought him around.

When she returned to Paris, her salon again became active, graced with the presence of Lafayette, Brissot, Barnave, Condorcet, and Narbonne-Lara. With the help of Lafayette and Barnave, she managed the appointment of Narbonne-Lara as minister of war. Marie-Antoinette reluctantly let this stand with a bitter comment on the good fortune of Madame de Staël, who now had the entire army at her disposal. Narbonne-Lara did not last long in his post, however. Advising the king to reject the aristocracy and support the propertied bourgeoisie to maintain law and order under a limited monarchy, he offended ministers of the crown, who orchestrated his dismissal.

On June 20, 1792, Germaine witnessed the storming of the Tuileries by a large, frighteningly violent crowd. The shouts, insults, and murderous weapons offered a horrifying spectacle. On August 20, she saw another such assault, and this time the palace was taken over by the mob, the royal family fleeing to the Legislative Assembly for protection. The frenzied rebels arrested every aristocrat they could find, and Germaine spent much money sheltering friends and helping them to escape. She hid Narbonne-Lara in the Swedish embassy and stood up to a patrol that wanted to search it. He was later secreted to England.

Worse was yet to come. On September 2, 1792, the rampant sans-culottes opened the jails and murdered the aristocrats and their supporters who they found there. Meanwhile, on the same day, Germaine set out in a fine six-horse coach accompanied by servants, the ambassador's insignia prominently on display. She headed for the gates of the city but had not gone far when the carriage was stopped by a menacing gaggle of women. Burly workmen appeared and ordered the carriage to drive to the section headquarters at the Hôtel de Ville. She was escorted through a hostile crowd brandishing pikes and lances and taken to an interrogation room. Her fate seemed sealed, but, as luck would have it, a friend who saw her in the headquarters of the Commune managed to secure her release, accompanied her to the embassy, and obtained a passport that allowed her to pass the city gate and turn the horses toward her family home in Switzerland. On September 7, she reached her parents' château and soon after gave birth to a son, Albert. She continued to give refuge to passing emigrants escaping France—noble or common.

Marie-Antoinette at the revolutionary tribunal where she was condemned to death. Bibliothèque Nationale de France.

Leaving Switzerland and making her way to England, she met Narbonne-Lara near London on January 21, 1793, to dissuade him from returning to France to testify in defense of Louis XVI. The day they met, the king went to the guillotine. Germaine returned to Switzerland in May and from there issued a plea to the revolutionaries to have mercy on Marie-Antoinette, a useless request that fell on deaf ears. The queen was executed on October 16, 1793.

After the death of her mother, in May 1794, Germaine moved to the château near Lausanne to form a new salon and enter the arms of Count Ribblin. Narbonne-Lara arrived later and, finding himself displaced, returned to a former mistress. In the autumn of 1794, Germaine moved on and again found a new love—Benjamin Constant, a 27-year-old Swiss writer.

She returned to Paris in May 1795, after the fall of Robespierre, made peace with her husband, and reestablished her salon at the Swedish embassy, which was attended once again by notable politicians and writers. Irritated by her political intervention, a deputy denounced her on the floor of the Convention and accused her of conducting a monarchist conspiracy as well as being unfaithful to her husband. She was ordered to leave France and by January 1, 1796, was back in Switzerland, where she continued her writing.

Germaine was notified by the Directory that she could return to France but could live no closer to the capital than 20 miles. Along with Constant, she moved into the abbey at Hérivaux and in the spring was given permission to visit her husband in Paris. On June 8, 1797, she gave birth to a daughter, Albertine, of undetermined paternity. Through Barras (a frequenter of her salon), she then secured the recall of Talleyrand from exile in England and his appointment, on July 18, 1797, as minister of foreign affairs. In 1798, her husband gave Germaine a friendly separation in return for a substantial allowance that permitted him to live comfortably in an apartment in what is today the Place de la Concorde until his death, in 1802.

Madame de Staël first met Napoleon at a reception given by Talleyrand on December 6, 1796, on the general's victorious return from Italy. She was enthralled by him, but, eventually, appalled by his policies, she left Paris again. She returned in 1802, and her salon became a center for anti-Napoleonic agitation. The emperor exiled her from the city in 1803, and she was not able to return until after his defeat, in 1815. She died on July 14, 1817.

## UNMARRIED MOTHERS

Unmarried women who became pregnant were supposed under the law to report the matter to the authorities and to present details of the circumstances to the courts. Failure to do so could lead to a charge of infanticide if the child was found dead for any reason.[16] The *Comité de Mendicité* believed this humiliating process made women reluctant to register their pregnancies to protect themselves and their lovers.

The committee also felt that to abolish the legislation and remove the stigma attached to out-of-wedlock births would encourage women to keep their babies. Those who required monetary assistance would receive it from the state. Children who were abandoned would also receive a state subsidy and be regarded as *enfants de la patrie* (children of the nation—precious human resources as potential soldiers or mothers).[17]

Most women who pressed paternity suits were of humble background. They sought monetary support for the child's upbringing and education. Sometimes this was awarded when witnesses (such as neighbors) saw the man in question courting the girl. Sometimes a woman had been promised marriage if she gave in to a suitor who then left her pregnant, or she might have been compromised by a married man. In the first instance, the young man might have gone off to the army, never to be heard of again. In the second, if she could prove her case, she had a good chance of winning some support. A law passed on November 2, 1793, outlawed the usual rights of unwed mothers and their children to pursue paternity suits for their support.[18]

## PROSTITUTION

The male nobility had their courtesans and set them up in luxurious apartments, lavishing costly gifts on women who had little to do except

LE SULTAN PARISIEN,
ou l'Embarras du Choix.

The Parisian Sultan. Prostitution under the Directory. Bibliothèque Nationale de France.

prepare themselves for their lover's visits. Many had started out as common prostitutes whose exceptional qualities had caused one or another aristocrat to single them out.

Despite being condemned as immoral, prostitution flourished and catered to all classes. Singers, dancers, actresses, and barmaids were all considered fair game, available to anyone who had the requisite money to treat them well. Such women were prohibited by law from seeking redress if they became pregnant. Those who worked in seedy brothels to make a little money or to help their families financially were the worst off. If they were lucky, the owner might offer them some protection from violence.

Young, pretty girls were often lured into brothels by offers of jobs as servants or by other false pretenses. Coaches arriving in Paris from the provinces were sometimes met by procurers looking for naive country girls in search of employment. The girls were soon to discover that the occupation into which they had been coerced was rather different from what they had expected.

Although they were considered outside the law, prostitutes plied their trade in public places and were manipulated by police, who used them as informants as well as sexual partners. Many also did other jobs, such as laboring in the linen industry or working as seamstresses, hatmakers, or laundry workers; prostitution was sometimes a part-time occupation that helped them to make ends meet. Some parents sacrificed one or more of their daughters to the trade in order to help feed the rest of the family.

Public morality was not seriously taken into account until the time of the Terror. The Constituent Assembly addressed the subject only once, when it decided, on July 22, 1791, that girls could not be arrested unless they committed offenses that outraged public decency or caused public disorder, thereby giving prostitution some legal standing. The problem grew, however, and when the Paris Commune and members from the various sections began making complaints, the Jacobins acted by passing laws that resulted in prostitutes being brought in for questioning about whether they were sympathetic to the republic. Libertinism was now declared suspect—ladies of the street might be in touch with antirepublicans and therefore might be enemies of the regime. They could be sheltering people wanted by the police such as priests, nobles, or other fugitives.

When no such enemies of the state were found, the situation settled down for a while. Then, suddenly, the attack against the street women began again. This time, the attorney-general for the Commune, Chaumette, decided that immorality was the last vestige of the corruption of society by royalty. He wished to reestablish morality, the fundamental basis of republicanism, asserting that by cleansing the moral environment, the government would save the country. A clean sweep of Paris was ordered, and all women considered to lead a loose life were subject to arrest. Police patrols circulated day and night to prevent soliciting (or even smiling at) the opposite sex. Virtuous citizens were recruited to aid the police, and old men were invited to become ministers of morals. All they had to do was give a sign and an arrest would be made. For a few months, the streets seemed clear of streetwalkers, and books and pictures considered obscene disappeared from shop windows. This crusade was as short-lived as the men responsible for it.

No sooner had Robespierre lost his head, than everything went back to normal.

## WOMEN OF THE PALAIS ROYAL

A man who knew his way around the city of Paris had no difficulty in finding the right girl, at the right price, for his amorous desires. Someone from the country, new in the city, on the other hand, would find a confusing collection of women, all with one aim—to get his money. At the time when the regions of France were preparing to send their delegates to the Estates-General, an enterprising Parisian publisher anticipated the problems that might arise and designed a newspaper, destined to go through several editions, in which he listed the names, average prices, physical characteristics, and addresses of the ladies of the Palais Royal, as well as those in other districts of the city.

He informed his readers that for anyone happening to have 25 livres, Madame Dupéron and her four lady friends would see to all their needs at

33 Palais Royal. However, if the client preferred the medium price bracket, he could not do better than Victorine, whose considerable favors could be won for six livres and a bowl of punch. The same price was in force at 132 Palais Royal for the charms of La Paysanne, who was not such a peasant as her name implied. The author advised the client to beware, however, as this young, healthy girl liked a good night's sleep. Georgette, it seems, was good but disgraced herself after drinking. La Bacchante, her rival, was superb and well known among connoisseurs for her daring eyes, electric body, and opulent locks. A fault was that she was scandalously lacking in notions of equality; her prices went up to six livres for young men and 12 for the more mature. She, too, had a rival, who styled herself Venus; she lived in the most elegant apartment and was not unworthy of the appellation.

Referred to as *les femmes du monde* (ladies of the world), these women formed a group of their own among the courtesans and lived in luxury, often on the second floor of the galleries in apartments that had views of or led into a garden. They gave excellent dinners and charmed their guests with graciousness and their variety of talents.

They took in strangers to introduce them to the pleasures of gambling. Many naive young men soon became addicted and often lost all their money. Madame de Saint-Romains, who, with her two attractive nieces, lodged above the Cafe Caveau, helped country boys empty their purses in card games. Two wild people from Canada known as the Algonquin and the Algonquiness exhibited themselves in the "costumes" of Adam and Eve in the garden of Eden.

Some establishments were open 24 hours a day. At a shop in the rue St. Honoré, for the gaping provincials, the women pretended to be nuns who had escaped from a convent without having time to put on any clothes as they recounted bizarre tales of how they were forced to take vows.

Various schemes were put forward, not to totally suppress prostitution but to control it. The popular writer Restif de Bretonne suggested that the girls, protected by the state, be accommodated in convenient houses where a council of 12 citizens of proven morality, such as the notary and the commander of the National Guard of the town, might watch over them. The council would select a matron-in-charge and a governess. Various entries between courtyards and gardens would permit clients to slip into the houses unseen, and ticket offices would be installed, similar to those at a theater. Presumably, the client would purchase his ticket and entered the house of his choice.[19]

## NOTES

1. Emmanuel Joseph Sieyès (1748–1836), a French statesman, attracted attention in the early days of the revolution with a pamphlet, *"Qu'est-ce que le tiers état?"* (What Is the Third Estate?). Cautious and moderate, he was a member of the Estates-General, the National Convention, the Council of Five Hundred, and the Directory. He helped launch the political career of Napoleon.

2. Germani/Swales, 128–29.

3. Schama, 324.

4. Andress (2004), 126.

5. Ibid., 253.

6. Ibid., 126.

7. See Pernoud/ Flaissier 22ff for more detail.

8. Rose, 110.

9. Ibid., 112–13.

10. Ibid., 114.

11. McPhee, 185.

12. Rapport, 15.

13. Wiesner, 139.

14. Robiquet, 33.

15. A noted liberal, Talleyrand became bishop of Autun in 1788. He served as president of the Constituent Assembly in 1790. Later, he gave up the clergy to serve in diplomatic posts under Napoleon, with whom he had a falling out. He died on May 17, 1838.

16. Hufton, 63.

17. Ibid., 64.

18. See Desan, 179, for details. This was a severe blow to many young women.

19. For other proposals, see Robiquet, 65–76.

# 11

# URBAN LIFE

## A ROYAL VISIT TO PARIS

On the morning of June 8, 1773, as Louis XV lay dying, the dauphin and dauphine, the future king and queen of France, prepared for their first visit together to Paris in what was termed the Joyous Entry.

In anticipation of the royal visit, all activities in the city were suspended, shops closed, livestock banned from the streets, and peddlers prohibited along the royal route. Babies left at the gate of the foundling hospital the night before were snatched up by nuns and taken out of sight. Thousands of beggars were cleared from the route or locked up for the day so that the royal sensitivities would not be offended by the sight of tremulous limbs, ragged clothes, and unwashed bodies. The multitude of prostitutes who plied their trade among the crowds of the Palais Royal were compelled to seek their livelihood elsewhere, although many could be seen among the spectators waiting for a glimpse of the royal entourage.

Among the cheering throngs, all the complexities of the Parisian population were evident: prosperous bourgeois—many of them doctors, bankers, lawyers, and businessmen—mixed with tradesmen and artisans. Now and again a colorfully dressed aristocrat appeared, his trailing sword and scabbard the mark of noble distinction.

Elbowing for room in the front rows were also lower bourgeois—craftsmen, grocers, vintners, tanners, and a legion of casual laborers and apprentices—given the day off from their workshops. Water carriers, street porters, bargemen from the river docks, and chimneysweeps all were present, the color of their work embedded in their skin. Prettily dressed embroiderers vied for front places, and fishermen abandoned their nets in the Seine to catch a view of the royal couple. Nuns and monks strove like the rest to push through the crowds to a desirable place. There were also pickpockets and cutpurses, anonymous in the crowd but greedily eyeing the more affluent. From villages near Paris, peasants had walked throughout the night for a glimpse of the future rulers.

When the first of the four royal coaches came into view, the cannon of the Invalides, as well as those of the Bastille and the Hôtel de Ville, announced their arrival, their discharges echoing across the city as black smoke rose into the clear, warm sky. The coaches rattled through the gate of the Porte de la Conférence, where the orchestra added its milder refrains to the general cacophony. Carriages filled with city officials and soldiers waiting at the gate fell into line behind the procession. The crowds, cheering and singing the songs printed on sheets especially for the occasion, drowned out the orchestra. Police and soldiers forced the people back with whips and the flat of their swords to keep them from overwhelming the royal coach as it headed for Mass at Nôtre Dame along the flower-strewn streets. Later, the royal couple was again mobbed when they went to dine at the Tuileries. Antoinette was only 17 years of age, and it was the first time she had seen Paris. She was excited. Little did she or anyone else anticipate the impending events that soon would overtake them all.

## CITY LIFE

A hub of activity, Paris was busy most of the time. At one or two in the morning, the day began for many farmers living in the outskirts. Along the main thoroughfares into the city, residents had to contend, long before daybreak, six days a week, with the plodding hooves of the farmers' horses and mules, echoing in the cobblestone streets as they pulled produce-laden carts toward the central market.

An earlier riser, strolling through the avenues in 1789 a little before the 5:00 a.m. Mass, would encounter lines of people already in front of the bakers' shops waiting for them to open. Those in line were mostly servants of the wealthy, poor working women, and the wives of laborers. Mingled with the pleasant aroma of fresh bread from the bakers' ovens—loaves of four, six, or eight pounds—was the scent of hot coffee from the carts of the streetside vendors.

Suddenly, one's attention would be captured by the tolling of bells of the numerous churches and monasteries in the city, each claiming a voice in the early dawn. The crow of roosters and barking dogs joined in. At this early hour, agreeable smells emanated onto the streets from the monasteries in which the monks were already cooking, and from the homes of the well-to-do, where servants were beginning to prepare the afternoon meal—the primary one of the day. Between six and seven, the streets were filled with laborers on their way to the workshops. About nine or ten, the wine shops opened for business, and workers emerged from their ateliers and shops to have a little bread and wine after putting in several hours on the job.

The fragrance of fresh apples, pears, peaches, and apricots filled the street, if the season was right, from a grocer's store or a corner market in the heart of the city, but then further on the powerful smell of fish already too long in the open air would take over, followed by the satisfying aroma of Brie or goat cheese from a *fromagerie* and, still later, that of roasting meat and stale beer. From a dark alleyway, the foul odor of urine and feces, human and animal, assailed the senses. Reaching Les Halles, the central market, everything combined into one homogenized essence of vegetables, grain, fruit, herbs, cheese, and fish, along with the odor from the sweat of hundreds of horses, donkeys, and mules, excrement, and decayed food. The pink carcasses of skinned hogs, speckled with black flies, hung from hooks above some stalls. Nearby, the overwhelming stench of rotting bodies from the *Cimetière des Innocents,* where a little lime covered the corpses decomposing in large pits, permeated the area. From the slaughterhouses in the city, the blood ran down the streets into the sewers, some drying on the pavements and giving off an appalling smell. The air was pungent along the Seine from the great sewers that flowed into the river, and, even in the lovely gardens of the Tuileries, by the river, multitudes of people defecated regularly.[1]

The flower market on the bank of the river presented an enjoyable interruption, radiating perfume and color. Markets specializing in specific products could be found throughout the city; for instance, on the left bank of the Seine stood the market of la Vallée, crowded with shoppers buying cooked or fresh poultry.

When the wind blew from the southeast, it filled the streets with smells from the distant Montagne Ste. Geneviève and the tiny river Biève, where breweries processed hops for beer and starch factories emitted their strong odor along with the rank of drying hides from the tanneries. On the slope of Ste. Geneviève was the University of Paris, with its faculty of theology, called the Sorbonne. Around the university were numerous bookshops, monasteries, and convents. The tomb of the patron saint of Paris, who inspired the city's defense against the Huns in 451 A.D., lay in the mausoleum on the summit. The site was important to Parisians as a place of pilgrimage.

Those people with money frequented the affluent areas of the western part of the city or the aristocratic faubourg St. Germain or the faubourg St. Honoré, close to the Tuileries palace. Here, they were ideally situated to attend the opera and the best theaters. They were also near the rue St. Honoré, with its shops selling luxury furniture and clothes, and a short carriage ride from the rue St. Denis and its displays of exquisite lacework and beautiful cloth.

Visitors and residents alike enjoyed the gothic cathedral of Nôtre Dame on the Ile de la Cité, an island in the river Seine reached by bridges. Nearby was the enormous central hospital, *l'Hôtel-Dieu,* and also on the island stood the ensemble of law courts, the Palais de Justice, home of the parlement of Paris.

Within working sections of the city, the residents were familiar with the sounds of cobblers hammering at their benches, lathes humming in the workshops of the woodworkers, and the raucous cries of the street vendors offering for sale tobacco, brandy, ribbons, religious objects, bracelets, earrings, necklaces, and sundry bits of food. Tables were set up for this purpose on busy corners. Even a deaf resident who lived close to the river would feel the vibrations of the blows of the 2,000 or so washerwomen hammering the linen with wooden batons. On the bridges over the Seine, musicians and ballad singers congregated, and makeshift outside theaters often drew a crowd. Sometimes citizens might amuse themselves tormenting the prisoners in the market pillories, where convicted criminals were forced to spend two hours a day in the stocks for all to mock.[2]

Shops that lined the poorer streets accommodated various tooth pullers, sellers of poultices and ointments, shoe menders, bakeries, and second-hand dealers of everything, including clothes, paintings, and books. The urban lower classes comprised laborers in building construction, carpenters, street cleaners and vendors, shop assistants, servants, water or wood carriers, street performers, men and women of the market stalls, factory workers, stagehands, laundry women, and a host of other poorly paid people with no skills and little or no education. They lived in the impoverished sections of the cities and were the first to suffer when food shortages led to higher prices, rents went up, or a cold spell increased the price of firewood.

To the east, beyond the huge fortress of the Bastille, lay the faubourg St. Antoine, where many thousands of artisans worked and lived. There, dingy workshops crowded into narrow streets; much of the city's manufacturing took place in neighborhoods seldom visited by most people, native or tourist. To leave the main thoroughfares and venture into the labyrinth of back streets was always a challenge for the uninitiated. Only those people who had lived in the area for many years could find their way around.

People in the city who were not employed in some kind of paid work often spent time on the streets of their neighborhoods. Women gossiped while waiting in line to collect water at fountains (about one-third of houses had wells, and the affluent had water delivered) or sat on chairs outside their doors, embroidering or sewing. Some kept an eye on their small children as they played in the street. The women of the quarter saw one another again and again at the fruit market, the baker's, the grocer's, or the pastry shop, where, for a couple of sous, they could indulge in a small cake.

The chatter would certainly have been about such things as the price of bread, who was pregnant, who had lost a baby, the plight of the woman whose husband had suffered an injury at work, who was unemployed, and who had found a job. The young lady down the street was seen with a soldier; she must be a whore, or she could have the pox. Women seldom ventured beyond the limits of their districts alone, and often it was with neighbors that they went to the big markets or down to the laundry boats on the river to wash clothes.

The neighborhoods were not unlike villages. Everyone knew everyone else's business, habits, daily activities, movements, and moods. Residents knew who was profiting, who was not, who was courting whom, and what progress was being made. Thin walls and narrow streets allowed for little privacy. Who drank too much, which couples fought all the time, when people went to bed, what time they got up—all was common knowledge in the quarter.

Quarrels and complaints between neighbors were often aired in the street, drawing a crowd that listened to the curses and insults and passed judgment. A neighbor had borrowed some firewood and never returned the equivalent. A young girl had snatched the doll of another and tried to keep it. The couple in the apartment above was always falling about drunk, causing great thumps in the night. The washing hanging from a window obstructed someone else's view of the street. Sometimes the arguments went on for years. The onlookers were often amused by the wrangling, but they were also ready to prevent physical encounters that might lead to injury.

In their leisure time, men could generally be found playing a card or board game at the local wine shop or spending time with the family sitting by the fire, but, with the price of wood, this could be more expensive than drinking with the boys. Some days, time might be spent visiting friends and relatives to dine and play cards, dominos, or backgammon or just to talk and catch up with the latest news. On holy days, they strolled along the avenues or beside the river with their wives or girlfriends. On Sundays, residents, especially courting couples, liked to leave the city for the villages a little beyond the customs houses, where prices in taverns were cheaper and the air and surroundings more pleasant. Neighborhood groups often went out together to the vineyards and open fields and enjoyed the quiet and serene environment.

An execution in the Place de la Grève was an occasion for fellow workers, as well as the women, to go in their groups to watch the gruesome public act. Even the back streets served as places of outdoor entertainment; men played skittles while the women watched. Children ran wild in the streets chasing each other or engaged in mock fights using sticks as muskets or swords or amused themselves with spinning tops or playing quoits, skittles, or ball games.

On feast days and Sundays, everyone disgorged from their dingy, crowded apartments and took to the streets, hailing friends and acquaintances as they passed. Most of the people in rundown quarters of the city were laborers—just above the beggars on the social ladder.

The people might be ground down by poverty and have their petty quarrels and lives exposed to the intrusive scrutiny of neighbors, but such closeness could be beneficial. A master craftsman and his wife who lived on the ground floor in comparative luxury, a journeyman on the next floor with his small family, a laborer on the third level with his working wife, and a penniless widow in the attic who made a few sous mending shirts— all were polite to one another and exchanged greetings. If the widow had not been seen on her daily walk to the grocer's, someone would check to make sure she was all right. If a violent quarrel seemed to put a woman in danger from a brutal husband, it would not be uncommon for the neighbors to knock on the door to inquire about her and even break it down if the situation seemed desperate for the woman. Bailiffs coming to seize goods or apprehend someone who could not pay his debts often encountered resistance from the neighbors who drove them off, forcing them to try another day. What appeared to be an unjust arrest in some quarters might well degenerate into a local riot in support of the victim. People also kept an eye on one another's property: a stranger in the building was cause for alarm and was watched closely.

The inhabitants of a poor quarter worked 14 or 15 hour days; a single shop girl might rise at four in the morning, spend all day in the shop, and come home about seven to prepare a little food and eat alone; but everyone put a high value on integrity and self-respect and generally addressed others using the esteemed terms *Monsieur* and *Madame*.[3]

## WORK AND LEISURE

To create a trade corporation, the king had to ratify the corporation's statutes by *lettres patentes*. With the king's sanction, it became a *métier juré*, or sworn trade, and anyone who became a master of the trade was required to sign an oath of loyalty to the corporation. To learn the trade, a young man or woman began as an apprentice; the ambition of most apprentices was to become a master of the craft. The apprenticeship usually began when the boys or girls were teenagers and lasted from three to six years. Apprentices were required to undertake a test of their skills by producing an original work judged acceptable by a jury of masters. For example, an apprentice seamstress had to create a pleasing dress or gown to fulfill the requirement.

In addition, candidates also needed sufficient money to buy the mastership from the corporate community. During the apprenticeship, filial subordination to the master was part of the process sanctioned by a legal contract.[4]

Journeymen, skilled workmen who had already served an apprenticeship, were hired for wages without long-term contracts to bind them to the master. Many were married and had families, and they retained their position in society as journeymen, usually for life, for, while they were hired to help the master, they seldom reached mastership themselves. Excluded from the confraternities of the masters, they formed parallel associations that had no standing in law but had elaborate rituals that were often kept secret. For itinerant young journeymen, the organization kept rooming houses in various cities and offered aid in times of sickness and when a member died.

It was expensive to set up in business. In Paris, a little before the revolution, the cost of a mastership ranged from 175 livres for a seamstress to as much as 3,240 livres for a draper. Most corporations charged between 500 and 1,500 livres, but often this was more than a journeyman could earn in a year.[5] Becoming a master offered many advantages, however. The master was assured of a place in the market and protection for his goods, which no one else was allowed to produce. His living standard was comparatively good, and in hard times he could draw on the charity of his trade's confraternity. Overall, a mastership meant prestige and security for one's family, and one's children had access to mastership at half the usual price. The master's position and privileges could be inherited by his widow until such time as she remarried or turned them over to a son. Because of his status, the master was able to get credit, and enhanced income often allowed him to buy property, which raised him even higher in his social milieu.

Then, on March 2, 1791, the revolutionary government dissolved the guild corporations. The corporate body and its regulations were no longer relevant. Former masters, who were now called entrepreneurs, could arrange contracts individually without corporate authority. There were also now no legal barriers preventing a journeyman from becoming a master and establishing a business for himself. If the business did badly, he faced the prospect of falling into the ranks of the wage earner, since there was no longer a corporate body to ensure him a place in the market or to lend financial assistance. Masters had to take their chances as employers in an unregulated open market.

For the working man or woman, the monotony of life on the job was regularly alleviated by local events. Besides religious holidays, secular festivities and celebrations took place in the quarters throughout the year, and one of the most elaborate and colorful was Carnival, when streets were replete with people wearing costumes and masks. Bonfires were not unusual, although the police discouraged them as a fire risk. Children marched around beating drums, and there was dancing, drinking, and socializing, with few settling into bed before the early hours of the morning. Itinerant actors presented bawdy plays and burlesque on makeshift stages, while magicians, acrobats, ballad singers, and puppet shows vied for the crowd's attention and its money.

Young country girls often found life on the family farm tedious and longed to go to the city to find jobs as clerks or apprentice seamstresses. This could, in fact, relieve the large family of the extra mouth to feed, and the girl also might be able to send a little money home once in a while. Paris was generally the preferred destination for such young people.[6] The working life of a single girl in the city was not an easy one. Girls who became apprentices worked hard for meager pay, slept in dormitories, and had little to eat. On Sundays, about half a dozen pounds of meat were stewed in a large pot; this had to feed everybody in the workshop for a week. The woman in charge sent the girls out on occasion to the local markets to purchase bread at a price much cheaper than in the bakeries, and it, too, had to last the week.

Walking through the streets of Paris during the time of the Terror could be a traumatic experience, especially for young girls or boys straight from the country. Cattle carts passing by on their way to the river were sometimes piled high with the bodies of men and women recently butchered. As the wagons bounced over the cobblestones, arms and legs dangled from the sides like puppets on a string, trickles of fresh blood falling on the roadway. At the river, the bodies and their separated heads were thrown into the water to drift downstream toward the ocean. Only a short time before, the victims had made the journey in the same tumbrels down the rue St. Honoré to the guillotine. Working in their shops as the carts passed, Parisians often didn't even look up, according to eyewitness reports, or turned their backs on the gruesome spectacle.

When people went into the streets of Paris, they made sure they were wearing the tricolor cockade on their hats, which identified them as patriots, whether they were or not. It was not wise to reveal any subversive characteristics or thoughts to anyone at anytime. To be denounced as a traitor could mean a place in the tumbrels.

## THE PARIS QUARTERS

Not unlike many other large European cities, Paris was composed of many districts or quarters, each with its distinct people and atmosphere. The wealthy middle class and the nobility occupied the faubourg St. Germain, as well as the Marais, the Temple, and the Arsenal districts.[7]

The working-class areas had their special occupations: the masons lived in St. Paul; the furniture and construction industries were situated in Croix-Rouge; and milliners, haberdashers, and producers of other fashionable goods inhabited the rue St. Denis and the rue St. Martin.

To the north of the city, the residents of the suburbs of Montmartre, St. Lazare, and St. Laurent were engaged mainly in the sale of cloth. In Chaillot, to the west, were ironworks and cotton mills, while the suburb of Roule, known as Pologne (Poland, as it was the home of many Polish immigrants) was one of the poorest neighborhoods in Paris. East of the city on both banks of the Seine lay the suburbs of St. Antoine and St. Marcel, where furniture workshops were situated, along with the Gobelins tapestry works, dye works, and Réveillon's wallpaper factory.

Doing the same jobs, frequenting the same taverns, and marrying local girls, the workers seldom ventured beyond their districts. Events happening in one section of the city were not even known about in others, as people were generally indifferent to what was going on elsewhere. Difficulties of transportation and traffic compartmentalized the city, and reactions to political events were different in the various sections.

Housewives shopping at the local market might be totally unaware that people were being massacred nearby. News, spread by word of mouth, could take several days to reach all parts of the city, and everything was extremely susceptible to exaggeration and rumor.

For those curious people willing to travel further afield to hear the most recent news, there were meeting places where discussions took place. The Jardin des Tuileries, earlier a fashionable parade ground, became the open-air anteroom of the Assembly, and the Place de la Grève was used for executions, mass gatherings, and parades of the National Guard. The most popular meeting place was the gardens of the Palais Royal. Here was the center of cafe life, restaurants, entertainment, and the favorite haunt of agitators, soapbox orators, rabble-rousers, scandalmongers, prostitutes, and demagogues. The galleries along the arcaded sidewalks had been rented out to tradesmen by the duke of Orléans some years before and had become the noisiest and, for the future of the royal crown, the most dangerous place in the city.

The marquis de Ferrières, a provincial nobleman, having visited the Palais Royal, stated:

You simply cannot imagine all the different kinds of people who gather there. It is a truly astonishing spectacle. I saw the circus; I visited five or six cafés, and no Molière comedy could have done justice to the variety of scenes I witnessed. Here a man is drafting a reform of the Constitution; another is reading his pamphlet aloud; at another table, someone is taking the ministers to task; everybody is talking; each person has his own little audience that listens very attentively to him. I spent almost ten hours there. The paths are swarming with girls and young men. The book shops are packed with people browsing through books and pamphlets and not buying anything. In the cafés, one is half-suffocated by the press of people.[8]

Most visitors never ventured into the old quarters but stayed in the hotels in the more affluent areas. However, that the capital was lively, noisy, and vivacious is evident from reports of foreigners who visited the city. A German bookseller and writer named Campe, who visited Paris in 1789, noted that not only were the people polite and animated in conversation but also that everybody was

talking, singing, shouting or whistling, instead of proceeding in silence, as is the custom in our parts. And the multitude of street vendors and small merchants trying to make their voices heard above the tumult of the streets only serves to make the general uproar all the greater and more deafening.[9]

Campe, a refined gentleman from a sedate and somewhat dull country compared to France, went one evening to watch the sunset from the Place Louis XV and suddenly found himself assailed by three old harpies who tried to kiss him and at the same time snatch his purse. Fortunately, he got away unscathed. Some witnesses found life in Paris harrowing, with the crowds, noise, smells, dirt, and abundance of people from the provinces looking for work, some of whom were desperate for a handout of a few sous. A lot of these wound up working in the quarries of the Butte Montmartre.

Some 4,000 of the nobility lived in Paris. The revolution brought about the first exodus of aristocrats from the city on July 15, 1789; the second and larger one took place after October. Those who remained found life rather boring, since there were no more grand balls and even concerts had been eliminated. Night patrols kept the streets peaceful and aristocrats indoors. As people left the richer districts for exile, trade slowed down and money became scarcer.

## A NOBLEMAN IN THE ESTATES-GENERAL

The marquis de Ferrières, a public figure in Poitou, divided his time between his chateau in Marsay and his grand house in Poitiers.[10] A student of the philosophers of the Enlightenment, he published three essays on the subject. His satire on monastic vows earned him a reputation as an intellectual and led the nobility of Poitiers to elect him as their representative to the Estates-General. He kept up regular correspondence with his wife after his arrival at Versailles. Like the majority of deputies, he deplored the move to Paris and complained that the streets of the city were rivers of mud in the constant rain and that he did not go out at night for fear of being run over by carriages. Instead, he spent the time alone and sad, seated by the fire. He invited his wife to join him in Paris, but they needed servants, so he asked if the cook at Poitiers would be able to dress her mistress? Would she sweep the floors and make the beds? If she was not agreeable, he would rather have the little chambermaid, who could help with the washing and manage some cooking. Madame de Ferrières arrived in Paris and passed two winters there, but in the summers of 1790 and 1791 she returned home and her husband continued to write to her about domestic affairs. In August 1790, the marquis stated that he was highly satisfied with Toinon, his servant, who gave him every attention, and wrote about his diet, which consisted of beans, haricots, cucumbers, and very little meat. He dined with another noble deputy from Béziers, who shared expenses with him helping to keep costs down. He declared that in the preceding month, the cost of provisions (butter, coal, vegetables, fish, and desserts) had amounted to 118 livres, and bread had cost another 30 livres. This sum did not include meat and wood, or lodging at three livres a day. Toinon was later replaced by a girl, Marguérite, who was excellent at making vegetable soup. The staff also included a man-servant called Baptiste, a short, jolly man who liked coffee and sneaked a cup whenever he could, ate too much meat, and spent his free time entertained by the marionettes in the Place Louis XV. The marquis said he had only one serious shortcoming: when he went down to the wine cellar, he always came back reeking.

## CAFE SOCIETY

In the summer of 1789, cafe society was in full swing, and there was more to discuss and argue about than ever before. The tables on the sidewalks were packed with people sipping everything from English and German beer to liqueurs from the French West Indies, fruit drinks, wine, Seidlitz water, and a host of other cathartic and herbal tonics, as well as coffee and chocolate-flavored drinks. Signboards advertising the cafes were on every corner, gallery, and arcade. In front of the famous cafe Caveau, great throngs gathered until two in the morning. Each establishment was well known for some specialty: the Grottes Flamande for its excellent beer, the Italien for its beautiful porcelain round stove, and the Café Mécanique for the mocha pumped up into patrons' cups through a hollow leg in each table. Of the many and varied places, the Café de Foy was the most popular of all, with its gilded salons and a pavilion in the garden. A fine brandy from the provinces was its trademark.

In the rue des Bons-Enfants stood the Café de Valois, frequented by many of the Feuillants reading the *Journal de Paris*, while the Jacobins were regular patrons of the Café Corazza, where François Chabot and Collot d'Herbois often held the floor. In the rue de Tournon was the Café des Arts, the focal point of the extremists from the Odéon district, while more moderate types congregated at the Cafe de la Victoire, in the rue de Sèvres. The differences in clientele could be striking. At the Régence, on the right bank of the Seine, Lafayette was greatly loved, but at the Cafe de la Monnaie, on the rue de Roule, the sans-culottes burned him in effigy. The Café de la Porte St. Martin attracted quiet, respectable people out for an evening stroll. As varieties of opinion were expressed, a man was judged by the cafe of his choice. Rarely seen in cafes before, women began to follow the example of the men and appeared in the evenings at the popular gathering places. They were welcomed, as it was good for trade—the cafe trade, which was to endure all upheavals and which persists until the present day.

Paris was not alone in the development of cafe society. All the major cities and towns of the country began to enjoy the companionship and the stimulation of discussion in their favorite bistros. Owners were exposed to certain occupational risks, as, on occasion, heated discussions led to dishes and cutlery being hurled across the tables. Major topics under discussion in the news sheets and by sidewalk orators were the revolution,

Reception of a Master Mason at a lodge meeting. Bibliothèque Nationale de France.

politics, members of the government, trade, colonies, finances, taxation, and the huge deficit.

## FREEMASONRY

Imported from England in the early 1700s, Freemasonry had by the end of the century reached 700 lodges, with 30,000 members, distributed throughout all the major cities. Many of the revolutionaries were prominent Freemasons. Louis-Philippe Orléans, cousin of the king, was Grand Master, and others included Georges-Jacques Danton, Marie-Jean Condorcet, and Jacques-Louis David. Individual Masons were very active within the new society, some working through the press and literary societies to make people aware of imminent political change. They were generally well educated, often drawn from the wealthier families and an important element, not unlike the salons, in spreading enlightenment ideas. Men of all shades of opinion were recruited by the lodges. The "Committee of Thirty," which contained many prominent men, met mainly at the house of Adrien du Port and put out pamphlets and models for petitions or grievances and gave its support to political candidates. How much Freemasonry influenced the course of the revolution remains to be clarified, however. The majority of members were bourgeois who approved of the Masonic abstract symbol of equality; yet the organization's hierarchical structure conflicted with the egalitarian principles of the revolution.

In the army, too, Masons were to be found, especially among the officers. Some claim that the election committees of the Estates-General consisted mainly of Masons. Freemasons were in general considered suspect by the Catholic Church, but although they preached a "natural" religion, they did not necessarily look for the separation of the church from the state. In general, Freemasonry attracted men who were interested in philanthropy, fraternity, and friendship (being open to greater social mixing than other old-regime groups), and in new political ideas.

The number of lodges reflected the strength of the bourgeoisie and other nonnoble groups of the Third Estate. Not all Masons became revolutionaries, but the lodges were present in many revolutionary municipalities, and their influence was palpable. Men who aspired to be politicians thus might have found it advantageous to join and benefit from the close personal ties available among the "brothers."[11]

## THE SANS-CULOTTES

The term "sans-culotte" referred to the men who did not wear the short knee trousers (breeches) and silk stockings of the nobility and the upper bourgeoisie but wore instead the long trousers of workers and shopkeepers.[12] They were generally from the lower and often impoverished classes, and "sans-culotte" was originally a derisive appellation. During the revolution, the sans-culottes became a volatile collection of laborers in Paris and other cities whose ranks soon included clerks, artisans, shopkeepers, goldsmiths, bakers, and merchants. They were easily manipulated by popular leaders such as Marat, Hébert, and Robespierre. The Jacobins used the sans-culottes to control the streets of Paris and other cities and to intimidate moderate members of the Assembly. The Committee of Public Safety under Robespierre was adroit at using the discontented masses, and in September 1793 a decree established a revolutionary sans-culotte army. In October of that year, this army participated in severe violence and brutality in Lyon against those it considered enemies of the state. The sans-culottes were associated with popular politics, especially in the Paris region, and were instrumental in the September massacres and in the attacks on the Tuileries palace. In January 1794, the sans-culotte army, having served its purpose, was disbanded by the Terror government.

Militant sans-culottes devoted much of their leisure to politics, even while holding no official post in their section of the city. Occasionally they would visit the Jacobin club, but they generally divided their evenings between the *société sectionnaire* and the General Assembly. In the section they would be surrounded by friends in their own social milieu. They wore the red bonnet, the *carmagnole,* and, in critical situations, carried their pikes in hand. The pike was a powerful symbol of the people in arms. It was not employed on the front against enemy armies but was extensively used to quell disturbances at home. When the death penalty was decreed,

A sans-culotte as seen by other sans-culottes. Bibliothèque Nationale de France.

on June 25, 1793, for hoarders and speculators, Jacques Roux said the sans-culottes would execute the decree with their pikes.[13] On August 1, 1793, the government authorized the municipalities to manufacture pikes on a grand scale and to provide them to the citizens who lacked firearms.

Besides attending meetings of the *sociétés sectionnaires* and the General Assembly, sans-culottes also found time to socialize in cabarets, cafes, or taverns, where they enjoyed singing patriotic songs.

The life of most sans-culottes was modest. Some bordered on the fringe of the lower echelons of society and lived in a perpetual state of desperation. It was not unknown for a family with three or more children to live in one sparsely furnished room on an upper floor of a building.

Bread, the primary ingredient in the sans-culottes' diet, was the principal source of nourishment for the poorer classes. The daily ration of the average adult has been estimated at three pounds, that of a child one and a half pounds. The sans-culottes demanded that their bread be of the same quality as that of the rich—made with pure flour. Under the old regime, a family of four or five would consume about 12 pounds a day at a cost of three sous a pound. The budget for bread, then, could be as high as 36 sous a day for a working man who made three livres a day, or about 60 sous. The remainder of the wage might go to rent and a little wine. The poor sans-culotte would return home to his attic after a day of backbreaking

A sans-culotte as seen by the English, along with comments such as "long live the guillotine!" Bibliothèque Nationale de France.

work, climb the stairs, and enter his one room to find his children crying or fighting and his wife perhaps pregnant and exhausted. He would sit down at a rickety table on a half-broken chair and eat his dinner of stale bread moistened by a little red wine before dropping onto a dirty cot, pulling a torn blanket over him. Often not even a newspaper could relieve his or his wife's ennui because neither of them could read.

Knowledge of the events of the day and of the revolution in general was gained at work sites or in city squares and, in small towns, by means of public readers who expounded on the events described in the newspapers to an audience of workmen gathered around for the occasion. In this way people learned something of the words of Rousseau and the philosophers and were inspired by the new ideas of liberty, justice, and equality. The newspapers were purchased with individual donations of the workers. For the man or woman who could read, there were ample posters, placards, and news sheets, as well as newspapers, to keep them informed. The patriotic papers of the popular societies were also read in the evenings.

Angered by their poverty and by their concomitant hatred of wealth, the sans-culottes insisted that it was the duty of the revolutionary government to guarantee them the right to a decent existence. They demanded an immediate increase in wages, along with fixed prices, and an end to food shortages. Further, they demanded that hoarders be punished and, most important, that the existence of counterrevolutionaries be dealt with. In terms of social ideals, the sans-culottes wanted laws to prevent extremes of both wealth and property. They favored a democratic republic in which the voice of the common man could be heard. Their ideology was not unlike that of Thomas Paine, the English-American radical who argued that the best form of government was the one that governed least. During the revolution, they were represented by Père Duchesne, an artisan and family man of the people whose name Hébert took for the name of his radical, generally vulgar, newspaper.

## NOTES

1. Garrioch, 18.
2. Ibid., 15ff.
3. Ibid., 28–29.
4. Sewell, 31–32.
5. Ibid., 118.
6. See Robiquet, 124.
7. Ibid., chapter 1, for more on the different districts in Paris.
8. Ibid., 4.
9. Ibid., 6.
10. Ibid., 16–19.
11. Ibid., 39–41.
12. Rudé (1988), 38; Hunt (1984), 199ff.
13. Soboul, 222ff.
14. Rose, 153. Roux was a popular parish priest of a Paris section and a member of the Cordeliers. He advocated death for the hoarders.

# 12

# RURAL LIFE

Up to the time of the revolution, agriculture provided some three-quarters of France's gross national product. Only about a million inhabitants lived in the large cities, and another 2 million populated the smaller towns. The remaining 23 million or so lived in the countryside, either on farmsteads or in small villages and hamlets around which they worked the land.

With no political power, the peasants were nevertheless heavily burdened by taxes—on income for the king (*taille*), on land and on their crops for the lord of the manor, and, through the *dîme*, for the church. In addition, there were taxes on wine, cider, tobacco, and salt. If a peasant sold a piece of land, he paid a sales tax. He also had to provide free labor about 10 days a year for the crown, a system known as the *corvée*. He was forbidden to kill any game animals, such as deer, boar, rabbits, and birds, even as they ate the crops and his family was starving. When his sons reached manhood and were needed on the farm, he could expect to see them forced into the army. Sometimes, desperation led to protests and violence.

Taxes had always imposed a hardship on the peasants, but toward the end of the eighteenth century peasants' growing resentment began to be aimed at the seigneurs, who often left the land in the hands of an agent while they lived in town. Frequently, peasants did not know their lord personally. Seigneuries could also be bought and sold, and wealthy bourgeois sometimes purchased them, being more interested in making the maximum profit possible than in honoring traditional obligations. Such changes were always a problem for the peasant, who then had to adjust to new ways and to new lords who, too often, raised the rents.

Relief from pressing duties and from taxes to pay for wars and courtly extravagance was the hope of every peasant. It was no secret that elegant and costly entertainment at Versailles filled the frivolous lives of the king's pleasure-loving courtiers while the peasants toiled from dawn to dusk in all weather to pay for it.

Visiting France not long before the revolution, Arthur Young noted that, in Salogne, "the fields are scenes of pitiable management, as the houses are of misery"; in Brittany, "the country has a savage aspect, husbandry not much further advanced, at least in skill, than among the Hurons,... the people almost as wild as their country, and their town of Combourg, one of the most brutal filthy places that can be seen; mud houses, no windows, and a pavement so broken, as to impede all passengers." From Montauban he wrote, "one third of what I have seen of this province seems uncultivated, and nearly all of it in misery." He thus described the condition of a large part of the French people and their deplorable lot, which he justly attributed to bad government and feudal exactions; he found only privilege and poverty.[1]

In the same vein, the Bishop of Clermont-Ferrand wrote that the people of the Auvergne were in terrible misery, living without furniture or any comforts and facing taxes so heavy that they could hardly feed their families.

To survive, much of the rural population undertook nonagricultural work when time permitted. While nearly half the land was owned by peasants (with certain restrictions), the land itself usually amounted to a small patch whose yield was barely big enough to feed the family. In the vicinity around Orléans, for example, some 80 percent of the peasants owned less than four hectares, and around Limoges about 60 percent owned and cultivated less than two hectares.[2] In winter, many went to the towns and cities in search of any kind of work to help sustain their families. Similar circumstances occurred in most regions of the country. The most fortunate peasants could find some kind of industrial work near home. By the end of the eighteenth century, textile manufacture for export had grown considerably; in Flanders, there was a long tradition of woolen manufacture, and, in southern Anjou, there was a center for the textile industries. In these and other places, peasants could find extra work.

Land use differed considerably from region to region. The Paris basin, the *pays de grand culture*, had a zone of about 100 kilometers extending out from the city of large farms where high-quality grain was grown for the city bread consumers.[3] These farms generally belonged to absentee landlords who rented them to farmers. They in turn hired landless laborers, who made up the majority of the rural population, to work them. Interspersed in this area, also within a day's travel from the city, were patches that grew fresh produce for the Parisian markets. Along the sides of valleys, there were vines growing on numerous small holdings whose proprietors, like the landless workers, were forced to buy their food from markets or farms. North of Paris, in the region of Beauvais, peasants cultivated small holdings of rye and oats for their own consumption and supplied cheese, hemp, flax, pigs, and cattle for the markets.

In the Cévennes, north of Nîmes, another kind of agriculture was practiced. Here, groves of mulberry trees produced the leaves that fed the farmed silk worms. Thousands of families reared these worms, unwinding the silk from their cocoons. This job was generally done by young women, who worked with their hands in the scalding water needed to soften the silk.[4]

Ancillary jobs associated with silk included mining coal from shallow pits to provide the fuel to heat the water. Wagon-men hauled the coal from the open mines to its place of use. Coal was also delivered to nearby lowland towns; on the return journey, the same horse-drawn wagons carried wheat to the hills to feed the silk-producing inhabitants.

The seigneurial regime of France had been steadily eroding, and, by 1789, only relics of it remained in existence. In most areas, the lords had become landlords, and the relationship of lord to tenant resembled a business transaction involving rent, a share of the harvest, and fees for transfer of property, rather than feudal obligations.[5]

In some outlying regions, remnants of the feudal system still applied, however. In Burgundy, for example, the villages had the obligation to give the tongue of every ox slaughtered to the lord of the manor for his table. In the Vosges, the bull's testicles had to be handed over. The concept of *mainmorte*, which required that a peasant obtain permission from his lord to sell his land or bequeath it to anyone but a direct relative who had lived on the land with him, was still alive in some regions.[6]

## AGRICULTURE

About 35 percent of the total area of France is arable, and some 7 percent of the labor force is engaged in agricultural pursuits today. In the 1780s, however, the vast majority of the population was thus engaged, and agriculture was the country's economic mainstay.[7]

Land cultivation was practiced in all sorts of climate and soils, from the high Pyrenees Mountains and Alpine homesteads to the flat marches of the Landes, from the open field farms of the Paris basin to the small enclosures of hedgerows in Normandy, and along the misty shores of the Atlantic Ocean and the sun-parched coasts of the Mediterranean.

Grain surpluses even in the most fertile regions were always rather small because of the outdated methods of farming, and production barely sufficed to feed the townsmen or the inhabitants of less productive regions. A number of areas were designated to provision Paris and its nearly 600,000 inhabitants, but, in years of poor harvests and shortage, riots erupted in the streets of the city.

The nobility, relatively few in number in comparison with the rest of the population, owned some 25 percent of the land, and the church owned around 10 percent. Much of the church's wealth came from urban property holdings, but the *dîme* made up a considerable sum. According to Young, who made inquiries in various parts of the country, the amount payable to the church was never 10 percent but always more—up to 20 percent of the peasants' income. The church did not collect on some new items of cultivation that did not date back to medieval times; these included potatoes, turnips, silk worms, olives (in some places but not in others), and cabbages. The peasant who owned cows paid nothing to the church, but, if he had lambs, the church took some of them in dues.[8]

There were swaths of common, uncultivated, or so-called waste land where the peasants used to graze their animals. Such land made up two-fifths of Brittany and much of the Alpine regions and the Massif Central but amounted to very little in more populated places such as the Ile de France.[9]

The Vendée (at the time part of Poitou) had only one road from Nantes to La Rochelle, and the land consisted primarily of waste, brushwood, heath, and morass, with patches here and there of cultivated rye and buckwheat. It was a region of large tenant farms that a family might occupy for generations. On some farms, mules were reared for export to Spain; on others, horses, cows, oxen, sheep, pigs, and poultry were raised to sell. In Languedoc, agriculture was very different, with vines, mulberries, and olive trees completely covering the hills.

Since wheat does not grow well on the same land two years in a row, it was rotated, the patch used for one year's crop remaining fallow the following year. The land was often divided into three sections—wheat, oats, and fallow—with the three uses applied in rotation so that the soil had a chance to replenish itself. In regions of poor soil, the land might be left fallow for far longer. Before planting, it was fertilized with manure; when that was not available, ashes, dead leaves, or whatever organic materials were available were applied. Then the plowing would begin. The land was tilled several times, depending on the crop. Wheat, for best results, might require four tillings. The plowing was generally accomplished by means of harnessed oxen or mules, and, sometimes, horses. It was not unknown for family members to pull the plow, itself often a primitive instrument of wood slanting down from a cross bar connected to two wheels. The pattern of everyday life in peasant communities revolved around tilling, planting, harvesting, threshing, and grazing the animals that supplied the manure to ensure a rich harvest. Since this kind of work was done by hand, seasonal laborers were an added requirement during harvest and threshing time. Most of the wheat grown in France was cultivated north of the Loire River.

The grass that grew on uncultivated land, such as in the foothills of the mountains, on rocky outcroppings, along the windswept coasts of the

Atlantic, and on marshy terrain, was productive for livestock. In these regions, animals were raised not only for food to feed the peasant population and to sell in the markets but also to serve as beasts of burden for the army, which always required horses and mules.

Maize (corn) was first introduced into Europe from the Americas in the sixteenth century. The first place in France to cultivate maize was the region of Béarn, in the southwest, where it was used as fodder for the animals long before the poorest of the peasants began to eat it in the form of cornmeal cakes in place of more expensive bread. By the eighteenth century, a large portion of the peasant diet was corn, but the wealthy seldom ate it. Soon it became evident that land planted with potatoes could feed twice the number of people as the same amount of land used to produce cereal crops. In addition, dried potatoes could be stored for a long time.

## BASTIONS OF FEUDALISM

In many out-of-the-way places such as Normandy, Burgundy, Brittany, and the Franche-Comté, peasants experienced brutal, arbitrary tyranny from aristocratic authority. There was no justice in the manorial courts in disputes between peasants and their lord, since the judges in such courts were dependent on the lord of the manor for position, power, and pay. The peasant paid fines or charges around every corner. Peasants had to pay the *banalité*, or rent for the use of the flour-grinding mills, which belonged to the lord but which the peasant farmer needed to process his wheat; he also had to press his grapes, as well as apples for cider, on the seigneur's press; bread could be baked only in the lord's ovens. For all of these activities, a fee was charged. In Brittany, the peasants were sometimes ordered to beat the waters of the marshes all night to keep the bullfrogs silent so that the lady of the manor could sleep peacefully.

The lord had the exclusive right, or banvin, to sell his wine at his price in his parish; there were many other rights particular to certain locations that weighed on the peasant—the *bardage*, or transport duty; the *fouage*, seigneurial taxes on fires; the *vingtaine*, or the seigneurial right to one-twentieth of the peasants' produce; a tax on fishing in the rivers and streams—all this in addition payments to the lord of the manor for every change of property.[10]

Most peasants were never full owners of land in the modern sense, but, nevertheless, the land they occupied may be regarded as their land, since it could be willed to the peasant's children or transferred to other occupants, usually for a fee.

A farmer could make various arrangements; the owner might hand over the land for an agreed amount of rent, for example, or the farmer could own outbuildings if they had been built at his expense, along with stock and crops. Both parties could separate under certain conditions, one being reimbursement of outlay.

## TERMS OF A LEASE

On August 1, 1779, in the town of Villefranche de Lauragais, a little southeast of Toulouse, Pierre and Mathieu Reynes, father and son, appeared before a notary and agreed to lease a farm called La Grave for one year commencing November 1. They were leasing it from Jacques Maurel, who was acting as agent on behalf of the owner, the powerful marquis d'Hautpoul. It was a large farm of about 35 hectares that seemed to offer a secure living. The lease was written in the form known as half-fruits—a kind of sharecropping contract. The stipulations were set out in detail.

For the use of the land, the two farmers were required to give to the agent in rent 36 chickens at Christmas and the same on St. John the Baptist's day, June 24, and a further 36 capons on All Saints' Day, when the lease expired. Besides the chickens, they were obliged to hand over 600 eggs during the course of the year and were expected to buy and raise pigs, geese, ducks, and turkeys, of which Maurel would take the half of his choosing when they were ready for sale. The rest of the livestock on the farm would be divided in the same way. The tenants were committed to keeping the property in good condition, providing their own tools and implements for their work, and they would pay for plows ordered from the village blacksmith. They were responsible for the hay and straw for the animals and would pay half the costs of any extra that was needed and could not be grown.

The three-field system applied. One-third of the land was for wheat, one-third was for beans or other vegetables and grains, and one-third was to lie fallow. If the tenants failed to utilize all the land, the agent could lease the unused portion to someone else. The father and son had to provide seed grain and pay the costs of cutting and threshing, which they could do by handing over part of the harvest, that is, paying in kind. While they provided the means necessary for farming and all the upkeep on the land, the owner took the lion's share of the result. Out of the little left over after paying the landlord, the father and son had to pay rents, as well as taxes to the crown and the dîme for the church. The half of the livestock that remained in the tenant's possession by the terms of the agreement could be sold to pay these and other obligations.[11] It has been calculated that the Reynes would have a profit of about 15 percent of the total yield at the end of the year. This did not produce enough money to buy bread sufficient to feed a family of five. There was no guarantee that the lease would be renewed, and the tenants were subject to the law if they broke any of the agreements. None of the parties was literate enough to write his name on the contract.

Another kind of farming, *métayage*, was based on a 50-50 split. It was in use primarily south of the Loire. In such a case, the owner supplied land, stock, and implements, and the manual laborer supplied his muscle. All produce was generally shared equally or according to the contract. Such farms were usually from 50 to 150 acres in size. The *métayer* (laborer) himself may have owned a small parcel of land.

## MIGRANT WORKERS AND DAY LABORERS

Peasants who held some land but not enough for their family needs (about four hectares) often had to find jobs on larger farms or perform nonagricultural work in factories, mills, or mines in order to subsist. They could find such work in the months that did not require planting and harvesting. For agricultural day laborers who possessed nothing more than a vegetable patch and a shanty, life was exceptionally difficult. They had to be mobile and travel where the work was to be found, and many hours of work (and pay) could be lost if bad weather ruined the harvest. Day workers could also seek employment as weavers and spinners in industry when there was no fieldwork, but such jobs paid a pittance.

Migrant workers from neighboring regions or countries who worked in the vineyards, olive groves, orchards, and wheat fields were particularly hard hit in bad times, with not enough money to feed their families or even to travel home again. Starving to death was a distinct possibility.

If a peasant farmer required help, he had to find someone to work for him, although it was not easy to produce the cash to pay him, and it sometimes turned out that the laborer had to work for credit. A male servant in Normandy was paid 60 livres per year, or roughly 100 sous per month.[12] Female servants on a farmstead were paid about a third of what a man earned. Typical daily salaries for short-term labor were 9 sous and dinner for an ordinary day worker, 12 sous for a thatcher, 13 sous for a plowman, and up to 15 sous for a reaper or a carpenter. Grain crops were taken in dues and rents, and surplus vegetables sold in the market brought in only trivial amounts of money. Stock rearing for urban markets brought in more. For instance, a single cow could fetch 60 or 70 livres, a sow 30 to 45. Lambs were worth 7 to 7 livres and a sheep about 15. The premature death of a peasant's cow or pig could bring on financial problems that might force him to sell off a little of his land to replace the animal.[13]

## RURAL LIVES

Peasants engaged in agriculture dwelt in isolated farmhouses or in hamlets, villages, or, sometimes, substantial small towns. Often the fields were some distance from their dwellings, and much time was spent going to and fro. Their households included a servant or two (if they were well off), unmarried children, elderly parents, or other relatives. Several families might share the same dwelling and work the same land. The majority, however, lived in stark, harsh, conditions very remote from those imagined by Marie-Antoinette in her little fairyland peasant village at the Petit Trianon. Most peasant families had to make do with a one- or two-room house with dirt floors, which they also had to share with any livestock. The houses, or hovels, were often dark, windowless, and poorly ventilated places where disease could easily breed, particularly when the walls were of dung and mud, as was often the case. If windows existed, they were without glass. Throughout the departments of Maine and Loire, many people lived in caves or troglodyte villages hollowed out of tufa rock.

Life was particularly hard for rural women, who often worked both in and outside the house, tending vegetables, which they sold along with eggs, gathering firewood, taking the cow or goat to pasture on common land, and feeding chickens or geese. In times of need, mother and daughters also helped in the fields and with the plowing. At other times, there were meals to be prepared and laundry to be washed and laid out in the field to dry in the sun.

Lack of privacy was taken for granted. A recently married couple usually had to sleep in the same room as other members of the household, and their emotional and sexual relationships were a matter of gossip. Village women gathered at the public well or at washing sites along streams to act as tribunes, casting moral judgment on the housekeeping, farming practices, or business astuteness of a young couple. Young unmarried men in the community also exercised their tongues in making fun of husbands suspected of being henpecked or cuckolded. Widows or widowers who married a second time, choosing a younger person as a mate, could be subjected to harassment by hostile young men and women who saw their supply of eligible partners in the village diminished.

The wealthier peasants could afford to educate their children, but for most, life was something to endure, with a constant worry about the future. A bad harvest meant little food and even starvation for those living on the edge of subsistence. Gathering the harvest was the dominant factor in their lives, for only if the harvest was successful could they pay their taxes and dues and feed the family. The entire household would be called upon when the harvest was ready, since all hands were needed to get the crops in before they rotted in the ground.

The men, meanwhile, worked in the fields repairing fences, cleaning tools, digging irrigation ditches, and tending to the animals. Depending on the type of farm, the man might have to spend months away with his sheep in the alpine pastures or weeks and months as a migrant laborer in addition to planting and harvesting his own field. He also had to leave to fulfill labor obligations to the seigneur and to the government—the detested *corvée,* buying or selling livestock, dealing with taxes, or negotiating a new lease. Children were put to work by age six or seven, or as soon as they could understand instructions.

## TALES AND LEGENDS

When the workday was finished, supper had been eaten, and the early winter night had descended, how did peasants in isolated farms and hamlets entertain themselves? One may never know the extent to which storytelling, sitting around the hearth, was part of family evenings, but it is clear that folk tales, passed down orally from one generation to the next, were recited for the benefit of children and adults. Stories in which a widow and her son, beaten down by poverty, leave the village, travel through a forest full of murderous brigands, and finally wind up in a filthy poorhouse before a magic bracelet rescues them demonstrate the terrible and dangerous conditions in which peasants lived and their desire to break free. The tale of a poor peasant who comes by a magic tablecloth that produces a fabulous meal whenever the peasant spreads it out reflects real life and the constant striving to satisfy hunger. Many French tales revolved around work in the fields, guarding sheep, gathering wood, carrying water, begging, or spinning wool or tell of young men setting out to find a better life. The wives of peasants in the tales are more often than not portrayed at the spinning wheel, gathering wood, hoeing, and, in some cases, yoked to plows. Such stories would have helped to relieve the tedium and bitter austerity of the peasants' daily life while at the same time serving as cautionary tales, warning that the world was a dangerous place in which they could expect only endless work and deprivation. They also offered a vague hope, depending on how much the peasant believed in magic, that his life of misery might be transformed for the better. Morality was not an issue in French tales, whereas quick thinking, cunning, deceit, and trickery were often themes; the peasant outwits the lord of the manor or even the king, and his life is improved. Escapism for girls might revolve around marriage to a horrible husband who then turns into a prince. Such themes occur over and over in the tales, and the magical acquisition of wealth by the peasant seems to take second place to the acquisition of food. Given three wishes by a benevolent fairy, the first is inevitably for a good meal—all one can eat. French folk tales also suggest that village life was not always as harmonious as it has been portrayed. Neighbors are often hostile, greedy, vengeful, spying, or thieving.

Cats have always been animals of superstition and are associated with witchcraft in many cultures; France was no exception. It was believed that cats possessed occult powers and that drinking their blood could cure various illnesses. If a man treated a cat well, he would have a pretty wife. On the other hand, to maim or kill a cat would prevent its association with witches, whose power would thus be diminished.[14]

## HAIL, HUNGER, AND HOSTILITY

Disastrous famines brought on by extreme bad weather occurred in France every decade or so, ruining the crops; other times, crops were lost to the devastation of war. Grain was the mainstay of the country and bread the most precious item of the diet. When food was in short supply, prices shot up, usually accompanied by riots, especially in the larger cities.

On July 13, 1788, black clouds rolled over central France and released a torrent of hailstones. The large pellets slammed into and destroyed the budding vines in Alsace, Burgundy, and the Loire Valley, decimating the wheat ripening in the fields south of Paris along with the fruit and vegetables. Bruised, split, and knocked to the ground, apples in Normandy rotted, and olives and oranges in the Midi were severely damaged.

Over vast regions of France, the storm was followed by drought, and the little that was left of the harvest was mostly parched and useless. The winter brought on the coldest spell in many years. It was said that birds froze in their nests. Rivers froze, watermills stopped working, and the little grain that remained could not be made into flour. Transportation came to a standstill in the deep snow that covered the ground in many areas as far south as Toulouse. Starving families in the Tarn and in the Ardèche regions boiled tree bark to make gruel. Provence was described by Mirabeau, in January 1789, as having been visited by the Exterminating Angel. Thousands of people froze to death, and many more died of hunger.[15] The cold was so severe that town and village councils kept bonfires blazing in the streets to keep the poor from freezing.

The spring thaw sent rivers over their banks, flooding fields and towns. The four-pound loaf of bread in normal times cost 8 sous in the summer of 1787, about half the wage earner's income; the price nearly doubled, to 15 sous, in February 1789. A family of four consumed two of these loaves each day, yet the manual laborer earned only between 20 and 30 sous per day.[16] Not only did the price of bread reach unheard-of prices, but another essential, firewood, nearly doubled in price. Thousands of cold and hungry people roamed the countryside looking for anything to eat or burn. The landless day laborers found themselves unemployed, far from home, and desperate; for the greater part of the rural population, small landholders or *métayers*, the situation was also dire. Being both producers and consumers, they immediately used any money made from selling their products to buy bread or wood. The steep rise in the prices of these items wiped out any profit the peasants might have had from the rising value of their crop. Many had to borrow money to make ends meet, using future crops as collateral. With much of the harvest virtually destroyed and taxes, which the peasants were unable to pay, owed to the seigneur and the state, creditors often called in the debt. Many were evicted from their plots and joined the growing ranks of the landless. This miserable mass of humanity shambled its way to the nearest church for a handout of a crust of bread and a little milk or headed for the big towns to try to find menial jobs or to beg in the streets. With migrant laborers also invading the cities looking for work, the peasants' prospects were bleak. Such conditions brought on hostile reactions and violence: bakeries and warehouses were raided, and hatred toward the well off and the monarchy, generally blamed for high costs and food shortages, intensified.

## MORTALITY

Death among the peasant population was as much part of daily life as everyday toil. The specter of death hovered above all beds in which a mother gave birth to a child. It was not uncommon for the mother to die or the child to be stillborn, or both. The fear of damnation after death was so strong that midwives were empowered by the church to baptize unhealthy infants if death seemed imminent and no priest was close by. If they could not save the baby, they could at least save its soul. An emerging hand or foot could be baptized if it was thought that the baby would die in the womb.[17]

If alone at the time of birth, the parents were permitted to perform the baptism. Complications with newborns were generally caused by the mother's overwork, poor diet, and illness. About one-fifth of all babies died within the first year or so, as many as one in three in the more impoverished areas of the country. Fewer than half reached their fifteenth birthday. With scant knowledge of hygiene, a multitude of diseases breeding in the unsanitary conditions, and no money for medicine, there was about a 50-50 chance that a baby would survive to adulthood; smallpox was one of the great levelers. The worst time to give birth was in the months of August through October, when breast-feeding mothers toiled in the fields and the only food was the fast-deteriorating remnants of last year's crop.

People tended to remain loyal to their villages and helped one another in times of need. Men often bonded through group drinking. When men of different communities met at fairs, hostilities could easily flare up, resulting in brawls, with the name of the village as a rallying cry. In some regions, violence among the men and a sense of solidarity among villagers resulted in vendettas in which knives or guns were used to even a score. Urban authorities showed little inclination and had little opportunity to investigate murders in remote, clannish, tight-lipped country communities.

## VILLAGE COUNCILS AND SOCIAL LIFE

The village or hamlet usually formed a parish of the Catholic Church, and the local priest looked on the inhabitants as his flock. The community might form the jurisdiction of a court and also regulate its own collective affairs. Some communities in the Pyrenees valleys, run by the elders of the village, joined with other villages to resist outside intrusion. In other regions, the communities were encouraged by the state to elect town officials and to meet regularly to conduct local business. Some of this had to do with state demands, such as the *taille;* the officials had to decide how much each resident owed to the king.

There was also a regular lottery for service in the militia, the country's military reserve. This service was loathed as much as the *corvée* by both parents and their sons, who, when their number came up, had to serve. Other duties of the villagers included helping with communal projects, such as making repairs to the church, wells, water troughs, laundry sites, and buildings, for which extraordinary local taxes might be assessed. The town council might also decide when the harvest, which required the participation of all village hands, would begin. As well, it managed the use of common land or woodland that fell under its authority. This sometimes meant entering litigation with neighboring communities. The stones of one village that were used to demarcate its common pastureland might be moved by the people of another village—an act that would lead to animosity. Open conflict could break out when a herd of animals strayed and was found eating grass that belonged to another village or when firewood was collected in woodland whose ownership was disputed. Young men sometimes took contentious matters into their own hands and attacked neighbors with fists or clubs. Sometimes the disputes went to court, where they often remained for decades.

Depending on the size of the community, one or more persons ran the administration and represented the local interest with regard to the seigneur, the state, and the church. More and more, however, throughout the eighteenth century, the state's regional official, the intendant, and his deputies supervised the work of the town councils, laying down the rules for their roles and managing tax assessments. In some places, the intendant appointed the town councils; in others, the seigneur appointed the members; and in still others, members were voted into office by the community.

As expected, village political life tended to be dominated by the wealthier members of the community. The village of Cormeilles-en-Vexin, north of Paris, with just over 200 households by the late 1780s, was in the habit of electing an official, the syndic, equivalent to a mayor and a town clerk, who might be a substantial farmer, an artisan, or even an innkeeper. The last syndic, in 1789, was Jean-Louis Toussaint Caffin, a *fermier de seigneurie*, a person who leased lands from the seigneur and then sublet them or hired laborers to work them. As he was also a flour merchant, he was very prosperous, and he and most of the others elected to the office were better off than the majority of the villagers. Tax records show that inhabitants paid less than 10 livres in taxes, while more than half of the syndics paid 50 livres. One, probably Caffin, paid 2,000 livres, a third of the assessment for the village.[18]

Besides having rights over common land and game, in many regions lords had other privileges, including the right to harvest timber on common lands, to ride over peasants' fields in pursuit of game, such as deer, without paying compensation for destroyed crops; the right to a special pew in the local church; the right to have special prayers said for his health and wealth; and the right to a weather cock on the manor house.

Sometimes his rights involved the dispensing of justice in a seigneurial court. In some places, he chose the village officials or convened the village meetings, with himself or his agent in charge.

By the late eighteenth century, more and more peasants were challenging their lords and taking them to court, backed by royal justice, to contest required payments such as those imposed to maintain the lord's fortifications, the exaction of extra dues for the use of the communal bread ovens, and the payments demanded for festivities and dowry when the seigneur's daughters were married.

It was in the royal interest to support the peasants, since the less they paid to the lord, the more the government could collect in taxes. Nevertheless, the peasants lost the great majority of their court cases but often found the money to continue pursuing them. As peasant resistance grew, especially among the younger generation, the landowners fought back. One case taken to court by a lord who charged his peasants with illegal sheep grazing dragged on from 1760 to 1784.[19] In the community of Villerouge-Termenes, the agent of the archbishop who owned the land began a lawsuit against the village in 1775 that continued sporadically on into the revolution. It concerned whether or not a relatively new food crop, the potato, was subject to dues and tithes.

## DEPUTIES, ESTATES-GENERAL, AND THE *CAHIERS*

Even in the poorest hamlets, the meeting of the Estates-General was looked forward to with some anticipation. Peasant *cahiers* were generally presented in simple, plain language and expressed not only peasants' distress and hopes but also their love and respect for the king.

While the nobility and the clergy elected their deputies directly, the Third Estate, made up mostly of provincial deputies, was more complicated. From January 1789, local assemblies under the medieval name of *bailliages* (bailiwicks) were convened, about 1 for every 100 voters, who had to be at least 25 years old and taxpaying residents. Usually held in the village church, the assemblies drafted their *cahiers* and elected deputies to represent them at a higher assembly, which then elected deputies to the Estates-General that would meet at Versailles. Those elected to the final prize were overwhelmingly lawyers and public officials, along with a few physicians and notaries and the occasional businessman. The rural *cahiers* were mostly concerned with the daily matters of taxes, justice, the draft for the militia, and the game laws.[20]

On February 25, 1789, the inhabitants of Ménouville, in the Paris basin, were called together, and the curate read out the king's letter summoning the Estates-General. These excerpts are typical of peasant *cahiers*:

We beg his Majesty to have pity on our farmland because of the hail we have had. Also we have a great deal of waste land which is covered with juniper, and this causes much trouble on account of the rabbits which are very numerous; it is that that makes us unable to pay the dues we owe to His Majesty. We have no help from anyone to bring us relief … we can expect help from no one but His Majesty. We have only a few good fields very remote from the village, the rest is wretched land very full of game and this causes very small harvests. We have one small meadow which only produces sour hay, the animals refuse to eat it, this is why we cannot raise stock.

The soil is so bad that you cannot plant fruit trees … they don't grow.

We state that salt is too dear for poor people. We state that there should not be any tax men. We state that there should be no militia duty because this ruins many families; it would be better if His Majesty laid a small tax on each young man. We inform His Majesty that our goods are too heavily burdened with seigneurial and other charges.

The *cahier* continued to complain of the bad main road, begun eight years earlier with *corvée* work. Eighteen months ago, however, a large pile of stones had been carted in and left in the road, with no one to do the work; travelers instead walked through the grain fields beside the road, causing much damage.[21]

From the Norman village of Vatimesnil, where spinning jennies threatened the livelihood of peasant households, came the following *cahier*:

We represent to His Majesty that food is too dear and that trade is not moving and that taxation is too heavy and that we can give no help to the State. And we would like to ask His Majesty for the good of the public to abolish spinning machines because they do great wrong to all poor people. And we present to his Majesty some ways which could restore the state to health: such as the clergy, because we have seen communities of four or five religious enjoying thirty or forty thousand livres without usually giving any of it away in charity; and fix a decent income for them and let His Majesty take the surplus. And we do not know of any other ways in which His Majesty could do good to all his people.[22]

It is from the *cahiers* that the complaints of people were made known to the royal court and the Estates-General. Some of the most pertinent suggestions presented in them were as follows:

The Estates-General should be called periodically.

Separation of powers should be instituted in the government, with legislative power held by a National Assembly.

Any new taxes should be agreed upon by the Assembly.

Liberty of person, thought, utterance, and publication must be guaranteed.

*Lettres de cache*t should be abolished.

No forms of arbitrary justice such as military tribunals should be permitted.

No censorship should be in force.

No interference with mail should be allowed, as this is an assault on liberty.

The annual publication of government budgets should be mandatory, with each department of state fully accounted for.

Venal office should be abolished.

No exemptions from taxes because of rank or privilege should be allowed.

Nobles and clergy should have no special privileges.

Tax farming or custom houses should be abolished.

All citizens should be equal before the law.

The *corvée* should be abolished.

Enlightened people hoped that increased prosperity on the land made possible by the use of updated methods of farming would create surplus and wealth, enabling the peasantry to become consumers of manufactured goods and materials.

A number of aristocrats shared similar views to those of the lower classes, agreeing that titles and privilege should be abolished, along with venal offices, but this was not the case with the poorer nobles in their chateaux out in the country who had little but their titles to cling to for the esteem they cherished. They refused to elect deputies to the Estates; they were not enamored of the idea of their inherited rank dissolving into the simple position of "citizen."

## THE GREAT FEAR

In late summer 1789, after the fall of the Bastille, and as harvest time approached, what became known as the Great Fear began to envelop the countryside. Many peasants were aware that the National Assembly was doing nothing to promote their interests, and rumors circulated that the aristocrats were sending an army of brigands against them. In panic, villagers armed themselves, attacked and burned chateaux, and destroyed the records of taxes and duties they owed to the local landlords. Nobles who resisted were killed or driven from their homes, and another wave of aristocratic refugees streamed across the borders of France to join other self-exiled *émigrés*.

During the afternoon of July 28, dust seen in the distance aroused the citizens of Angoulême. Every able-bodied man was called upon to defend the city. Thousands took up arms (whatever they could find) and scoured the areas for culprits. There were rumors that nearby towns had already been burned to the ground. When no brigands were found after several days of searching, it was concluded that the swirl of dust seen earlier had been created by the mail coach on the high road to Bordeaux.[23]

The alarm created by this incident induced the city of Angoulême to take steps toward the formation of a citizens' army to protect itself and the countryside. Other towns followed suit, putting themselves on a military footing. It was also brought home that the nobility had failed to perform its traditional role of protecting the peasants, who, turning against their masters, called again for the abolition of noble privileges, which were no longer justified.

From then on, everyone anticipated the arrival of bandits coming to ravish their fields and steal their property. As rumors spread from village to village, peasants fled into the hills at any sign of strangers approaching their farms and hamlets. The numbers grew in the telling, with as many as several thousand (imaginary) renegades on the move in some areas. Armed with pitchforks, axes, and knives, the inhabitants of one village went to the aid of another nearby that they had heard was under attack. The inhabitants of the village supposed to be under siege thought those coming to help them were the anticipated brigands. Those who fled the besieged village rushed on to the next one to report the attack. And so panic based on rumor and mistaken information spread throughout entire regions.

The Great Fear was an illusion, but nevertheless it was very real to the people. The aristocrat brigand or the vagrant in his pay was a phantom figure, but revolutionaries nonetheless helped spread the rumors of an aristocratic plot. The threat helped cement national cohesiveness by uniting peasants and their villages against the aristocracy and giving the people some idea of their strength in the event that it became necessary to defend their hearths.

On August 4, 1789, the viscount de Noailles, brother-in-law of Lafayette, proposed the abolition of seigneurial feudal rights. The Assembly wasted no time in passing the legislation. By late August, the chaos in the countryside had eased, and the Great Fear had passed. It had left its mark, however: revolutionaries in the towns had sent out their newly created National Guard to protect crops and property, and the rebellious peasants had forced the National Assembly to take notice of, as well as action on, one of the fundamental issues of the revolution—the ancient privileges of the nobility.

## A CHANGE IN PEASANT SOCIETY

The new regime became somewhat organized in 1790, and the country people's lives underwent a degree of transformation. The peasants now stopped removing their hats, lowering their heads, and addressing their masters as *Monsieur le comte*. They often increased their small plots of land by confiscating and taking over parts of abandoned noble estates and began killing the rabbits, chickens, geese, and ducks that had eaten their cabbages and lettuces in the past while they watched helplessly. Similarly, they began to hunt wild animals and birds, all once the property of the lord of the manor, with newly acquired firearms that they had up to now been forbidden to possess.

The rents on land were just as legal under the revolutionary government as they were under the old regime, but under the new circumstances they were not paid regularly. Young says that in August 1791 he was informed by a person of authority not to be doubted that "associations among tenantry, to a great amount and extent, have been formed, even within fifty miles of Paris, for the non-payment of rent."[24] The obvious feeling among these peasants was that they were now strong enough to resist payments and that the landlords were powerless to collect them.

The revolution had changed France and its country people in other ways. The peasant could now be governed by an Assembly that he had helped elect. He could take his grievances to courts that would, at least in concept, respect all men as free and equal. He could work when and where he chose and no longer paid duties to an aristocratic overlord or to the church. In the eyes of the law, the peasant was as respectable as the priest or the highborn. Anyone could buy and sell land if he had money enough. The lowborn could now play a role in village life and even aspire to elective positions. In theory, the peasants had achieved a great step forward, although there was little obvious improvement in their general standard of living.

## WAR, CONSCRIPTION, AND UPRISINGS

The French government's declaration of war on Austria, in April 1792, and Prussia's declaration of war on France less than two months later, on June 13, had strong repercussions in rural areas. France needed soldiers. The lottery system used to induct young men from the regions became a nightmare for many families. Farmers struggling to make a living could ill afford to lose the labor their sons provided, and the young men of the country did not want to go to fight in a distant war.

Preparing for the upcoming struggle, on February 24, 1793, the Girondins ordered the recruitment of 300,000 more troops. Enrollment began in March in the Vendée, the department on the Atlantic coast at the mouth of the Loire. The region was one of the most wretched in France, with rocky hills, deficient soil, and poverty-stricken, illiterate inhabitants. The locals were also fiercely religious; they protected nonjuring priests, supported the monarchy, and wanted no part of the revolution or the despised republic for which they were being forced to fight. Enraged and encouraged by their priests, they rose in revolt on March 11, 1793, a few days after France declared war on Spain. At first using only farm implements for weapons, the rebels defeated a detachment of National

Guardsmen sent to deal with them. The aristocrats of the Vendée, many about as poor as their peasants, joined the movement and helped shape the rebels into a fairly efficient army of irregulars who, supplied with hunting guns or stolen or captured weapons and knowing well the rugged terrain, engaged in guerrilla tactics and easily put to flight additional National Guard units sent to crush them. The counterrevolution spread rapidly as the Vendeans cut the Guard to pieces in several towns, raided supply depots, and disrupted enemy communication lines before retreating to their isolated farms and hamlets. The Girondist government was faced with an internal threat as dangerous as the foreign enemies of the revolution. The rebel force that called itself the Royal and Catholic army was defeated by government troops in December 1793; the army then carried out a scorched-earth policy against the remnants of the peasant resistance. In Nantes, some 3,000 people accused of participating in the rebellion were executed. Scattered conflicts continued for years; the region lost a third of its population through fighting and the subsequent Terror, with peace completely restored only in 1801, under Napoleon.

## NOTES

1. Young, 19 (Salogne), 123 (Brittany), 125 (Montauban).
2. Andress (2004), 8.
3. Ibid.
4. Ibid., 9–10.
5. Ibid., 23.
6. Schama, 319.
7. Aftalion, 32.
8. Young, 320.
9. There are no precise figures for the distribution of land, and various writers give slightly different estimates based on tax returns and other records.
10. See de Tocqueville, General Notes, 289ff, for feudal rights.
11. See Andress (2004), 6–7, for this contract and more detail.
12. Ibid., 15.
13. For these figures, which apply mostly to the situation in Normandy in the 1780s, see Andress (2004),16. For an overview of the peasantry, see Lefebvre, chapter 9.
14. For more on French fairy tales see Darnton/Roche (1999), passim.
15. Schama, 305.
16. Ibid., 306.
17. Andress (2004), 3.
18. Ibid., 19.
19. Ibid., 26.
20. Schama, 309.
21. Cobb/Jones (1988), 38.
22. Ibid., 42.
23. Robiquet, 29.
24. Young, 326.

# 13

# MILITARY LIFE

For some, life in the military was stimulating and carried out with purpose—to do one's duty and strive for advancement. As the baron de Besenval, commander of the king's Swiss Guard, expressed it, *"La guerre est une passion"* (war is a passion).[1] Through his taxes, the peasant bore the brunt of this passion when the monarchy required an army both for foreign wars and to prevent civil unrest.

About 1 in 20 men served in the army under the old regime, and even in Paris there were barracks in the faubourgs, for about 8,000 soldiers patrolled the city at night.[2]

The size of France's armed forces had steadily declined from the superb million-man army of Louis XIV, about a third of whom were mercenaries, and much public dissatisfaction was focused on the dismal record in the wars of the mid-eighteenth century. Under Louis XVI, soldiers were volunteers, and 23 regiments were made up of foreigners, including Italians, Germans, and Irish. The best regiments, the Swiss Guards, formed part of the king's household. But, swept from the seas by the British and far outclassed on the battlefield by the Prussians, the military inspired little confidence.

Conscription was used only to recruit for the militia, a reserve army for use in wartime. Potential recruits drew lots in each district, and the unlucky ones were forced to enroll. Exemptions abounded, however, and only the poorest of men were actually obliged to sign up; any military commitment was bitterly resented in the rural areas. These reserve units, comprising about 75,000 men, performed a few weeks' training a year in peacetime. Military life and its so-called benefits seem to have had no appeal for even the most destitute peasant.

A volunteer force, the regular Royal Army, contained about 250,000 men assigned to cavalry, infantry, and artillery units. Most of them were drawn from the lowest echelons of society, generally from the northern border districts, where invasion was most likely and where the recruiting sergeant used the inducements of a life of adventure, better wages than many were used to, the excitement of wine and women, and maybe even a chance to plunder.

Before the revolution, it was nearly impossible for a poor commoner or even for the poorer members of the provincial nobility to enter the officer caste. In 1789, out of a total of nearly 10,000 army officers, more than 6,500 were of noble birth.[3] Many who had the appropriate ancestry simply bought their commissions. In fact, the army law of 1781 *(Loi Ségur)* stated that anyone promoted to the rank of captain or above must have at least four quarters of aristocratic blood in his veins, which excluded all commoners as well as the newly ennobled.

## REVOLUTION

The Royal Army was intimately involved in the events of the revolution from the beginning. Regular troops that were in sympathy with the revolutionaries often disobeyed the orders of their aristocratic officers, setting the pattern for insubordination and conflict. Defiant behavior became a political issue tied to patriotism and was sanctioned by the revolutionary government in the summer of 1789. Mutinies broke out in several places. In Nancy, a revolt was put down by extreme force after bitter fighting. The king's flight to Varennes, in June 1791, and his subsequent arrest and suspension led to a great exodus of military officers, who resigned, deserted, or emigrated. Those that remained at their posts were subject to more intense resistance from the soldiers, which encouraged a further exodus of officers. The defections were worrisome for the revolutionary government and the military as the danger of a foreign war intensified in early 1792. The three military field commanders, Luckner, Lafayette, and Rochambeau, knew that the army was not ready for war. When it came, on April 20, 1792, when France declared war on Austria, they were proved right. The French assault on Tournai, in the Austrian Netherlands, was a disaster. On April 29, the French troops panicked and streamed back into Lille in an attempt to escape the slaughter.

Invading armies now entered France, and more officers became *émigrés*. Noncommissioned officers with solid military experience replaced the aristocrats, and there was a large influx of recruits from urban areas to fight against the foreign threat to the revolution. Nearly every aspect of

Marquis de La Fayette (Lafayette), a French general who had fought in the American War of Independence. Courtesy Library of Congress.

daily life in France during this period of the revolution was deeply influenced by war and the concomitant military demands.

The sans-culottes did all in their power to prevent the wearing of any distinctive uniform in the army. They believed that privileged units, such as the grenadiers and infantry, should not be singled out by their special clothes—equality was the rallying cry. Both militants and journalists emphasized the importance of equality in the army. In his newspaper, *L'Ami du Peuple,* on August 14, 1793, Jean-Théophile-Victoire Leclerc suggested that the revolutionary army provide the same pay for commanders, officers, and soldiers, who should all eat the same bread so that differences in rank would not lead to vanity on the part of those who had the better situation.[4]

## THE NATIONAL GUARD

The National Guard was formed by popular mobilization in the early summer of 1789 and was ratified by decree of the Constituent Assembly a few months later, on August 10, inspired by the Great Fear and by the gathering of the king's troops in the vicinity of Paris. Municipal councils were ordered to oversee the creation of National Guard companies. Made up of volunteers, they were created as a defensive force against counterrevolutionary backlash and also served to keep order among the unruly masses. Placed in charge of this body was the popular and liberal marquis de Lafayette.

All over France, the district municipal councils were charged with recruiting, equipping, and organizing the volunteers. On Sunday, June 26, registers were opened at town halls to record the names, ages, professions, and residence of those wishing to join. The frenzied activity went on for several weeks as young men and their families discussed the pros and cons of enrolling and made their decisions.

The recruit supplied his own uniform of royal blue with scarlet and white trimmings, as well as his own weapons. The guard was made up primarily of sons of the bourgeoisie and, at first, only active citizens, those who each year paid the equivalent in taxes of at least three days' work. Many rushed to join. This patriotic gesture posed little threat to their well-being. They could strut around wearing the national cockade on their caps, stop civilians for questioning, and attend the fêtes looking smart in their uniforms. They elected their own officers, and each battalion carried a flag reading on one side "For the People of France" and on the other side "For Liberty or Death."

When little skirmishes, fracases, or street demonstrations occurred in Paris, the National Guard was sent out to quell the disturbance. They were responsible for firing on the crowd in the Champ de Mars, July 17, 1791, killing about 50 people. Most of the time they were idle, spending time in their favorite cafes, where they congregated.

Other cities and towns soon created their own National Guards, especially during the Great Fear of late summer 1789. In the provinces, they were used to parade at local celebrations, show a martial spirit in accordance with the changes taking place in the capital and in the government, and, if required, protect the town officials and local property.

Following the king's attempt to escape the country, in 1791, the National Assembly ordered mobilization of all National Guardsmen in the frontier zones and asked for a further 100,000 Guard volunteers from other regions to mobilize and protect the nation.

When the dispatch calling for volunteers reached the villages of the northern frontier, church bells rang. The National Guard assembled there, bearing arms; police and detachments of regular army blocked the roads; many people barricaded themselves in their houses or fled to the woods— all expecting an invasion of Austrians, which royalist sympathizers had predicted was imminent.

In the west, the danger seemed less threatening, and the recruiting went on in a festive atmosphere. The mayor of one village, for example, went down to the meadow where the townsfolk were dancing (since it was the feast day of the town's patron saint). Beating a drum, he read the mobilization order, exhorting the young men to enlist. They were promised good pay, higher than that of the regular army, a one-year tour of duty, relaxed discipline, holidays, and rapid promotion.[5] Within a few months of the king's attempted flight, the 100,000 had been enrolled. Many could not afford to buy their boots, rifles, and clothes, so collections were taken to help them, while administrators from city to hamlet tried to find money and purchase equipment. Once outfitted, the men were given a little training by former military men, and, with the blessings of constitutional bishops (those who had signed loyalty oaths) and supplied with their new flags and colorful uniforms, the men were sent off toward the frontier, finding a party in every town on the way to welcome them.

The volunteers now included the spectrum of society, from middle-class lawyers, merchants, artisans, priests, and workers to even a few noblemen, but few young farmer peasants answered the call. Taking care of their land was more important than fighting in distant places.

The regular army (or whites) and the volunteer army (the blues) were generally hostile to each other. The regulars considered the volunteers overpaid, inept, poorly trained, badly equipped, and, sometimes, incompetently led. In the opening campaigns against Prussia and Austria, in the summer of 1792, they proved to be correct. The blues were driven back in Belgium, and the fall of the fortress town of Longwy opened the road to Paris. The popular slogan *"la patrie en danger!"* swept the nation, and the sans-culottes joined the army and the National Guard in droves. Forty thousand enlisted in the departments close to the frontier, and another 20,000 were brought from Paris to halt the Prussian advance.[6] The famous battle of Valmy, on September 20, 1792, turned the tide and saved France and the revolution.

Other victories soon followed, leading to the conquest of Belgium by General Dumouriez in the winter of 1792–93. In December, many retired from the volunteer army, as they were entitled to do, despite appeals to their patriotism from the government. On February 1, 1793, France declared war on England, and again the military situation gradually reversed. On February 21, another critical time for France, the regular army and the volunteers were amalgamated. Their previous differences in recruitment, promotion, pay scales, and uniforms were now all standardized into one armed force.

## MOBILIZATION

On August 23, 1793, the Convention ordered a *levée en masse* of the entire French nation. The youth would go to battle, married men would forge arms, and old men were to engage in repairing public buildings and squares of the cities and inspire the young to bravery by preaching unity of the republic and hatred for the monarchy. Women were to stitch tents and uniforms and work in military hospitals, while children were expected to make bandages. State workshops were set up to produce arms for nearly a million men. Everything was subject to requisition, from gold to grain. Even church bells were melted down into cannon. On June 26, 1794, in the decisive battle of Fleurus, the army soundly defeated the Austrians, who were driven from French soil. But there was trouble brewing on the home front: the Girondist citizens of Lyon and other sections of the south over-threw their Jacobin authorities and took up arms against the Convention.

## REVOLUTIONARY ARMY

Organized for the most part in the fall of 1793 in Paris, a new force evolved at the initiative of the popular societies, the most influential of which were the Jacobin clubs. This revolutionary or people's army *(armées révolutionaires)* was not associated with the regular army but consisted of militias formed from ordinary citizens, mostly sans-culottes, to combat counterrevolutionary activities and grain hoarders as bread prices rose and to enforce the policies of the Terror in the provinces. They scoured and despoiled villages for hidden caches of wheat. The largest was the army of Paris, which contained more than 6,000 men of sans-culotte extraction and a mixture of civil servants and ex-soldiers. More than 50 such so-called armies were organized in the provinces, but most numbered under 100 men. They were paid a generous daily wage. Their mission was to enforce the Maximum (price controls on wheat and flour), to supply the urban food markets with grain (often requisitioned from hostile peasants), and to supply the military commissaries of the regular army. Because of the policy of de-Christianization, they also indulged in appropriating parish churches to use as stables and supply depots and destroying the idols. As conflicts with peasants became more common as the local inhabit-ants fought back to protect their crops and their Catholic faith, the Monta-gnard leadership in the Convention decided that these people's armies were causing more trouble than they were worth. They were abolished in December 1793.

## A SOLDIER'S LIFE

There were, of course, some men who preferred the military life, enjoy-ing the glory of belonging to what they considered the finest army in the world. Others found having generally regular meals and pay more desir-able than having to think for themselves as civilians, in spite of the hard and, at times, dangerous life of a soldier.

Recruits spent a little time in the barracks (usually a converted monas-tery or church) learning the basics of warfare before joining their regiment.

On the campaign trail, the soldier passed most of his time in the open, sleeping in tents. Officers might find lodging in the house of a wealthy bourgeois, where they ate well and often had company in bed.

The men almost never changed their clothes and often slept on the same patch of ground for several months. Military life could be extremely monotonous, more so perhaps for those who were illiterate, with the boredom alleviated now and then by card games and gambling and, sometimes, by the intense adrenaline rush of battle, which could result in tremendous slaughter. Tactics of the time included massed musket fire and case shot with cannon rounds at close range, followed by a bayonet charge. For many, the trauma of killing or the threat of being killed changed their lives, and they were never the same after having been in battle.

Long marches from one zone to another in all weather, carrying a rifle, ball, powder, and other necessities such as water and biscuit left soldiers exhausted, hardly able to put one foot ahead of the other; yet rest was out of the question until the new camp was made secure and livable, with pickets posted, latrines dug, and tents erected. Guard duty required the soldier to stand or walk for many hours along the perimeter of the camp, sometimes in freezing weather, blistering winds, or the unpleasant heat of the afternoon sun, and was one of the most onerous duties. At night the sentries struggled constantly between the need to be alert and the overwhelming desire to sleep. Desertions were frequent.

When supplies were slow in arriving or did not come at all, soldiers were often compelled to live off the land and eat whatever they could find. The Convention passed a law in 1793 that included the death penalty for soldiers found guilty of indiscriminate pillage and repeated desertion—a penalty that was sometimes carried out by officers as an example to the rest of the men. Usually, however, a blind eye was turned to pillage on long marches when supplies lagged behind and the men were hungry.[7]

Angry citizens sometimes complained to their mayor about the behavior of soldiers camped in the vicinity or in the villages, where drunkenness and attacks on peasants were rampant while the soldiers were stealing food. Theft and even rape were all too often considered by soldiers to be part of their unofficial wages.

Efforts to supply the army were not wanting. From 1793 on, with the nation under arms, the French people were nearly permanently in a state of requisition. The wealthy were forced to loan money to the government, bells were taken from the churches, and the peasants had to provide horses, mules, and donkeys. Everything was nationalized. In Paris, workshops hammered out bullets and rifles and cast cannons. People were told to search in their cellars and outhouses for saltpeter, which was needed to make gunpowder.[8]

Behind every regiment stretched a lengthy line of women. Some were washerwomen, some provided food and drink for the soldier with a few coins in his pocket to pay for them, some were wives who on occasion gave birth along the route, and others were prostitutes, whose numbers swelled when the pay arrived. Most women did not shun battle, and they were there in the heat of the fight, giving a sip of brandy here or an encouraging word there. They, too, lived a difficult and precarious existence.

## WOMEN IN THE MILITARY

Some women were determined to do what was then considered a man's job, and at least 40 women and perhaps many more donned the uniform and went off to fight in the army. When some soldiers were identified as women, a decree of April 30, 1793, ordered all women home from the ranks. This order was widely ignored, and some women managed to continue without being found out. Some were praised for their bravery even after they were identified, and one fought on even when her husband perished in the battle beside her. Citizenness Favre was captured by the enemy and taken to the rear, where prisoners were slaughtered by sword cuts to save gunpowder. When her turn came, her clothes were ripped off, and she was revealed as a woman. Fortunately for her, the captain commanding the unit of Prussian light cavalry rescued her from his men. Later, back in France, she appeared before the Convention to complain on behalf of the army about poor equipment, a lack of arms and boots, and the incompetence of the high command. Her criticisms were similar to those of other soldiers, who were not in a position to voice their views.[9]

## MEDICAL SERVICES

With France at war with most of Europe and employing huge conscript armies to defend its revolution, French soldiers fought bloody battles and suffered enormous casualties. Young men had a good chance of being killed, severely maimed, or dying of infected wounds. Disease was a constant threat to men living in close quarters. Without good knowledge of medical treatment, physicians employed drugs in combination, often in excessive amounts, and resorted to harmful procedures such as bleeding, purging, and sweating to treat fever.

Medical provisions were always in short supply, and troops could expect nothing more than the most elementary care for wounds and illnesses and nothing at all for traumatic mental disorders. Proper hospitals, antiseptics, and anesthetics were then not available, and there was only alcohol to help lessen the pain. Every regiment had a surgeon with a few assistants, and the usual treatment for a severe leg or arm wound was amputation before gangrene set in.

Much of the French military medical service had fallen on hard times during the revolution; although a number of military hospitals had been built on the northern frontier during the old regime, many were no longer usable. Those that were usable were not sufficient for the large number of casualties, and nearby homes were often commandeered to billet the patients.

On November 19, 1793, on a visit to Strasbourg, Saint-Just was appalled by the terrible conditions in the hospitals there. He ordered the municipality to find 2,000 more beds in the next 24 hours, and they were rounded up from wealthy households.

The medical command was divided between a physician-in-chief, Jean-François Coste, and a surgeon-in-chief, Pierre-François Percy. Both were career medical officers. Surgeons treated wounds by incising them and feeling around with their fingers for the musket ball or shell fragments, which they pulled out; they then sewed the patient back up. As with other wars, it was not the wounds that took the greatest toll; it was the ensuing infection.

Coste and his colleagues tried, with little success, to follow the teaching of John Pringle and others on camp diseases and hospital sanitation.[10] No surgery was done on the battlefield. Sick and lightly wounded soldiers were simply left there to fend as best they could until the fighting was over, at which time they could be collected and evacuated. This might mean a wait of three or four days. The more seriously wounded were taken by their fellows to a collection point, where they remained until they were loaded into large, cumbersome wagons that were the only ambulances available. There were never enough of these wagons, and they were usually kept far from the battle zone. The men would then be transported to a military hospital behind the lines, often a full day's journey of three or four miles. The miserable, jarring passage was often fatal for the gravely wounded, who ended up at the cemetery instead of the hospital.

The evacuation process resulted in the loss of many strong, healthy men, since it required about six soldiers to carry one injured man, his weapon, and his equipment from the battlefield. The wounded might be taken on an improvised litter made of guns, branches, or coats or by farmers' carts pressed into service.

Percy, the chief surgeon, attempted to address the problem by organizing litter bearers to work on the battlefield to bring in the wounded. Because of the misery he observed, Percy was eager to get the men out as quickly as possible. In 1792, he wrote:

In retreat before the enemy there is no more frightful a spectacle than the evacuation of mutilated soldiers on big wagons; each jolt brings the most piercing cries. They have to suffer from rain, from suffocating heat or freezing cold and often do not have aid of food of any sort. Death would be a favor and we have often heard them begging it as a gift from heaven.

It was another French surgeon, Dominique-Jean Larrey, who actually developed a system of rapid evacuation. Larrey joined the French army in

1792 and served in northern France. Recognizing the need to get wounded soldiers off the fields of battle as soon as possible, as well as to be able to conduct some treatment on the battlefield itself, he developed several new types of horse-drawn carriages, which he called "flying ambulances," that were constructed especially for wounded men.

Delayed amputation had been the rule, but military surgeons noted that the wounded bled more and had a great deal more pain as their muscles became rigid, making amputation more difficult. Gangrene, sepsis, and death were more common in patients who were evacuated to the rear with untreated wounds. Larrey noted that soon after being wounded, when a patient was in neurogenic shock, the bleeding was not as great, the muscles were more relaxed, the limb was numb from bruised nerves, and the pain of amputation and the agony of the saw were much reduced. In addition, he realized that if the injury was cleaned and surgically dressed, evacuation would be more comfortable and infection less likely.

Slowly, a better system was developed in which lighter, faster, and more comfortable carriages were kept closer to the fighting, with first-aid kits attached. On the basis of his observations, Larrey established new surgical guidelines. Immediate amputation was indicated if:

a.  The limb was shattered or the joints smashed.

b.  Small bones, joints, and nerves were all broken up.

c.  There was too much muscle tissue damage or major arteries were missing, even if the bone or joint was sound.

He stopped the use of liniments and ointments, ordered that wounds be washed only with water, and required that, if amputation was required, the stump was to be dressed with new adhesive bandages so that the wound could drain.

Larrey's surgical skills became so efficient that he was able to sever a leg in one minute, an arm in 17 seconds. He gave much of the credit for saving lives to his ambulances, which allowed wounds to be dressed first on the battlefield and the wounded to be quickly evacuated afterwards.

Those who had been wounded in the war had first claim on the resources of the state. Further, pensions for invalid veterans were increased, with the lowest-ranked being given the same as an officer. Needy families of military men were promised more help, and war widows were promised increased pensions and a less cumbersome way to apply for them, under the terms of a law passed June 1, 1794.[11] The promises to the wounded veterans and their families sounded impressive, but everything was massively underfunded and months in arrears. In addition, resistance to pensions for those wounded in war and for war widows came from all quarters. All funding was finally suspended, a bitter shock to many of the sufferers.

## AVOIDANCE OF DRAFT, AND DESERTIONS

Conscription first became mandatory on February 14, 1793, and was extended in August by the mass callup. By 1794, the republic theoretically had more than a million men under arms—an exceptional number for the times. Conscription was not popular in France, and placards and graffiti immediately appeared everywhere crying out against it. In the west, the compulsory enrollment helped provoke massive uprisings, especially in the countryside. The 1790s were difficult for the country's lower-class youth. While politicians dreamed of liberating Europe from oppressive monarchies, their lofty ambitions were not shared by those who were called upon to do the fighting. The years of heavy callup for the army were the spring of 1793 and 1795 (and, later, 1808 and 1810), and in many village communities where the inhabitants were deeply attached to the soil, there was no tradition of military service. Sowing seeds and harvesting the crop were more important than marching across Europe to fight for abstract concepts like freedom and liberty. For peasant families, anywhere away from their immediate environment was generally considered foreign, a place where things were strange and of little consequence for their own daily lives. The local community was often all the peasants knew or wanted to know, and their resistance to recruitment took a variety of forms.

Many conscripts did not appear at the recruiting stations. A useful subterfuge was for an eligible son to use the documents of a younger dead brother to conceal his age or even for parents to send a younger child in place of an older brother, knowing he would be turned down for failing to measure up to the height requirement.

Since only bachelors were expected to serve, marriage was one way out of military service, and records show that the stratagem of a convenient marriage was often used. There was a large increase in marriages hastily contracted during times of callup. While the government could do nothing about it, officials were probably not surprised when they found that a potential conscript of 20 had married a woman of 74. The revolutionary laws permitted divorce. Not until 1808 did a new law on marriage stipulate that a recruit had to prove at least three months of marriage before he could be considered ineligible for military service. Marriage certificates were often falsified, however. There were other methods of avoiding the draft; some men forged birth certificates to appear younger, sons mysteriously "passed away," and young men chopped or shot off trigger fingers. Town representatives from the mayor down in many places helped falsify medical documents for their local men and sometimes even hid them in their houses.[12] If the family of a dissenter had the money, a medical doctor might prescribe a concoction hat would produce high fever and difficulty in breathing for a short period of time so that the recruit would be rejected as unfit for military duty.[13]

When looking for deserters in the countryside, the police or soldiers often ran into a wall of silence as the people of the village protected their sons and even resorted to violence to do so. Desertion was rampant. In March 1795, the country had 1.1 million men enrolled in the army, but probably not more than half that number were actually under arms as they were supposed to be.[14] Few in rural France considered it a crime to desert or to find some other way out of military service. While pamphlets extolled the virtues of the army, with the benefits of pay and regular food, and the chance to participate in the glorious fight to preserve liberty and the revolution while freeing others still under the yoke of despotism, these claims made little impact on young rural men. There was always someone in the village or a stranger passing through who had been to war and knew what the government propaganda failed to say. Booty, adventure, and glory were set against the realities of war—intestines hanging out from a stomach ripped open by an enemy bayonet, blindness and burns suffered in an explosion, shattered bones from musket shot; the real possibility of lying wounded on a battlefield for days before the end finally came, loss of a leg, an arm, or both to gangrene, and amputation that could be expected even from lesser wounds. Where was the glory here?

Desertion in the 1790s did not always mean a life on the run; often young men simply returned to their villages, where friends and neighbors would welcome the runaway and protect him. Officials of small localities felt more loyalty to the deserter than they did to the government in Paris. Often local mayors failed to submit lists of conscripts to the government as they were legally required to do. Even larger towns in the Gironde failed to comply with the law.[15] Male villagers and relatives of deserters were known to attack soldiers or police who came to arrest the runaway.

Reacting to this, the government billeted soldiers in the family home of a deserter, causing a burden on the family and inhabitants until the man gave himself up. The soldiers, generally drunk, noisy, and prone to harassing the women, also sometimes made the villagers demand that the deserter give himself up. In the area of the Tarn, however, locals refused to feed the soldiers, motivating the military to withdraw rather than face the prospect of sending in food for their men. On some occasions, entire households left their cottages, joining their sons or brothers in the hills, rather than submit to what they considered to be arbitrary injustice.[16]

In principle, desertion could be punished by death after 1793, but this was not put into practice. The death penalty was reserved for those who deserted to the enemy and fought against France.

## LETTERS FROM SOLDIERS

Soldiers' memoirs and letters home cast a little more light on what life was like in the army.[17] Sergeant Friscasse, son of a gardener who had already enlisted, signed up at age 19 on August 24, 1792, in the first regiment of the Haute-Marne. He seems to have spent much of his time in arms drill and marching. Not until September 12, 1793, did he see his first action while engaged in the defense of Mauburg. French troops defending the city suffered hardship from hunger, since the enemy had taken or destroyed all the grain. There were no provisions in the town, and the surrounding countryside was devoid of food sources. The water, drawn from ditches close to the latrines, was foul, and many suffered from typhoid fever. Wine was scarce, and life was extremely tedious. Later, his regiment moved on to winter quarters in other towns, always close to the enemy. Marching and boredom seem to have been an integral part of a soldier's life, interspersed with physical contact with the enemy. Sergeant Friscasse, however, occupied some of his time writing descriptions of the places he was stationed.

Another young man, Xavier Vernère, started out with a miserable life that began to improve when, at age 14, he walked right across France to Rochefort, where an uncle helped him enlist in the naval cadets. Having come down with a fever, however, he was unable to sail to India with the rest of the cadets of his school, and the navy now did not want him. In 1790, he made his way to Tours to another uncle, a sergeant-major in the Anjou regiment. Here he learned a little about life in the army. He followed the regiment to St. Malo and eventually was able to join. His uncle was promoted to second lieutenant, and Xavier, now 16, was to serve under him.

War had been declared, and the supplemented Anjou regiment was ordered to join the army in the north. On July 15, 1792, the division was camped on the plain of St. Denis, near Paris. The soldiers were forbidden to enter the city, but, climbing up the hill of Montmartre, Xavier and his companions could see the entire city. The temptation was too great. They crossed the barrier and entered Paris. The experience was exhilarating: the boulevards, the Place Louis XV, the Seine and its bridges, the Legislative Assembly, and especially the Palais Royal were astonishing sights for country boys.

Orders were now changed, and the division left St. Denis, not for the north but instead to join the army of the Rhine, going via Nancy and Lunéville. Here Xavier met a young lady at the house where he was lodging, and they spent many hours together talking in the garden. The following morning, at sunup, the troops were buckling on their packs, preparing to leave for the next stage of their march, when the young woman came to wish Xavier goodbye. They slipped off together to hide in a doorway, Xavier ignoring the demands of the army. Their passionate embraces were interrupted by an officer, who ordered the young man to join his troop. In spite of looking longingly back at the town where he had left behind his new love, Xavier soon found the realities of war occupying his thoughts as the troop reached Haguenau. Carts transporting the wounded to the rear passed regularly, the cracks between the floor planks dripping blood onto the road. The lines were reached, but no attack from either side was in the offing, and the French troops spent the winter encamped near Rudesheim and Bingen, on the Rhine. Xavier was greatly delighted when he was promoted to quartermaster-sergeant and confessed that no Marshal of France

ever received his bâton with greater pride than I felt when I put the silver galoons on my sleeve. Ideas above my station fired my mind and I fatuously calculated that, at seventeen and a half, I had a rank which raised me well above nine-tenths of the entire army.[18]

Xavier survived and eventually became a Colonel of the Empire under Napoleon.

Born in 1770 at Nancy to well-off farmers, Gabriel Noël received a good education. Having volunteered for the army, he was sent to the town of Sierck, in Germany. He found it a tiresome, wretched hole and spent his time studying German and reading. From there the troop moved on to another German-speaking village in Lorraine that was worse. He noted that they had two beds for five men and wrote, "Fate has decided that I should be in the one containing three persons. Our beds are made of straw with a sheet spread over it." On top of the sheet was a feather quilt. But, he adds, "what makes it even less inviting is that every detachment in France seems to have used our sheets." He mentioned that the bugs were rampant, that he slept in his clothes (apart from his overcoat), and that he had difficulty communicating with the Germans.

Another volunteer, Etienne Gaury, quartered at Fort Vauban during the early months of 1793, used to march along the bank of the Rhine with the band playing in view of the enemy. He comments that they did not shoot at them; had it been the other way around, the French would certainly have done so. Life for Etienne was not too unpleasant except for two things: high prices and the stupidity of the inhabitants, whom he found brutish and coarse. Nor did Etienne like the food. Pork, vegetables, and potatoes were in abundance, but, he complained that the staples of the French soldier, wine and bread, were too expensive.

Other letters from soldiers record this common complaint. They detested the beer drunk by the locals and longed for a good bottle of wine or brandy from home.

Such was the case also in the south. On February 4, 1795, Captain Gabriel Auvrey, stationed at Mauberge, received a letter from his two brothers who were at Fort l'Aiguille, near Toulon, complaining that everything was too costly: 20 sous for a bottle of wine that five months before had cost 5, and a loaf of bread cost 3 livres. They reported that cloth also was too expensive for them to buy. "To make a pair of trousers and a waistcoat of Nankeen or Siamese calico you have to put down seventy-five livres." As the war continued, troops complained more and more of the shortage of food and rising prices.

## *ÉMIGRÉ* ARMIES

The defection of numerous officers from the regular army and from France led to the formation of an *émigré* army, the first of which was created in Baden in September 1790. Called the Black Legion, it was commanded by the younger brother of Mirabeau. This unit was absorbed into the army led by the counts of Provence and Artois—brothers of the king—who had their headquarters at Koblenz. Other units were formed by the prince of Condé and by the duke of Bourbon. The three forces reached their maximum strength of nearly 25,000 by the summer of 1792. They were financed, in part, by the courts of Spain, Austria, and Prussia, but the funds were never adequate. A major problem was the lack of rank and file to serve under the aristocrats, who all insisted on being officers. The result was companies of gentlemen who demanded the same pay that they had received in the French royal army, a bone of contention with the donor countries. Insolent and irresponsible behavior reduced their effectiveness as a fighting force. For example, some 200 *émigrés* were dismissed for pillage in the winter of 1791.

The *émigrés* gave advice to the duke of Brunswick, commander of the Austro-Prussian armies, that was pure wishful thinking. They drafted a manifest that was issued by the duke on July 25, 1792, threatening the people of Paris. This only strengthened Parisians' resolve to fight and precipitated the overthrow of the monarchy two weeks later. They also petitioned the duke to allow them to spearhead the assault on France, assuring him that they would have the full support of the peasantry and would be able to rally loyal regiments of the French frontline army to their cause. In the summer of 1792, they invaded France, failing in even the simplest missions, such as the capture of the small town of Thionville. Instead of attracting popular support, they alienated the peasantry, arousing determined resistance and increased national patriotism.

The haughty *émigrés* refused to follow orders, and, on one occasion, Brunswick put the prince of Condé under arrest for insubordination. They proved so incompetent that the emperor Francis II ordered the dissolution of their army.[19] By the end of 1792, only 5,000 men remained in the army of Condé.

## AFTER THE REVOLUTION

A law of September 5, 1798, enabled some young men to buy their way out of conscription by paying a replacement, and many did. Those who did fight in the Revolutionary Wars, which for many stretched into the Napoleonic Wars, were disillusioned and resentful. The alien and distant government and its laws had made an unwelcome intrusion into their lives in villages where there was little or no sentiment of nationalism. Many who returned after the wars found the local economy in worse shape than when they left, and their long absences had been detrimental to the upkeep of the land, buildings, crops, and livestock. Those who came back with disabilities, mental and physical, and unable to work joined the destitute. Most had spent what would have been the best years of their lives in military uniforms and regarded the experience with bitterness, well aware that they had missed the chance to perhaps acquire some land and build a modest life for themselves and raise a family. Their youth had been wasted serving their country, while others with money had evaded that obligation. Everyone knew that the system of conscription was grossly unfair. The high rate of desertions also fed the increasing threat of banditry.

In the words of one ex-soldier,

Six or seven years of lost youth … and all that because we had bad luck in the lottery and that we lacked 3,000 francs to pay for a replacement.[20]

## THE NAVY

Like the army, the ranks of officers were theoretically restricted to those of noble birth, but most nobles were not interested in the navy, preferring not to risk the rigors of the sea. Competition for places in the navy was

A French shipyard ca. 1774. The hull of a new ship under construction can be seen in the background. In the foreground is a dry dock into which the ship will later be moved and floated. The large building is where the head shipwright oversees all the work.

thus much less keen than that in the army, even though there was no purchase price—at least for ranks below that of admiral. In times of shortage, officers had to be selected from commoners.

There was a type of naval conscription according to which men under 60 years of age who lived in coastal districts or along navigable rivers had to register in the naval reserve if they had any experience afloat. They also had to be available for call-up in times of crisis. The system was as unpopular with fishermen and bargemen as was the militia lottery with the peasants.

A good deal of money was spent on the navy, for Louis XVI wanted to keep France a strong sea power. Building new frigates and ships of the line was not cheap, and a new naval harbor under construction at Cherbourg, employing 3,000 men just before the Revolution, played its part in the huge and growing deficit.[21]

## NOTES

1. Behrens, 119.
2. Garrioch, 310.
3. Lewis (1972), 140–41.
4. Soboul, 229.
5. Lewis (1972), 143.
6. Ibid., 144–45.
7. The city of Rome was unnecessarily sacked by French troops in February 1798, but General Massena, the French commander, took no action against the soldiers. His own loot was said to be worth well over 2 million francs.
8. Lewis (1972), 158.
9. Pernoud/Flaissier, 284–85; Andress (2006), 158–59.
10. Pringle was an English physician general (1707–1782). He is known as the founder of modern military medicine for his reforms in army hospital and camp sanitation; he recognized the various forms of dysentery as one disease and coined the term "influenza."
11. Hufton, 78.
12. Forrest, 157.
13. Ibid., 158.
14. Lewis (1972), 152.
15. Forrest, 156–57.
16. Ibid., 162.
17. For the following and other letters, see Robiquet, chapter 19, 161ff.
18. Ibid., 168.
19. Francis II was the last Holy Roman emperor (1792–1806).
20. Quoted in Forrest, 163.
21. Doyle, 32.

# 14

# LAW AND ORDER

The administration of justice in prerevolutionary times was "partial, venal, infamous" in the words of Arthur Young.[1] It was generally agreed that there was no such thing in France as a fair and impartial verdict. In every case that came before the court, judges favored the party that had bought them off.

In instances of land dispute, a party in the argument might also be one of the several dozen judges of the court, all of whom had bought their high positions. To counterbalance control in the provinces by the local nobility and the 13 local parlements, the crown sent out intendants to each area to enforce royal authority (especially taxation), and these officials often came into conflict with the local courts and aristocracy.

The 13 regional parlements were judicial bodies of appeal; they also were supposed to register royal edicts, although they sometimes did also make laws. They might defy the king by refusing to register his edicts, in which case the king could issue a *lit de justice,* forcing registration. If this failed, he could exile the parlement to a provincial town where its voice would be diminished, as Louis XVI did to the powerful parlement of Paris in 1787 when it refused to register a new land tax. The members became heroes to the people for defying the despotic king, who backed down, and the parlement returned to Paris. It soon lost its popularity at the beginning of the revolution when it opposed both the doubling of the number of members of the Third Estate and voting by head in the Estates-General. All the parlements played little or no role in the early months of the revolution and were abolished by law on September 6, 1790.

A Revolutionary Committee in session. Bibliothèque Nationale de France.

The royal system of justice contained about 400 provincial (or *bailliage*) courts.[2] In the towns there were also municipal courts, while throughout the countryside there were thousands of seigneurial and ecclesiastical courts. The king still presided over all justice, but the further one got from Versailles, the less influence he had, since royal demands could take weeks to reach all corners of the country.

## CRIMES AND THE FRINGE SOCIETY

The old regime wanted social stability and hierarchy, but absolute order had not been attained. There were riots from time to time in the cities and insurrections among the peasants in the countryside. There was also a fair amount of crime in the streets of the larger towns, where underworld vagrants, thieves, and other marginal people posed a threat to established society. Strict regulations were set out to curb their habits and to produce order, backed by the police and, if necessary, the army. State control over workers' guilds (in theory if not so much in practice) and the regulation of the wet-nursing trade and of prostitutes, among others, were attempts to bring about order. Paris police inspectors responsible for keeping a check on criminals operated a network of secret agents generally recruited from the criminal class itself. The police were feared for their arbitrary capability to snatch people off the street and, in the course of a few minutes, confine them to a prison cell.

Physical pain formed a large part of the justice system. A period in the pillory, which entailed great discomfort and public abuse, was in itself unpleasant enough, but this might be followed by routine whippings and even branding. A weekly occurrence in major cities, hanging of criminals for aggravated crimes was a spectator sport. Prior to death, the condemned person was subject to excruciating pain caused by tortures such as the breaking of all four limbs with an iron bar, and the hanging itself was a prolonged ordeal of strangulation.

## *LETTRES DE CACHET* AND LAW OF SUSPECTS

Introduced about the middle of the eighteenth century, the *lettres de cachet* were anathema to the people. By royal decree, anyone could be arrested and imprisoned without trial for an indefinite period of time. A husband could have his wife incarcerated if he even suspected her of infidelity. Unruly or uncontrollable sons and daughters might go to prison at the request of their parents. Family honor was important, and the police and government were ready to help protect it. Under Louis XVI, some 14,000 *lettres de cachet* were issued.[3] The king simply signed the forms and had them sent to the police or ministers who had requested them; these officials then filled in the name of the person to be arrested.

This administrative arrest posed a continuous threat to everyone, even nobles such as the duke of Orléans, who, by such a letter, was exiled for disagreeing with the king. The system of *lettres de cachet,* which promoted arbitrary arrest, was often condemned in the *cahiers* by members of the Third Estate as an abuse of the people. The use of the *lettres* was abolished by the Estates-General except in cases of sedition and family delinquency.[4]

One of the most draconian laws for the French people, enacted on September 17, 1793, was the Law of Suspects, which formed the underlying code of the Terror by giving the Committee of Public Safety broad powers of arrest and punishment over the masses of humanity. It also gave wide-ranging powers to local revolutionary committees. The Surveillance Committees that had been constituted according to a law of March 21, 1793, were responsible for drawing up the lists of suspects and for issuing arrest warrants.

The proof necessary to convict the enemies of the people is every kind of evidence, either material or moral or verbal or written.... Every citizen has the right to seize conspirators and counterrevolutionaries and to arraign them before magistrates. He is required to denounce them when he knows of them. Law of 22 Prairial Year II (June 10, 1794)

Anyone who had by speeches, writings, associations and conduct shown himself or herself hostile to the revolution was considered suspect and subject to arrest. This standard applied to anyone who appeared to favor monarchy or federation, as well as to those who were unable to prove their means of livelihood; those who could not demonstrate that they had fulfilled their civil duties; and those who had been refused a certificate of civil loyalty, an official document vouching for the bearer's civic virtue. The surveillance committees throughout the country, generally under the guidance of the Jacobin clubs, were responsible in overseeing the issuance of arrest warrants signed by six citizens in good standing.

Any public official who had been stripped of his post by the National Convention, former members of the nobility or clergy who had not consistently demonstrated devotion to the revolution, and all *émigrés* were on the list of suspects. A person could be challenged for the most trivial of reasons, such as addressing someone as *monsieur* instead of "citizen" or employing the *vous*, the polite form of "you," instead of the familiar *tu*. A neighbor could report another neighbor for making a derogatory statement about the government, whether he had done so or not, for reasons of spite or jealousy, and an arrest warrant would be issued. Under these extreme, harsh conditions, no one was safe from imprisonment and even death, yet few dared complain.

## POLICING TOWN AND COUNTRY

Police informers and spies attended nearly all political meetings, watched over the ports, and pretended to be inmates in the prisons in order to keep an eye on other prisoners. The Committee of General Security gave the Jacobin government the most effective police service in the history of the country. The work of the Revolutionary Tribunal was watched over by Fouquier-Tinville, the public prosecutor, a man totally lacking in compassion. He developed the technique of condemning prisoners to the guillotine in batches; innocent or guilty, all stood together in the dock and received the same sentence of death.

The detention centers were suspected bastions of conspiracy against the government. During the Terror, they were overcrowded, and the prisoners were in constant danger of *les moutons* (the sheep), that is, government secret agents who were quick to report anything suspicious.[5] The sansculottes never wearied of conjuring up visions of plots hatched in the prisons.

Executions with drums rolling were a carryover from the old regime, but what was now different was the revolutionary rhetoric, the uniforms, and the scale of the executions. In Lyon, for example, Fouché and Collot d'Herbois, perhaps finding the guillotine too slow, ordered hundreds of victims to line up before open graves and dispatched them with cannonshot. Dead or alive, the bodies were covered over. Carrier, at Nantes, maybe short of gunpowder, drowned 2,000 prisoners, many of whom were priests, in the Loire River.[6]

In the vast countryside, policing was less well organized than in the cities. Unlike in Paris, where the head of the police was a high government official, in the provincial towns he and his men were only a part of the municipality and were generally short of money. The national network of mounted police, the *maréchausée*, a kind of highway patrol, was thinly spread, and four or five men had to cover hundreds of square miles. A report shows that, in the 22 years between 1768 and 1790, the *maréchausée* detained some 230,000 individuals in government workhouses.[7] They were not prepared to handle mass civil disorder, however. The king could, of course, call upon the army from the local garrisons to quell disturbances in the countryside, but, as the government realized, sending troops against the population too often would only cause lingering resentment and further problems.

Most men and women incarcerated in French prisons before the revolution were small-time thieves; in many cases, their crimes had been motivated by desperation. A piece of fruit stolen from the market, some clothes ripped from a drying line, an armful of firewood taken from its owner, an attempt at pickpocketing among an urban crowd at a fair or festival were all offenses that could lead to the whipping post, prison, or even an appointment with the hangman.

Violent crimes were probably no less frequent but often were not subject to judicial punishment. Up to and into the period of the revolution, domestic servants, children, and apprentices could be physically or mentally punished for any perceived misconduct. Wives were subject to abuse, verbal or physical, by their husbands, who acted with no fear of legal retribution.

Among the noble classes, male servants could be sent to inflict pain, usually by beating someone who might have insulted a member of the family. The law and the force of arms in the country were on the side of the seigneur. His right and that of his agents and even his servants to go around armed rendered the unarmed peasantry impotent. The laws to keep the peasant disarmed were designed to maintain the power of the nobility, as well as to protect its hunting monopoly. Before the revolution, there were occasional sweeps through the countryside by soldiers and mounted police, who scoured the areas for illegal arms. There were a few places, such as eastern Languedoc, far from Versailles and Paris, where armed peasants flouted authority and the seigneurs were the ones reluctant to leave their châteaux.[8]

## DAILY LIFE IN PRISON

Under the old regime, most prisons were abominable places. The poor, especially, could not pay the price to the warders for the few available luxuries and thus were obliged to sleep on filthy straw mattresses in rat-infested cells. The threat of disease was always present. As usual, prisoners with money were treated especially well.

Under the Terror, conditions grew worse because of the overcrowding. The old-regime prison, the Conciergerie, on the Ile de la Cité appears to have been one of the worst. Smelling of ordure and disease, plagued by rats, it was an appalling place where residents slept on the floor in the same spot where they had to relieve themselves. Those who could afford the outrageous prices for a bed were more comfortable, and the money was a source of revenue for the Revolutionary Tribunal, which supplied the beds. Perhaps as bad as anything was the trauma of waiting each day for the roll call of those destined to see the public prosecutor, with small chance of being found innocent, or of those already destined for the guillotine.

There were about 50 prisons in Paris during the Terror, many of which were converted monasteries, convents, schools, or former poorhouse prisons such as *Salpêtrière* and *Bicêtre*. Some held only a score or so of inmates, but others, such as the Conciergerie, held about 600 in 1793.[9]

The former monasteries of Paris that had been transformed into jails lacked the security found in other institutions built for the purpose of housing prisoners. The inmates were relatively free to wander around and socialize with each other. They lacked beds but were allowed to bring their own. Some brought in entire bedroom suites. Windows without bars and doors without locks made incarceration more tolerable. Mail and packages were not censored or even opened, and food could be sent in to be cooked on portable stoves placed in the corridors for the purpose. Games such as chess and cards were organized, and there were ballgames in the courtyard. Poets wrote, painters sketched and applied their brushes. It was not unknown for children to share a cell with their parents and to keep pets. The previous home of the Ursine nuns housed the actors of the *Comédie Française* who had been confined for playing emperors, kings, queens, marquises, and other members of the aristocracy on stage. The duke of Orléans, while confined in the prison of the *Abbaye*, was able to order in oysters and white wine for his final meal. On one occasion, the fanatical gatekeeper at *Les Recollets* prison insisted that the crowns on the heads of the kings and queens in a chess set be broken off before he would allow the pieces into the prison area.[10]

In some places, men and women were not strictly segregated, and sexual liaisons were not unusual. If a woman was or became pregnant, she was allowed, at least, a stay of execution. The Conciergerie prison was the staging ground for those on their way to meet the prosecutor, as well as the depository for those already convicted. It was here that the condemned awaited the tumbrels to take them on their last journey, and it was here that Marie-Antoinette awaited her appointment with the Revolutionary Tribunal. The hatred of the high nobility knew no limits. On the same day that the queen entered the prison, the Commune sent her eight-year-old son a toy guillotine.[11]

## VAGABONDS

Many honest citizens believed that jobs were available and that vagabondage was the result of an unwillingness to work. Some thought that beggars, rural or urban, had neither morals nor religion and were all potentially thieves and assassins. This belief was tot always unfounded. If handouts were not forthcoming in a village, derelicts passing through might try extortion by threatening arson.

Initiatives were put in place in 1768 in which the *maréchausée* were issued new orders to arrest those who had not worked for six months in a profession or trade and who had no property or position to help them subsist and no one worthy of trust to vouch for their respectability. Individuals caught in these circumstances received three years at hard labor or in the royal galleys, which meant, in effect, imprisonment in a royal naval base, since men were no longer chained to the oar.

A network of state-controlled institutions, *Dépots de Mendicité*, was established to house the indigent in each of the 32 prerevolutionary administrative districts. Throughout the years heading into the revolution, the police continued their policy of detaining socially marginal people.

Vagabondage often led to brigandage. The Great Fear was inspired by the threat of hundreds of beggars who banded together in gangs to raid, loot, and ravish communities. Later, the Revolutionary Army, sent out from Paris to police the gathering of food for Parisians, gave brigands an opportunity. The basin around Paris had been the home of robber bands throughout the eighteenth century. Now they could plunder anonymously wearing the revolutionary uniform of the army. In October 1793, at Corbeil, a gang of 25 thieves robbed isolated farms at gunpoint.[12]

## ARMY DESERTERS

Bands of brigands were augmented by deserters from the army. Worn down and disillusioned by long service, many soldiers drifted away from their units. Some were reintegrated into their home villages, but this was not possible for everyone under threat of arrest for desertion. For these people, there was little alternative but to take up a life of crime on the road that also sometimes had political overtones. Throughout the last decade of the eighteenth century, individuals and groups created severe local problems by attacking property and persons. Buildings that held administrative documents were targets for arsonists seeking to destroy birth records, which were used for conscription.

Violent crime increased dramatically after 1789. The near-collapse of public welfare and the many new military deserters, in conjunction with

Brigands on the rampage, plundering an inn. Bibliothèque Nationale de France.

the thousands of unemployed, greatly inflated the number of thieves and bandits. Some of these pillaged the state services such as mail coaches, while others raided granaries to eat or sell the contents. Blackmail and extortion were common. Farmers and their wives were sometimes tortured by having their feet roasted over an open fire by thieves trying to force them to reveal their cache of hidden stores and valuables.

In the west, armed gangs of deserters from the Vendée gathered. In the southeast, gangs of counterrevolutionary brigands were reinforced by army deserters. Some of the bands grew quite large, numbering more than 60 men, and ranged the countryside at will between the Pas-de-Calais and Belgium.

Another group that menaced the population in the Beauce, south of Paris, was not disbanded until 1799. In this case, about 120 people, 38 of whom were women, were charged with 95 crimes in the year 1796–1797. Children as young as 10 had been recruited to spy out likely targets. Among this motley crew, most were from rural society, some were military deserters, and some had mutilations and deformities. Some walked with canes or crutches. To this gang, the *Band d'Orgères,* were attributed some 75 murders. They sometimes camped in wooded areas and operated by night, but more often they slept in country inns and ate well on their stolen spoils. They were also charged with killing entire households in isolated farms before sitting down to eat the victims' dinner. Drunken entertainment among the corpses followed. Further, they were prone to killing each other. Disobedience or failure on some mission might result in an individual's murder; a woman's refusal of sex to a male leader could and sometimes did result in her demise.

Smaller gangs, too, kept entire villages on edge and in some cases mixed their robberies with outright vandalism. In the Vosges, a farmhouse door was smashed in one afternoon, the house robbed, and all the crockery and windows broken; the thieves then cooked a meal with the provisions available, eating it at leisure, and walked away with all the valuables they could find. Villagers were too afraid to attempt retaliation against bandits, and these kinds of assaults paralyzed whole towns, villages, and hamlets, where any passing stranger was treated with the utmost suspicion.

When the centralized power of the Terror was formally abolished, in April 1795, the National Guard again took up its original duties of protecting property. In December 1795, the government in Paris empowered itself to send agents to all towns of fewer than 5,000 people and created a Ministry of General Police. Military action sometimes put whole departments under martial law. Some of the most lawless areas then were pacified. Nevertheless, the Directory continued to be faced with gangs of royalist rebels in the Haute-Garonne region and in the Atlantic western provinces.[13]

## HOMOSEXUALITY

The church considered sexual acts that were not specifically to procreate a mortal sin. There should be no sex before marriage, the sole purpose of which was to have children. Anything else, homosexuality or masturbation, was strongly denounced as a sin against God and nature. On the other hand, the philosophers believed that anyone who had cast aside the burdens imposed by the church, including restrictions on sexual activity such as abstention or repression, had become enlightened; hence, homosexuality was known as *le crime des philosophes*. Many rationalist and humanist philosophers who discussed such matters as sodomy considered it to be a depraved practice, however.

It seems that homosexuality and transvestitism were not uncommon, especially among the upper classes. In the 1780s, a police register in Paris recorded the arrest of several hundred men from every social level who had been found either in homosexual acts or in places that homosexuals were known to frequent, as well as others who made their preferences obvious by wearing certain kinds of clothes or hairstyles. The reports mention male prostitution for cash and parties and other gatherings where homosexuals could meet people of like mind, as well as sincere relationships between men. Harassment by the police was common. Anyone identified as homosexual or lesbian could face the death penalty by burning if the case was pursued. Most such cases never saw the inside of a courtroom, but if a case did go to court, exile or a short stay in prison was generally the result. The marquis de Condorcet, who was elected to the Legislative Assembly and who was known as the last of the philosophers, argued that the base vice of sodomy should not be a criminal offense since it violated no man's rights. Because court cases were few, the extent of homosexuality may never be known. Those that were prosecuted usually involved transvestite dress or women who had tried to pass as men.

During the revolution, the Constituent Assembly, in the interest of usurping political power from the church, drafted a new penal code that decriminalized all forms of consensual adult sexuality as long as such activity did not take place in public. This code was ratified in 1791, and France became the first modern western country to overturn the ban on homosexuality, so long perpetuated by the church. This penal code, however, was more liberal in theory than in practice, as persecution by police continued as it had in the past.[14]

The authorities were even less diligent when it came to women and were likely to ignore reported acts of lesbianism; priests did the same, perhaps because procreation was not involved. If the women involved were nuns, however, the penalties could be severe. The most notable person to be executed for, among other accusations, debauched sexuality was Marie-Antoinette.[15]

## SMUGGLERS

Under the old regime, punishment was often erratic or out of proportion to the crime. Groups of five or more armed smugglers of salt in Provence were sentenced to a fine of 500 livres and nine years in the galleys. In the remainder of the kingdom, the penalty for smuggling was death. Groups of fewer than five armed men assembled for the purpose of smuggling paid a fine of 300 livres and served three years in the galleys. Unarmed smugglers who used carts, horses, or boats for their illicit traffic were fined 300 livres, and, if this was not paid, they were sentenced to three years in the galleys. Sentences thus varied from region to region but were drastically increased for those condemned for a second offense. Unarmed smugglers who carried salt on their backs were subject to a fine of 200 livres, and, if the fine was not paid, they were flogged and branded. A second offense carried a penalty of 300 livres and six years in the galleys.[16]

Women and children were treated with lesser fines, but repeat offenders were flogged and banished from the kingdom. Parents were responsible for fines incurred by their children and were flogged for defaulting on payments. Nobles caught smuggling were deprived of their nobility, and their houses were razed. Soldiers who used arms while smuggling were hanged; if they had not used arms, they received a sentence of life in the galleys. Death was the punishment for any employee who worked in the salt works or who was involved in the transport of salt and who was caught smuggling; their houses, even if they were of the privileged class, could be entered and searched for incriminating evidence.

Smuggling salt was considered to be the same as stealing from the king, since the tax on salt went to him. On average, about 3,500 people a year were arrested for the offense. Evasion of the tax on salt was most prevalent in the west.

In a country crisscrossed by internal district boundaries and customs houses and in which the cities charged taxes on items entering their confines, smuggling was bound to be a big business. Forbidden objects, such as antiregime or pornographic books, magazines, and pamphlets from foreign presses were carried through various customs checks with the aid of a good bribe.[17]

## OTHER CRIMES AND PUNISHMENTS

Prior kings had given princes of the blood and other nobles grants of land that covered all the game animals on that land. A desperate peasant living on the land who killed an animal often went to prison. Numerous edicts were passed to prevent any disturbance of game. For example, it was prohibited to weed or hoe the ground during nesting time lest one disturb the young partridges or to spread manure of night soil lest the flavor of the birds be inferior to that of birds that fed on the peasants' grain, and mowing hay before a certain time of year was banned because it could expose the birds' eggs to danger. Removing stubble too early deprived the birds of shelter.[18] These matters often came up in the *cahiers*.

The revolutionaries swept away these noble rights and the judicial system of the old regime, instead establishing a criminal court in each department, a civil court in each district, and a justice of the peace in each canton. The judges of all the tribunals were elected. Buying and selling of offices, preferential treatment of the wealthy, and bribes to judges became a thing of the past. Trials by jury, honest courts of appeal, and free legal counsel for those who could not pay for it were instituted. Torture was abolished, and sentences were less harsh than before.

## NAPOLEONIC CODE

The task of preparing a code of law was entrusted, in July 1800, to a commission, named in honor of Napoleon, that consisted of the most eminent jurists of France. The code enacted in March 1804 is still in force in France today. The term applies to the entire body of French law as contained in five codes dealing with civil, commercial, and criminal law that were promulgated between 1804 and 1811. This code was a compromise between the customary law of the northern provinces of France, which was basically Germanic, and the essentially Roman law of the southern region of the country. Among its merits are its simplicity and clarity. It has required many judicial interpretations, however, and has been frequently modified by legislative amendment. As a result of Napoleon's conquests, the code was also introduced into a number of European countries. Some Latin American republics adopted it, and it also became

EXIT LIBERTÈ a la FRANCOIS! — or — BUONAPARTE closing the Farce of Egalité, at St Cloud near Paris Nov'10th 1799.

Bonaparte ending the farce of égalité at St.-Cloud, 1799. Courtesy Library of Congress.

the model for the civil codes of the Canadian province of Quebec and the state of Louisiana.

The rise to power of Napoleon no doubt eased the fears of many people who lived in the areas where brigandage and terror had reigned for years. His efficient centralized administration, with its effective police and military, cleansed France of lawlessness, often, however, to the detriment of liberty.

## NOTES

1. Young, 320–22.
2. Lewis (2004), 13–14.
3. Rudé (1988), 14.
4. Schama, 362.
5. Lewis (1972), 129.
6. Ibid., 131.
7. Andress (2004), 54.
8. Ibid., 69–72.
9. See Cobb/Jones, 216, and Schama, 793ff.
10. Robiquet, 151.
11. Scurr, 186.
12. Andress (2004), 218–9.

13. Ibid., 248–49, for more on roving bands of robbers and deserters.

14. For these examples and others see Lewis (2004), 153–54.

15. The word "homosexual" had not yet been coined in the eighteenth century; the French used the word "pederasty" to describe sexual acts between same-sex couples.

16. Young, 315–16.

17. For more on salt, see Kurlansky. Schama, 75, states that between 1780 and 1783, 2,342 men, 896 women, and 201 children were convicted in one region of Angers, along the Brittany border, for salt smuggling. Dogs, too, were trained to smuggle salt, but there are no figures on canine arrests.

18. Young, 317.

# 15

# AFTERMATH

By 1795, the people of France had had enough of revolutionary government. The decade that began in 1789 was a time of high hopes for many millions of people, who anticipated a golden age of political liberty, social equality, and economic freedom. For hundreds of thousands, it was also a time of bitter despair and bloody civil war. For the 300,000 or so nobles and clergy, the revolution was a disaster, as it was for those who depended on the upper classes for employment or the church for charity and for the untold numbers of families who lost fathers and sons in the brutal wars defending the revolution.

Direct results were the abolition of the absolute monarchy, the abrogation of the feudal privileges of the nobles, including the total eradication of the remaining vestiges of serfdom, the elimination of feudal dues and church tithes, the breakup of large estates, and the principle of equal liability for taxation. Career advancement became open to those with talent rather than to members of a particular class, and the bourgeoisie gained access to the highest positions in the state, which itself was no longer a federation of provinces or the private property of a monarch. Instead, it now belonged to the people.

Other social and economic reforms included the elimination of imprisonment for debt and the abolition of the rule of primogeniture in inheritance. The revolution managed to give practical application to the ideas of the philosophers: equality before the law, trial by jury, and, ultimately, freedom of religion, speech, and the press. It transformed the institutional structures of France and led to lasting changes in the nature of the church and the family. The principles of freedom of religion as enunciated in the Declaration of the Rights of Man resulted eventually in the separation of church and state and freedom of worship for Protestants and Jews.

Yet memories of the Terror and mass conscription for the military were never far from the minds of many citizens. The civil war in the Vendée, which cost around 400,000 lives, turned the inhabitants against republicanism for generations. The great mass of working people in both urban and rural settings continued to live in much the same manner after as they had before the revolution. Their lives in fact changed little before the middle of the nineteenth century, when migrations to the urban communities increased and production in large businesses became more efficient. City dwellers and the sans-culottes were eventually transformed into the working class of the industrial revolution, while the upper bourgeoisie remained the dominant element in society. A new social class of capitalists emerged, distinguished from workers by their ownership or control of the means of production. The poor and the destitute continued to make up a major and growing underclass. The local city or village councils could not cope with relief for them, and the series of work schemes and relief measures proposed by the government were piecemeal and never adequately financed.

The initial staunch supporters of the revolution, the urban workers and the sans-culottes, had sacrificed much and gained little in concrete benefits.

The system of the old regime was replaced by one in which cash became the important ingredient between a new generation of capitalist farmers and the workers they employed. Costly wars still took their money in taxes and their sons off to battlefields, thwarting the farmers' dreams of self-sufficiency. Landless laborers remained the most vulnerable to depredation and hunger.

Women emerged from the revolution with the right to inherit equally with their brothers and to sign legal contracts if they were unmarried; but precious little else changed. The divorce laws of 1792 were sharply curtailed in 1804 and abolished in 1816.

The registry office for births, deaths, and marriage was passed from church to state; the sale of offices ended. Administrators of the old regime were largely maintained, but some official offices were eliminated, including the one that oversaw collection of the salt tax (later reinstated). The military changed little; the majority of the officers, once *émigrés*, had served the old regime.

In the coup d'état of November 9, 1799, Napoleon Bonaparte joined a conspiracy against the government, seizing power and establishing a new regime—the Consulate. Under the Consulate's constitution, Bonaparte, as first consul, had dictatorial powers. On February 16, 1800, he issued a decree that effectively reduced local government councils to rubber stamps, and three days later, he took up residency in the royal palace of the Tuileries.

Mayors and deputy-mayors of towns of more than 5,000 inhabitants were now to be directly appointed by the First Consul himself; officials for other towns were appointed by the department administrator, the prefect, who himself had been sanctioned by Napoleon. It was much the same as under the old regime, when the king had appointed the intendant to administer the districts. Candidates for local councils, appointed for 20 years, were selected on the basis of property qualifications. Judges also were appointed rather than elected.

Napoleon had himself crowned emperor in 1804; he established a court and made counts, dukes, and even kings of his relatives and friends. For many who had lived under the old regime, it must have seemed like a case of *déjà vu*. The reform and codification of the diverse provincial and local laws culminated in the Napoleonic Code. Press censorship was reintroduced, along with a new salt tax, an efficient spy system, and a police force. Custom houses at the gates of the cities were reestablished. The revolution did not meet the high hopes of the working people that they would be given power. It was not until 1848 that all men of age were given the vote, and not until 1944 did women gain the franchise. Workers waited until 1864 for the right to strike and twenty years beyond that for the right to form trade unions. Free, secular, and compulsory education came only in the 1880s, and welfare provisions for the infirm, the elderly, and the unemployed were not instituted until the twentieth century. The new hierarchy under Napoleon, which after 1799 was based on the criterion of wealth, retained many nobles of the old regime. Those who had escaped the guillotine and others who returned from exile again began to play a major economic and political role. Of the 281 men Napoleon appointed to administrate the departments, nearly half were from old aristocratic families. In 1815, after the downfall of Napoleon, a limited monarchy was restored that endured until 1848.

# Appendix 1

## DECLARATION OF THE RIGHTS OF MAN AND CITIZEN

The Declaration of the Rights of Man and Citizen adopted by the National Assembly on August 26, 1789.

**Articles:**

1. Men are born and remain free and equal in rights. Social distinctions may be founded only upon the general good.
2. The aim of all political association is the preservation of the natural and imprescriptible rights of man. These rights are liberty, property, security, and resistance to oppression.
3. The principle of all sovereignty resides essentially in the nation. No body nor individual may exercise any authority which does not proceed directly from the nation.
4. Liberty consists in the freedom to do everything which injures no one else; hence, the exercise of the natural rights of each man has no limits except those which assure to the other members of the society the enjoyment of the same rights. These limits can only be determined by law.
5. Law can only prohibit such actions as are hurtful to society. Nothing may be prevented which is not forbidden by law, and no one may be forced to do anything not provided for by law.

6. Law is the expression of the general will. Every citizen has a right to participate personally, or through his representative, in its foundation. It must be the same for all, whether it protects or punishes. All citizens, being equal in the eyes of the law, are equally eligible to all dignities and to all public positions and occupations, according to their abilities, and without distinction except that of their virtues and talents.

7. No person shall be accused, arrested, or imprisoned except in the cases and according to the forms prescribed by law. Any one soliciting, transmitting, executing, or causing to be executed any arbitrary order, shall be punished. But any citizen summoned or arrested in virtue of the law shall submit without delay, as resistance constitutes an offense.

8. The law shall provide for such punishments only as are strictly and obviously necessary, and no one shall suffer punishment except it be legally inflicted in virtue of a law passed and promulgated before the commission of the offense.

9. As all persons are held innocent until they shall have been declared guilty, if arrest shall be deemed indispensable, all harshness not essential to the securing of the prisoner's person shall be severely repressed by law.

10. No one shall be disquieted on account of his opinions, including his religious views, provided their manifestation does not disturb the public order established by law.

11. The free communication of ideas and opinions is one of the most precious of the rights of man. Every citizen may, accordingly, speak, write, and print with freedom, but shall be responsible for such abuses of this freedom as shall be defined by law.

12. The security of the rights of man and of the citizen requires public military forces. These forces are, therefore, established for the good of all and not for the personal advantage of those to whom they shall be intrusted.

13. A common contribution is essential for the maintenance of the public forces and for the cost of administration. This should be equitably distributed among all the citizens in proportion to their means.

14. All the citizens have a right to decide, either personally or by their representatives, as to the necessity of the public contribution; to grant this freely; to know to what uses it is put; and to fix the proportion, the mode of assessment and of collection, and the duration of the taxes.

15. Society has the right to require of every public agent an account of his administration.

16. A society in which the observance of the law is not assured, nor the separation of powers defined, has no constitution at all.
17. Since property is an inviolable and sacred right, no one shall be deprived thereof except where public necessity, legally determined, shall clearly demand it, and then only on condition that the owner shall have been previously and equitably indemnified.

Prepared by Gerald Murphy (The Cleveland Free-Net—aa300). Distributed by Cybercasting Services Division of NPTN.

# Appendix 2

# THE REPUBLICAN CALENDAR

A new calendar was introduced by the Convention on October 5, 1793, to date from September 22, 1792, the day after the proclamation of the First Republic. It replaced the Gregorian calendar and rejected the Christian view of reckoning time and events from the birth of Christ. It was to represent a new start. The new names of the months were inspired by nature, and although their aspirations may have been universal, the revolutionary calendar was based on the seasons of northern France. The first year under the new system was called An I (Year I), the second An II, and so on.

The year was divided into 12 months, each of which had 30 days. Each season comprised three months, named according to their natural characteristics. Thus, September 22, 1792, became the first day of the Revolutionary Calendar, 1 Vendémiaire year I.

The names of the months were:

1. Vendémiaire (vintage)
2. Brumaire (fog)
3. Frimaire (frost)
4. Nivôse (snow)
5. Pluviôse (rain)
6. Ventôs (wind)

7. Germinal (seed)
8. Floréal (blossoms)
9. Prairial (meadows)
10. Messidor (harvesting)
11. Thermidor (heat)
12. Fructidor (fruit)

The month was divided into three decades, of which the final day was a day of rest. This was an attempt to de-Christianize the calendar, but it was unpopular because now there were now only three days of rest in a month instead of four. The 10 days of each decade were called, respectively, Primidi, Duodi, Tridi, Quartidi, Quintidi, Sextidi, Septidi, Octidi, Nonidi, and Decadi. The five or six remaining days following the last day of Fructidor at the end of the year (September 17–21 in the Gregorian calendar) were designated national holidays and called by these names:

1. Fête de la vertu (virtue)
2. Fête du génie (genius)
3. Fête du travail (work)
4. Fête de l'opinion (opinion)
5. Fête des récompenses (rewards)
6. Jour de la révolution (leap-year day)

The conversion of a Republican date to a Gregorian one is as follows:

Year 1:      September 22, 1792
Year 2:      September 22, 1793
Year 3:      September, 1794
Year 4:      September 23, 1795
Year 5:      September 22, 1796
Year 6:      September 22, 1797
Year 7:      September 22, 1798
Year 8:      September 23, 1799
Year 9:      September 23, 1800
Year 10:     September 23, 1801
Year 11:     September 23, 1802
Year 12:     September 24, 1803

Year 13:       September 23, 1804
Year 14:       September 23, 1805

A new clock was also established according to which the day was divided into 10 hours, each consisting of 100 minutes composed of 100 seconds.

# GLOSSARY

**Armée Révolutionnaire**—An armed force of Jacobins and sans-culottes raised in late summer 1793 to propagate the revolution in the countryside and to force farmers to release their stocks of grain for Paris and other towns. Disbanded after the executions of the Hébertists.

**Assignats**—Interest-bearing bonds based on the value of confiscated church property that after April 1790 became paper money. They rapidly lost value and by 1795 were almost worthless.

**Bourgeoisie**—Term pertaining to the urban upper middle class of the Third Estate; professionals such as lawyers, doctors, bankers, brokers, manufacturers, and office holders in the royal bureaucracy. Other members of the bourgeoisie lived on investments from property or other holdings.

**Cahiers de Doléances**—Lists of grievances drawn up in early 1789 in specially convened meetings of citizens in regional districts and cities and representatives of each of the three orders of the Estates. They exposed problems inherent in the political and social system that could be acted upon by the deputies elected to the Estates-General.

**Certificat de Civisme**—Documentary proof of civic virtue and revolutionary purity; generally demanded of applicants before employment could be obtained in the Paris sections during the Terror. The documents were issued first by the municipality and then by the surveillance committees. Denial of a *certificat* meant that one was suspected of antirevolutionary thoughts or activities. Their issuance came to an end after the Terror.

**Champ de Mars**—Originally the main military parade ground of Paris on the left bank of the river Seine (the Eiffel Tower stands today at one end of it.) Site of the Festival of Federation on the anniversary of the fall of the Bastille and the massacre of July 17, 1791.

**Committee of General Security**— A body charged by the Convention with surveillance of state security throughout the country, issuance of passports, and prosecution of foreign agents and counterfeiters. Essentially a police committee, it was second in power only to the Committee of Public Safety, and the functions of the two committees overlapped somewhat. It oversaw revolutionary justice.

**Committee of Public Safety**—The more important of the two leading government committees of year II (1793) (see Committee of General Security); responsible for both internal and external affairs. Its powers overlapped those of the Committee of General Security in police and judicial matters. Consisting of a dozen members, it functioned as the executive power of government from April 1793 to October 1795 and was presided over by Robespierre during the period of the Terror.

**Constituent Assembly**—A body made up of members of the Third Estate and their noble and clerical allies of the Estates-General. It drafted a constitution and acted as a provisional legislature from 1789 through 1791.

**Convention**—The National Convention, a revolutionary single-chamber parlement elected in September 1792 to write a constitution following the downfall of the monarchy. The 745 deputies were divided between Girondins and the more radical Montagnards, with a large number of uncommitted members (the Plain) in between. It remained in session until October 1795.

**Cordeliers**—The ultra-revolutionary club of the Cordeliers, founded in April–May 1790 under the leadership of Danton, Marat, Hébert, and Ronsin, attracted many members because of the low dues (two sous per month) and its radical rhetoric. It also welcomed women to its meetings, which were each attended by about 400 people. Hebert's newspaper *Père Duchesne* became its mouthpiece. It lost power and influence after the Terror and was discredited and closed in March 1794.

**Corvée**—Unpaid work on land or roads or aid given to troops by peasants for a specified number of days each year. the corvée was a kind of royal tax paid in manual labor to the government. It was abolished in 1790.

**Council of Ancients**— Made up of 250 married or widowed men, priests excluded; all were over 40 years of age. It served as the upper house of the legislature during the Directory. Members could accept motions of the Five Hundred, which would then become law, or veto them. Members were elected for three-year terms, one-third of which were renewable every year.

**Council of Five Hundred**—Made up of 500 members, it and the Council of the Ancients served as the legislative branch of government during the Directory. Created by the constitution of 1795, it served as the lower house of the bicameral legislature. Members served three-year terms, with one-third of the seats renewed each year. The council had the power to initiate laws, which then had to be approved by the Council of Ancients. Stability in government was not achieved, however.

**De-Christianization**—General government policy of eliminating Christianity by defrocking priests, closing churches, and instituting the worship of the secular abstractions of reason and a supreme being. See Deism.

**Deism**—Deists held the view that religious knowledge or natural religion is either inherent in each person or accessible through the exercise of reason. They denied the validity of religious claims based on revelation or on the church teachings.

**Dîme**—Tithe collected by the Catholic Church for its own uses under the old regime. Levied on peasants, mainly on their crops or animals, or both, it varied from region to region and according to the type of crop or animal but could be anywhere from 8 to 20 percent. Abolished in 1790.

**Directory**— A board of five directors chosen by the Council of Five Hundred and approved by the Council of Ancients as authorized by the Constitution of 1795 to serve as the executive branch of government. It was in power from October 26, 1795, to November 10, 1799, and was supposed to be a safeguard against dictatorship.

**Émigrés**—Antirevolutionists, mostly aristocrats, who went into exile outside France and plotted against the revolutionary government. They numbered about 150,000.

**Estates**—The three orders of society: clergy, nobles, and commons.

**Estates-General**— The consultative assembly summoned by Louis XVI in 1789 to consider taxation and government debt. It consisted of deputies from the three estates. They met at Versailles in May 1789, in a session attended by 1,139 delegates, of whom 291 were clergy, 270 were aristocrats, and 578 were commoners.

**Farmers General**—A company of financiers, 40 to 60 men, under the old regime who paid the crown a specified sum in return for which they were granted the right to collect taxes—by force if necessary.

**Faubourgs**—Suburbs once outside the walls of Paris but within the city limits by the time of the revolution. The two most famous at the time of the revolution were Saint-Antoine and Saint-Marcel. They were mostly working-class districts and strongholds of the sans-culottes. Saint-Antoine, located east of the Bastille, accounted for about 70 percent of the besiegers of the Bastille. Saint-Marcel, situated on the left bank of the Seine in the southeast section of the city, included the many tanneries and dye shops along the Bièvre stream and was the poorer of the two.

**Federalist Revolt**— Reacting to the proscription of Girondin deputies from the National Convention in June 1793, 13 departments began resisting the Montagnard leadership in the Convention. The revolt centered around Bordeaux, Caen, Lyon, and Marseille. These cities withdrew recognition of the Convention in Paris and all decrees issued after May 31, 1793. They called on their citizens to march on Paris and restore the deputies. The revolt failed. The struggle was fundamentally about the provincial cities' reaction to the hegemony of Paris, but the rebellions were crushed by government troops. Lyon held out for two months, and 1,900 rebels were executed.

**Fédérés**—Citizen soldiers, mostly National Guards, who came to Paris from the provinces for the Festival of the Federation in July 1790, and again on July 14, 1792. Many were from Marseille and participated in the uprising of August 10, 1792. Some returned home, and others went to join the regular army at the front.

**Feuillants**— Constitutional monarchist deputies and journalists who split of from the Jacobins over moves to depose Louis XVI after the flight to Varennes in June 1791. They formed their own club, named after the monastery in which they met. Resurgent Jacobins forced their decline and closure by the end of 1791.

**Girondins**—Left-wing deputies. mostly from the Gironde, in southwest France, in the Legislative Assembly. They were one of the two major factions in the National Convention (along with the Montagnards); they opposed, and were largely eliminated by, the Jacobins in 1793.

**Hébertists**—Followers of Hébert, a writer turned revolutionary who was a prominent member of the Cordelier club. Anti-Christian, his followers turned several thousand churches, including Nôtre Dame, into temples of reason. Falling afoul of Robespierre, Hébert was guillotined on March 24, 1794.

**Hospitals**—Before 1789, hospitals served the poor and were funded by the Catholic Church. Eventually the state took them over and tried to create a welfare system. There was never enough money to maintain them, and by 1793 they were in bad condition. Local authorities who distributed funds to hospitals were always short of money. While all French people were guaranteed free medical care, the declining value of assignats and the continuous wars led to overcrowding and a shortage of funds.

**Hôtel de Ville**— City hall.

**Hôtel-Dieu**—General hospital.

**Jacobins**—Paris revolutionary popular club that met in a former Jacobin (Dominican) monastery, the primary center of increasingly left-wing discussions. Jacobean clubs, the most important of the popular societies, were also located in the provinces. Members were mostly middle-class professionals; they numbered about 1,000 in 1790, but membership more than doubled the following year, There were about 934 such clubs around the country by July 1791. The Jacobins rose to political dominance in Paris and in some provincial cities. Because of its association with the policies of the Terror, the Paris club was ordered closed by the Convention on November 12, 1794.

*l'Ami du Peuple*—(Friend of the people) The popular newspaper put out by Marat for Parisian readers, mostly sans-culottes, printed scandals and articles on conspiracies against the revolution and attacked the king and his ministers, the deputies of the Assembly (of which he became a member), and any perceived treason to the revolutionary cause. Marat rallied against the Girondins and was considered responsible for the September massacres, of which he approved.

**Legislative Assembly**—Single-chamber parlement elected under the constitutional monarchy, 1791–1792, that ended with the declaration of the French Republic.

**Lettres de Cachet**—Sealed orders by which the king could incarcerate or exile anyone without charges or trial. Voltaire was a victim of such a *lettre* and was imprisoned in the Bastille. The *lettres* were abolished by the Constituent Assembly in January 1790.

**Levée en Masse**—Mobilization of the nation's total manpower and material resources for war; issued on August 23, 1793.

**Liberty Tree**—An early and enduring symbol of the revolution, the liberty tree grew out of the ritual of the maypole at the time of spring planting but, as a living tree, came to represent regeneration. It could be any kind of hardy tree and was present at all revolutionary festivals. Under the Terror, it became a capital offense to cut one down.

**Lit de Justice**—Royal session of the Paris parlement at which the king presided to force acceptance of his edicts.

**Livre**—Unit of weight and a unit of monetary value. See Money.

**Maximum**—Laws of May 1793 that fixed the price of grain and of September 1793 that did the same for the price of basic foods, such as bread. The part of the law that covered fixed wages was never rigorously imposed.

**Métayage**—Share cropping, most widespread in the south; the farmer usually split his crop equally with the landowner.

**Money**—There were 12 deniers in a sou and 20 sous in a livre. The louis d'or was a gold coin first struck in 1640 and issued until the revolution. The franc was established as the national currency in 1795 as a decimal unit, and in 1796 it was set at about 1 livre 3 deniers. It contained 4.5 grams of fine silver and was made up of 100 centimes. A 20-franc gold piece was issued after the revolution.

**Montagnards**—Occupying the highest seats at the National Convention, the Montagnards (the men of the mountain) were the primary faction that opposed the Girondins. Estimates of the number of Montagnards (often referred to as Jacobins, since most were members of the Jacobin club) vary considerably, from 135 to 270. They were supported by a strong base in Paris and by the sans-culottes. Of the 24 deputies elected from Paris, 21 sat on the mountain. They came to dominate the Convention but lost influence with the demise of Robespierre.

**Muscadins**—Anti-Jacobin youth from upper-middle-class families. They wore flamboyant clothes of the earlier court style and reacted to the Terror after the fall of Robespierre by smashing busts of Marat and violently attacking former supporters of Robespierre and the Terror. They were repressed when their usefulness against former radicals was over.

**National Guard**—Citizens' militia formed in the spring and summer of 1789 in the Paris districts and other cities to maintain order, protect property against mob violence, and guard against counterrevolutionary plots.

**Nobility of the Robe**—Magistrates and bureaucrats, mostly wealthy, who acquired their aristocratic status by service to the king from the seventeenth century onward.

**Nobility of the Sword**—The oldest aristocratic families, who traced their lineages back to the Middle Ages and owed their status and privileges to their service to the crown on the field of battle.

**Paris Commune**—Revolutionary municipal government of Paris formed in July 1789 by an insurrectional committee composed of 144 delegates—three from each of the 48 sections of the city. It was challenged by the Girondins, who tried to curb its growing influence in the political affairs of the Assembly. The Commune and the Jacobins then ousted Girondin members from the Assembly.

**Parlements**—The function of the parlements was the administration of justice. The 13 parlements of France were the highest courts of justice in their areas. They had wide-ranging powers of police and administration and some political clout, in that they had to register any edicts from the king in order to make them into law.

**Père Duchesne**—Hébert's impious popular journal, which appeared three times a week between 1790 and and his death in 1794. It catered to the sans-culottes, using foul language of the street. The government had the paper sent to soldiers in the field. After the death of Marat (see *L'Ami du Peuple*), the paper became the mostly widely distributed in France, with a readership of some 50,000.

**Philosophers (Philosophes)**—The rationalist writers of the eighteenth century, such as Voltaire, Montesquieu, Diderot, and d'Alembert, who advocated the use of reason instead of custom, tradition, faith, or superstition as the basis for the organization of society and state.

**Plain or Marais**—Name of the center-aligned group in the Convention, which sat in the flat middle area of the chamber and generally remained uncommitted to the opposing Montagnards and Girondins. It comprised about 250 deputies. Sometimes they did hold the balance of power; by opposing Robespierre, they made it possible for his enemies to isolate, arrest, and execute him and his followers.

**Représentant-en-Mise (Representatives on Mission)**—Agents sent out by the National Convention who were entrusted with considerable powers of repression in the provinces, especially during the Terror. Their job was to recruit men for the army. After June 1793, they were appointed by the Committee of Public Safety. One of their tasks became the suppression of the Federalist revolt.

**Sans-Culottes**—Revolutionaries who made a virtue of their plain dress, in contrast to that of the nobility and the upper bourgeoisie. They were workers, shopkeepers, petty traders, crafsmen, and the poor and wore trousers instead of the breeches and stockings of the higher classes.

**Sections**—Forty-eight areas into which Paris was divided for political purposes, replacing the former 60 Districts. Each was run by a revolutionary watch committee and was able to organize armed men (sectionnaires), mostly sans-culottes. Other cities also had their sections. Section assemblies played a major role in shaping uprisings and influencing the government. They were instrumental in the uprising of August 10, 1792 (the attack on the king's residence at the Tuileries that toppled the monarchy) and in the campaign that led to the downfall of the Girondins.

**September Massacres**—Between September 2 and September 6, 1792, sans-culottes and Federalists stormed a number of prisons in Paris and indiscriminately massacred more than 1,000 prisoners, some after summary trials, some with no trials.

**Sociétés Populaires**—Term applied to local clubs and societies after the summer of 1791. Many were affiliated with the Jacobin club. Because of their independent and radical policies, many were disapproved of by the revolutionary government of the year II. Some were closed after the fall of Hébert, others after Thermidor. A few survived into 1795.

**Sou**—(Earlier, sol) See money.

**Surveillance Committees**—Watch committees formed in each commune in March 1793 to observe officialdom and maintain public security and order. They often took the place of local government in the districts and were controlled by extreme Jacobins. Later they became known as *Comités Révolutionnaires* and, after Thermidor, as *Comités d'Arrondissements.*

**Taille**—The basic direct tax of the old regime, paid by the commoners and peasants. The amount due varied between provinces.

**Terror**—The term describes the period from September 1793 to July 1794, during which the Jacobin government imposed its authority through terror by economic, military, and judicial means. It was a reaction to war, both foreign and civil, and to the threat of antirevolutionary conspiracies.

The guillotine was kept busy eliminating real or imaginary revolutionary dissenters. The Terror ended when it claimed the head of Robespierre.

**Thermidorians**—The politicians who took power after the fall of Robespierre on 9 Thermidor (July 27, 1794), ending the Reign of Terror.

**Third Estate**—The common people, as opposed to the clergy (First Estate) and the nobility (Second Estate).

**Tuileries**—A royal palace and gardens in Paris that had not been used by the royal family for nearly a century. Louis XVI and the queen occupied the Tuileries palace after they were forced to move to Paris from Versailles. After their death, it was occupied by the National Convention for its meetings, by the Committee of Public Safety, by the Council of Ancients, and, in 1800, by Napoleon.

**Vendée**—A mostly rural department in western France with no major cities; residents of the Vendée were loyal to the monarchy and to local priests, most of whom refused to swear the civil oath of the clergy. The peasants revolted against the government in March 1793 when recruitment began to fill a levy of 3 million men for the army. The revolt spread and turned into full-scale rebellion and civil war, which was not crushed completely until 1801.

# BIBLIOGRAPHY

Aftalion, Florin. *The French Revolution. An Economic Interpretation.* Martin Thom, trans. Paris: Editions de la Maison des Sciences de l'Homme (1990).
>A treatment of the French economy at the end of the old regime, including the economic thought of the Enlightenment, followed by the financial problems that faced the Constituent Assembly, such as the assignats, property rights, prices, and the Maximum. 226 pages and chronology.

Andress, David. *French Society in Revolution 1789–1799.* Manchester: Manchester University Press (1999).
>A social history of the revolution in narrative form. The failings of the revolution in the treatment of poverty and gender issues are underscored.

———. *The French Revolution and the People.* London and New York: Hambledon and London (2004).
>The book is primarily about the common people of France and how they experienced and coped with revolutionary events.

———. *The Terror. The Merciless War for Freedom in Revolutionary France.* New York: Farrar, Straus and Giroux (2006).
>The author revisits the Terror, taking into account the events and economic problems in the provinces as well as in Paris. This revisionist work also has a chronology, a glossary, and a cast of characters and their occupations.

Behrens, C.B.C. *The Ancien Régime.* London: Thames and Hudson (1967).
>A view of the class structure, ideology, finances, and reform failures under the old regime, accompanied by many paintings, drawings, and maps, including colonial territories.

Bosher, J. F. *The French Revolution.* New York and London: W. W Norton (1988).
>A history of the revolution and its effect, coupled with a chronology of events and a who's who of the period.

Braudel, Fernand. *The Structures of Everyday Life. Civilization & Capitalism 15th–18th Century.* Vol. I. New York: Harper & Row (1981).

This 623-page volume of facts, figures, and pictures covers daily aspects of life on an international scale from the fifteenth through the eighteenth century, with many references to France.

Brockliss, L.W.B. *French Higher Education in the Seventeenth and Eighteenth Centuries.* Oxford: Clarendon Press (1987).

A study of the structure and content of the college and university curriculum of the seventeenth and eighteenth centuries. The conclusion specifically deals with the period of the French revolution.

Brockliss, L.W.B., and Colin Jones. *The Medical World of Early Modern France.* Oxford: Oxford University Press (1997).

This volume deals with the full range of medical practitioners and provides a thorough discussion of the evolution of the medical profession and its relationship to its rivals—surgeons, apothecaries, and folk healers.

Burke, Edmund. *Reflections on the Revolution in France.* London: Scott, Webster and Geary (1790).

This work condemns the revolution as a blind incarnation of the Enlightenment: sanguinary, violent, and a formula for disaster. Burke's views turned the British public against the revolution. He refuted the ideals of 1789, predicting that the outcome of the turmoil would be a nation of atheists under a military dictatorship.

Cameron, Rondo, ed. *Essays in French Economic History.* Homewood, Ill.: American Economic Association (1970).

Part II, pages 107–82, discusses French guilds, industry, monetary circulation, and agriculture in the early modern period, with references to tables and graphs.

Campan, Madame de. *Mémoires de Madame Campan. Première Femme de Chambre de Marie-Antoinette.* Anglo, Carlos, et Jean Chalon, eds. Paris: Mercure de France (1988).

A firsthand account of the intrigues at court, the relations between highborn families, and the personality of the queen. The original edition of the *Mémoires* appeared in 1822.

Carlson, Marvin. *The Theater of the French Revolution.* Ithaca: Cornell University Press (1966).

Plates and drawings complement this history of the stage from 1789 to 1799, which includes a chart of the major theaters of the time.

Church, William F., ed. *The Influence of the Enlightenment on the French Revolution.* Boston: D. C. Heath and Company (1964).

A series of essays in 108 pages in which the authors discuss the degree of enlightened influence on the revolution. The essays embody a spectrum of opinion.

Cobb, R. C. *The Police and the People 1789–1820.* Oxford: Clarendon Press (1970).

Divided into three sections totaling 393 pages, the book examines police records to assess assumptions and attitudes of the authorities toward sansculottes, prostitutes, popular violence, and many aspects of daily life in both town and country.

———— and Colin Jones, eds. *Voices of the French Revolution.* Topsfield, Mass.: Salem House Publishers (1988).

With short biographies of revolutionary participants, glossary of terms, and numerous pictures, the book covers revolutionary events from 1789 to 1795. The narrative history is accompanied by contemporary memoirs, newspaper reports and other primary sources.

Cooke, James J. *France 1789–1962.* Modern History Reference Series. Hamden, Conn.: Archon Books (1975).

An alphabetical reference to the men, women, events, laws, and concepts that shaped modern France.

Darnton, Robert, and Daniel Roche, eds. *Revolution in Print. The Press in France 1775–1800.* Berkeley: University of California Press (1989).

A series of essays on the printing trade, its organization, censorship, pamphlets, and role and impact on the revolution, with many pictures and documents.

———. *The Great Cat Massacre.* New York: Basic Books (1999).

The author examines the nature of eighteenth-century French folk tales and superstitions and their relationship to the lower classes of society.

Desan, Suzanne. *The Family on Trial in Revolutionary France.* Berkeley: University of California Press (2004).

This work looks at the relationship among family, politics, and state during the French revolution. The author analyzes the continual interaction between family members, revolutionary politics, and state building and argues that the revolution transformed the most intimate relationships and challenged the patriarchal structure of old-regime families.

Dowd, David L. *The French Revolution.* New York: American Heritage (1965).

A history of the revolution, liberally illustrated with drawings and paintings of events and notables of the time.

Doyle, William. *The Oxford History of the French Revolution.* Oxford: Oxford University Press (2002).

In 481 pages, this work traces in detail the history of the revolution from the accession of Louis XVI in 1774 through the rise of Napoleon in 1802 and examines the impact of events in France on the rest of Europe.

Dwyer, Philip G., and Peter McPhee, eds. *The French Revolution and Napoleon.* London and New York: Routledge (2002).

A sourcebook of events in 213 pages, with extensive chronology and a wide selection of primary texts from 1787 to 1815, commentary, and seven illustrations.

Erickson, Carolly. *To the Scaffold.* New York: St. Martin's Griffin (1991).

A historical novel firmly based on fact and covering the life of Marie-Antoinette.

Forrest, Alan. *The French Revolution and the Poor.* Oxford: Blackwell (1981).

This work examines the good intentions of the men in power in their efforts to alleviate the sufferings of the poor and needy and looks at how well they succeeded in these endeavors.

Francois, Patrick. *Social Capital and Economic Development.* London and New York: Routledge (2002).

Largely unexplored by writers on the French revolution, the principles of trust and social capital discussed in this book could lead to their application in a new chapter on revolutionary developments.

Frangos, John. *From Housing the Poor to Healing the Sick. The Changing Institution of Paris Hospitals under the Old Regime and Revolution.* Madison, N.J.: Fairleigh Dickinson University Press (1997).

The author maintains that the revolution transformed the hospital system from a collection of religious institutions that cared mostly for the poor and elderly to a system of institutions that treated the sick as the religious orders lost their control and authority was transferred to medical adiministrators.

Furet, François. *The French Revolution.* Antonia Nevill, trans. Oxford: Blackwells (1996).

The work covers the period of Louis XVI (1770) to the fall of Napoleon (1814). The author discusses two revolutions: the first, egalitarian, begun in 1789, and the second, authoritarian and dictatorial, under Bonaparte.

Garrioch, David. *The Making of Revolutionary Paris.* Berkeley: University of California Press (2002).

A general history of Paris prior to and during the revolution. Well endowed with illustrations, this book covers many aspects of city life, its benefits and problems, in 383 pages.

Germani, Ian, and Robin Swales, eds. *Symbols, Myths and Images of the French Revolution.* Regina, Saskatchewan: Canadian Plains Research Center (1988).

Twenty-three papers make up this collection of 342 pages, treating a wide range of subjects with numerous pictures. Several papers discuss the English, Russian, and Chinese revolutions to provide a broad perspective of the subject. Some papers are in French.

Greenlaw, Ralph W., ed. *The Economic Origins of the French Revolution.* Boston: D. C. Heath and Co. (1958).

In 95 pages and 12 essays by noted writers, the work describes economic conditions during the old regime and the revolution.

Hampson, Norman. *The First European Revolution 1776–1815.* New York: W. W. Norton (1969).

A highly illustrated work covering the period 1776–1815. The book is primarily concerned with ideology and deals with the impact of the revolution and Napoleon's reign on the rest of Europe.

Hanson, Paul R. *Historical Dictionary of the French Revolution.* Lanham, Md.: Scarecrow Press (2004).

The dictionary includes important events, significant institutions, a bibliography, and more than 400 entries, plus a chronology.

Harris, Jennifer. "The Red Cap of Liberty. A Study of Dress Worn by French Revolutionary Partisans 1789–94." *Eighteenth Century Studies,* 14 (1981), 293–312.

The author shows the symbolic importance of the red Phrygian cap, often referred to as the *bonnet rouge* or the *bonnet de la liberté,* which permeated every aspect of the revolution. Pictures accompany the article.

Hibbert, Christopher. *The Days of the French Revolution.* New York: Quill William Morrow (1980).

A narrative history from the meeting of the Estates-General to the coup d'état that brought Napoleon to power. The concentration is on events and people, rather than on ideas and concepts.

Hillam, Christine, ed. *Dental Practice in Europe at the End of the 18th Century.* Amsterdam and New York: Rodopi B.V. (2003).

Part 1 of the book (pages 37–168) is dedicated to dental practice in late-eighteenth-century France, covering selected areas and Paris. Besides detailed descriptions of instruments and procedures, there are a number of biographical sketches and advertisements for contemporary dentists.

Hoffman, Philip T. *Growth in a Traditional Society. The French Countryside 1450–1815.* Princeton: Princeton University Press (1996).

In 361 pages, the book explores the economic development of France in both countryside and cities, from the complexity of land leases and community rights to agricultural production. The work is accompanied by many charts, graphs, and models.

Hufton, Olwen H. *Women and the Limits of Citizenship in the French Revolution.* Toronto: University of Toronto Press (1992).

A series of four lectures given by the author on the role of women in the revolution and their reaction to events.

Hunt, Lynn. *Politics, Culture, and Class in the French Revolution.* Berkeley: University of California Press (1984).

Signs, symbols, and language are brought to the fore, demonstrating the political nature of the revolution. The rhetoric of the revolution, its imagery and symbolic forms, make up the bulk of this study.

———. *The Family Romance of the French Revolution.* Berkeley: University of California Press (1992).

The author draws on newspapers, novels, paintings, speeches, and pornography to frame a picture of the collective psyche of the people of the French revolution.

Jones, Colin. *Charity and Bienfaisance. The Treatment of the Poor in the Montpellier Region 1740–1815.* Cambridge: Cambridge University Press (1982).

This work discusses the problems of poverty, begging, relief, popular attitudes toward the poor, and movements toward a welfare state and the retreat from it.

———. "Médicins du Roi at the End of the Ancien Regime and in the French Revolution," in Vivian Nutton, ed., *Medicine at Court in Europe 1500–1837.* London: Routledge (1997).

———. "Pulling Teeth in Eighteenth-Century Paris." *Past and Present,* 166 (May 2000), 100–45.

The paper begins with the famous tooth-puller *Le Grand Thomas* on the Pont Neuf and takes the reader into the realm of eighteenth-century charlatans and qualified dentists who began to take care to preserve teeth rather than just pull them.

Jones, P. M. *The French Revolution 1787–1804.* Harlow: Pearson (2003).

A concise narrative history, glossary, chronology, 22 documents, and who's who in 154 pages.

Kurlansky, Mark. *Salt.* New York: Penguin Books (2002).

A history of salt, with a section dedicated to France.

Lefebvre, Georges. *The Coming of the French Revolution.* R. R. Palmer, trans. Princeton: Princeton University Press (1947).

The book, first published in 1939, covers the beginning of the revolution. Some of the author's conclusions have come under criticism by new research; nevertheless, his analysis of events, even though disputed by revisionist views, demonstrates the complexities of the times.

Lewis, Gwynne. *Life in Revolutionary France*. London: B. T. Batsford, Ltd. (1972).
    This work goes beyond the historical narrative and describes the effects of
    the revolution on peasants, artists, priests, and the common people. The
    text is well endowed with pictures.
———. *France, 1715–1804: Power and the People*. Harlow: Pearson (2004).
    Divided into three parts, this work (with three maps) discusses conditions
    under the old regime, the influence of the enlightenment on the people, and
    the social background of the revolution.
Loomis, Stanley. *Paris in the Terror*. New York: J. B. Lippincott Company (1964).
    The book treats the period of the Terror with emphasis on the major person-
    alities that shaped the period.
Lough, John. *France on the Eve of Revolution. British Travellers' Observations 1763–
    1788*. London and Sydney: Croom Helm (1987).
    Accounts by English travelers in France over a period of 25 years, ending in
    1788, with background notes on those mentioned in the book in the appen-
    dices.
McPhee, Peter. *The French Revolution 1789–1799*. Oxford: Oxford University Press
    (2002).
    In 234 pages, the author surveys the repercussions of the revolution on
    rural communities, the environment, and city life and discusses the role of
    women. Six maps are included.
Morton, J. B. *The Bastille Falls*. London: Longmans (1936).
    This work covers the period from the beginning of the revolution to the
    fall of Robespierre, highlighting the major events in an informal, novelistic
    style.
Pernoud, Georges, and Sabine Flaissier. *The French Revolution*. London: Secker &
    Warburg (1961).
    A series of eyewitness stories on aspects of the revolution, especially in
    Paris, between 1789 and 1794. The sources for the accounts are given at the
    end of the book.
Rapport, Michael. *Nationality and Citizenship in Revolutionary France: The Treatment
    of Foreigners 1789–1799*. Oxford: Clarendon Press (2000).
    At the beginning of the revolution, foreigners were welcomed to France,
    but, with the Terror, this altered. The book discusses the change of attitude
    with reference to the development of national identity and the concept of
    citizenship.
Robiquet, Jean. *Daily Life in the French Revolution*. James Kirkup, trans. New York :
    Macmillan (1965).
    In an informal and familiar style, the author covers most aspects of daily
    life, along with pictures and personal letters of the period.
Root-Bernstein, Michèle R. *Boulevard Theater and Revolution in Eighteenth-Century
    Paris*. Ann Arbor, Mich.: UMI Research Press (1984).
    In 324 pages and 14 plates, the work describes the value of the theater, its
    role in the revolution and its transformations in accordance with events,
    as well as actors, playwrights, plots, the people who attended, and censor-
    ship.
———. "Popular Theater in the French Revolution." *History Today*, 43 (February
    1993), 25–31.

The author discusses the content of the plays, changes in their dramatic presentation to conform to the revolutionary movement, and the reaction to these changes, as well as censorship, actors, and playwrights.

Rose, R. B. *The Making of the Sans-Culottes. Democratic ideas and institutions in Paris, 1789–92.* Manchester: Manchester University Press (1983).
In 200 pages, the author delves into the origins of the sans-culottes, the Paris sections, popular societies and popular politics, and the relationships between them and the revolution.

Rudé, George. *The Crowd in the French Revolution.* Oxford: Clarendon Press (1959).
The author examines the nature of the crowds that took part in the revolution, their social identity, aspirations, and relationships. The appendices show prices and wages in Paris at the time, populations of the Paris sections, and other information on insurgents and rioters.

———. *The French Revolution.* London: George Weidenfeld & Nicolson Ltd. (1988).
A chronological account of revolutionary events, with detailed examples, maps, and chapters on the impact of the revolution both in France and in the wider world.

Schama, Simon. *Citizens. A Chronicle of the French Revolution.* New York: Vintage Books (1989).
A massive, sprawling overview of 948 pages, well endowed with pictures and maps, that concludes with the fall of the Jacobins.

Scurr, Ruth. *Fatal Purity. Robespierre and the French Revolution.* New York: Henry Holt and Company (2006).
Essentially a biography of Robespierre, his bourgeois background, rise to power, friends and enemies, personality, and morals.

Sewell, Jr., William H. *Work and Revolution in France. The Language of Labor from the Old Regime to 1848.* Cambridge: Cambridge University Press (1980).
The structure of masters' corporations and journeymen brotherhoods under the old regime and their destruction by the revolution. Later chapters deal with labor organizations through 1848.

Soboul, Albert. *The Parisian Sans-Culottes and the French Revolution 1793–4.* Oxford: Clarendon Press (1964).
The study discusses the importance of the sans-culottes between 1793 and 1794 during the Terror and their organization into 48 Parisian sections.

Tannahill, Reay, ed. *Paris in the Revolution. A Collection of Eye-Witness Accounts.* London: Folio Society (1966).
Excerpts of various and sundry revolutionary events, including some accounts by those who narrowly escaped death by revolutionary tribunals.

Tench, Watkin. *Letters from Revolutionary France.* Gavin Edwards, ed. Cardiff: University of Wales Press (2001).
These letters to a friend in London were first published in 1796 and recount the author's experiences and observations while a naval prisoner of war after the capture of his ship by the French, on November 6, 1795, off Brittany.

Tocqueville, Alexis de. *The Old Regime and the French Revolution.* Stuart Gilbert, trans. New York: Anchor Books (1955).

The first volume of a proposed but unfinished major work on the French revolution, published in 1856. For the most part it deals with the period of the old regime.

Tour du Pin, Madame de la. *Memoires.* Felice Harcourt, trans. New York: McCall Publishing Company (1971).

The remembrances of an aristocratic woman associated with the royal court, written between 1820 and 1853, the year she died. She covers her childhood, the court of Louis XVI, the revolution, during which she spent much time in hiding, and her escape to America.

Wiesner, Merry E. *Women and Gender in Early Modern Europe.* Cambridge: Cambridge University Press (1993).

The work includes topics such as literacy, artistic creations, piety, witchcraft, and women as consumers between 1500 and 1750.

Wilcox, Turner R. *The Mode in Costume.* New York: Charles Scribner's Sons (1958).

A history of clothing, accompanied by drawings, in the Near East and the West, with four chapters devoted to the French revolutionary period.

Wrigley, Richard. *The Politics of Appearances. Representations of Dress in Revolutionary France.* Oxford: Berg (2002).

This book explores the relationships between how people dressed and their political allegiances and beliefs.

Young, Arthur. *Travels in France during the Years 1787, 1788, 1789.* Miss Betham-Edwards, ed. 4th ed. London: George Bell and Sons (1892).

An agricultural specialist, Arthur Young traveled in France just prior to and during the revolution. Although he was primarily interested in farming, he recounts the revolutionary events and describes the state of villages, farms, industry, lodging, and prices along with many of the people he met there.

# INDEX

**ABOUT THE AUTHOR**

JAMES M. ANDERSON is Professor Emeritus at the University of Calgary, Canada. He has spent many years in Spain, Portugal and France both as a Fulbright Scholar and as the recipient of Canada Council and SSHRC grants, contributing numerous articles and books to the field of European studies. He is author of 13 books, including *The History of Portugal* (Greenwood, 2000), *Daily Life during the Spanish Inquisition* (Greenwood, 2002) and *The Spanish Civil War* (Greenwood, 2003).

**DATE DUE**

12/10/09